The Altitude Experience

The Altitude Experience

Successful Trekking and Climbing Above 8,000 Feet

MIKE FARRIS

Professor of Biology
Hamline University

FALCONGUIDES®

GUILFORD, CONNECTICUT
HELENA, MONTANA

AN IMPRINT OF THE GLOBE PEQUOT PRESS

FALCONGUIDES®

Photos by Mike Farris
Text design by Nancy Freeborn

Library of Congress Cataloging-in-Publication Data
Farris, Mike, 1955-
  The altitude experience: successful trekking and climbing above 8,000 feet/Mike Farris.
    p. cm.
Includes bibliographical references and index.
ISBN: 978-0-7627-4358-2
1. Mountaineering—Health aspects. 2. Altitude, Influence of. I. Title.
RC1220.M6F37 2008
616.9'893—dc22

                                                                    2008008831

Printed in the United States of America
10 9 8 7 6 5 4 3 2 1

A trekker approaches Gasherbrum IV, Pakistan.

Contents

Chapter 6: Experiences at Altitude: Circulation, Respiration, Nervous System, and Immunity

Chapter 7: Experiences at Altitude: Food, Digestion, Hydration, and Hygiene

The trekking on Mount Kilimanjaro isn't difficult until the altitude affects you.

Acknowledgments

This book would not be possible without the contributions of the researchers, climbers, and explorers listed near the end of the book. I hope you'll read some of these publications and gain your own insights. To the several hundred people listed in the Literature Cited, thank you for your work.

Several individuals took the time to review sections of the manuscript. Cindy Kermott, M.D. (Mayo Clinic) and Stephen Lawler, M.D. (Allina Medical Clinic) provided feedback on several of the medically related chapters. Marty Knight, Ph.D. (Hamline University) and Chris Daymont, M.S. (St. Olaf College) provided suggestions on the exercise physiology and training sections. Eric Bergh, M.A./Licensed Psychologist (St. Olaf College) helped me clarify my thoughts about psychology and stress. David Dahl, Ph.D. (St. Olaf College) and Roland Hunter (The Mountain Company) made suggestions from a climber's perspective.

I would especially like to thank Sue Hopkins, M.D., Ph.D (University of California, San Diego), who provided invaluable feedback on subjects ranging from pulmonary vasoconstriction to cutting boards.

The students in my high-altitude physiology seminar helped me realize how little I actually knew about the subject; special mention to Vanessa McClellan, Sarah Burich, and Kristina Haycraft.

My climbing partners for a variety of altitude adventures have included Dave Gillette, Ed Burrell, Mike McCombs, Kevin Martin, David Dahl, and Bruce McDonald. To these guys and the others not mentioned here, thanks for keeping me in one piece.

While traveling in Nepal and Pakistan I've learned from many people. Special thanks to Stu Findley, Chris Grasswick, Francis Slakey, Mike Roberts, Jamie McGuinness (Project Himalaya), Dan Mazur (SummitClimb), Deb Robertson (M.D.), Chris Warner, Mario Panzeri, Sue Fear, Piotr Pustelnik, Artur Hajzer, and Krzysztof Wielicki. While in Minnesota, I've listened carefully to Scott Backes, our resident hard man.

While in Pakistan, I've always been well cared for by Ashraf Aman, Niaknam Karim, Essar Karim, Deedar Karim, and the rest of the staff of Adventure Tours Pakistan.

The American Alpine Club Library was an essential resource that more of you should use; join the AAC today.

Emily Niemczyk was very helpful with text entry, proofreading, and other administrative tasks. Thanks to Hamline University for computer hardware and software, and to my colleagues there for conversations and insights.

Julie Selmo, Allie Holdhusen, and Jerry Glantz graciously served as photo models, and thanks to Rozemarijn Janssen for allowing me to use my photo of her on the cover.

Kudos to the staff at Globe Pequot Press for their hard work during the production of this book. Copyeditor Laura Daly expertly cleaned up the mistakes in the manuscript and fixed my sometimes peculiar syntax. Editor John Burbidge served as shepherd, keeping me moving in the right direction with gentle prodding. Thanks, John.

My family has endured my travels with patience and understanding. My wife Kathy has borne the brunt of both the travel and the writing, for which I will always be grateful.

Mike Farris
Northfield, Minnesota
March 2008

Introduction

This book had its genesis at 7,900 m (26,000 ft) on Broad Peak, Pakistan, in 2004. I was only about three hours from the summit but moving very slowly due to dehydration. I was stopping to eat snow every 20 to 30 feet—not very thirst-quenching—but finally I had to decide whether to turn around or continue. Was it dehydration? Or cold? Or altitude sickness? Should I take a caffeine pill? Or acetazolamide or dexamethasone (altitude illness medications)? Or should I go down and try again? I chose the latter and never got another chance at the summit due to bad weather.

At Base Camp I realized that the dehydration had started several days prior to the summit attempt when storms had slowed our summit push. I also realized how little I actually knew about the interactions among altitude, cold, fatigue, and dehydration. The more I thought, the more questions I had; hence this book.

The person who understands life at altitude will have a better chance of having a successful and enjoyable trip. The best way to gain this understanding is through experience, but most folks don't have the freedom to spend years cultivating their comprehension of life in thin air. Another way is to learn from others by reading about their experiences in accounts of expeditions and exploration. Unfortunately, the nuggets of wisdom about life at altitude are often scattered throughout hundreds of pages of text. You can also read the medical and biological research literature and attempt to apply it to your own real-life situations.

This book does all of this for you. I've identified the major physical and mental issues you may confront at altitude—not just those related to altitude illness—and discussed the medical and scientific explanations/solutions for these issues. I've tried to "dejargonize" and "undorkulate" the science so that anyone who took high school biology should be able to understand the important issues. At the same time I've sifted through the written accounts of more than one hundred high-altitude climbers and explorers to extract the useful, practical information related to life at altitude. You'll find their contributions liberally sprinkled throughout this book. Finally, I've applied my 30 years of altitude experience to make recommendations and provide advice. I've tried to indicate what is accepted fact, what is possibly correct, and what is speculation or personal opinion.

This isn't a medical text, it's an educational text (Fig. 1). My goal is not to solve problems, but to prevent them from happening through education. In a few instances I have provided some diagnosis and treatment recommendations, but everyone traveling high should have a true medical resource available, such as a doctor or at least another book

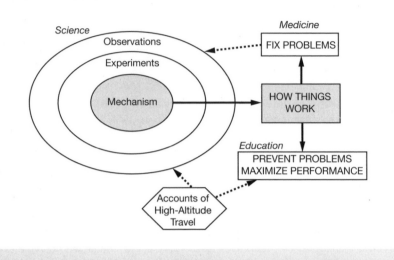

Fig. 1. Science leads to an understanding of the biological mechanisms through a process of observation and experimentation. Physicians use these mechanisms to fix malfunctions of the body and mind. The goal of this book is to help you prevent problems where possible and to help you maximize your performance at altitude. I'll use both the results of scientific research and the wisdom of visitors to altitude in this book.

on medical issues at altitude. (See the list at the end of this chapter and Appendix E: Recommended Reading.)

As you read through this book, you'll see many explanations of the ways in which the body responds to altitude. Beware! There's a reason why doctors go to school for years and years—reality is very complicated. Far more complicated than I'm letting on, but that's an inevitable tradeoff with accessibility. I've simplified, omitted, and generally squashed complexity in the hope that the more general biological issues can be understood.

The easiest approach to this complexity is to eliminate it by dividing all bodily responses into two categories: "altitude illness" and "not altitude illness." This is a reasonable approach from a medical perspective, but it limits our ability to improve performance at altitude by understanding the "not altitude illness" category. A primary goal of this book is to take a broader approach and deal more with performance at altitude than with altitude illness.

It's said that "a little knowledge is a dangerous thing." I can't condense years of medical and scientific training into a few pages, so keep in mind that there are many topics left completely uncovered. I'm trying to open a couple of doors in a skyscraper, knowledge-wise.

HOW TO USE THIS BOOK

The text is organized into four sections: Chapters 2 and 3 cover the scientific background of altitude biology, Chapters 4 through 8 cover the body's responses to altitude, Chapters

9 through 11 cover social/psychological issues and extreme altitude, and Chapters 12 and 13 cover practical issues related to preparing for altitude and visiting altitude.

As you read, you'll sometimes notice a gray number in superscript (like this[1]). This tells you the source of the information just before or after it. All of the references are included in Appendix D: Literature Cited, allowing you to explore further if a particular topic catches your attention.

The quotations scattered throughout the book come from the mountaineering literature. Scientists draw conclusions after conducting formal experiments, while high-altitude travelers draw conclusions by observing their responses and the responses of those around them, that is, through experience. Although this anecdotal information isn't adequate for scientific purposes, it's quite frankly the best information we have for some important questions about altitude.[360] I have used mostly scientific evidence to discuss the why and how of the body's response to altitude, along with the knowledge of past travelers, when I discuss what to do while at altitude.

Writing a book for an American audience leads to an inevitable problem with the metric system: We don't know it. So for altitudes up to about 14,000 ft, I'll use the familiar units. For higher altitudes I'll use meters, primarily because you'll never hear these altitudes expressed in feet (except in Alaska). But never fear, I've included a handy conversion table in the back of the book that will get you back to feet if you need it.

For each chapter, I have recommended some additional resources in case you want to pursue a topic in more detail. (See Appendix E: Recommended Reading). I've tried to pick sources that are accessible and readable, but some topics are by nature very technical.

Throughout this book I sometimes used he to indicate she, *he,* or it, as English doesn't have a gender-neutral third-person singular pronoun.

Lastly, no book is perfect. If you find errors or want to make suggestions, write to me c/o The Globe Pequot Press, Box 480, Guilford, CT 06437 or send an e-mail to editorial@GlobePequot.com.

FOR THE NON-SCIENTIST

I've spent a good chunk of my career teaching science to people who thought they were too dumb to understand science. Anybody who's smart enough to want to travel to altitude is smart enough to understand almost all of the scientific topics in this book. Some topics are quite complex, but if you follow the suggestions below, you should be able to get what you need from this book.

- Visit www.TheAltitudeExperience.com and download any corrections.

- It's not necessary to read everything in this book. If you're not interested in the science, skip it until you need it. If you're reading the science and it gets too tricky, skip to the next section and come back later. Chapters 2 and 3 contain the bulk of the science discussion.

- Maximizing your performance at altitude requires a working knowledge of the major topics in this book. The serious altitude traveler will need to spend more time on the science sections.
- There is a list of key concepts at the end of each chapter to help you understand the major issues. Read those if nothing else.
- Appendix A contains biological and chemical concepts that may help you better understand some of the concepts discussed in the text.
- Many topics are dealt with in more than one chapter. Sometimes you may want to go back and visit an earlier chapter to gain the background needed to understand a particular topic.
- The graphs and other figures are there to help you understand the science. Some people may find them easy to understand, others may find them more challenging. Use the text, figures, photos, or whatever combination works best for you.

FOR THE SCIENTIST

Please keep in mind that I've cited only a few examples of the literature available on any topic. I've used a mixture of primary literature and secondary sources such as review articles and books. My goal is to provide an entry into the literature, with an emphasis on the newer publications. Practical considerations prevented me from including all of the information that might be of interest to scientists. Consult the cited sources (Appendix D) to obtain more in-depth explanations for the phenomena discussed in this book.

RECOMMENDED READING

Below are books that I feel are invaluable for the serious high-altitude traveler. They are listed in order of importance. The first three should be considered required reading.

Bezruchka, S. 2005. Altitude Illness: Prevention and Treatment. 2nd edition. The Mountaineers, Seattle. *This is the best reference to altitude illness that I've seen, and it fits in your pocket. I never travel without it.*

Twight, M., and J. Martin. 1999. Extreme Alpinism: Climbing Light, Fast, and High. The Mountaineers, Seattle. *Excellent advice on physical and mental training that applies to anyone, and a wealth of additional information for the technical climber. Worthwhile for all high-altitude travelers.*

Coffey, M. 2003. Where the Mountain Casts its Shadow. St. Martin's Press, New York. *The best coverage of tragedy, family, and motivations of climbers. A must-read for anyone interested in high-altitude climbing.*

Boukreev, A. 2001. Above the Clouds. St. Martin's Press, New York. *A collection of writings by one of the top high-altitude climbers of this generation which contains much useful advice for the climber striving for extreme altitude.*

Noakes, T. D. 2003. Lore of Running. 4th edition. Human Kinetics, Champaign, IL. *A veritable cornucopia of information on training and exercise physiology, though it sometimes disagrees with the establishment viewpoint.*

For the scientist, add the following:

Ward, M. P., J. Milledge, and J. B. West. 2000. High Altitude Medicine and Physiology. 3rd edition. Arnold, London. *An expensive but thorough scientific summary of the area, written at the advanced undergraduate to graduate level.*

Hornbein, T. and R. B. Schoene (eds). 2001. High Altitude: An Exploration of Human Adaptation. Marcel Dekker, New York. *An even more expensive summary and technical treatise, written at the advanced graduate level.*

www.ncbi.nlm.nih.gov/entrez/query.fcgi?db=PubMed. This free public database known as PubMed contains abstracts of most of the papers cited here and often contains links to free full-text copies of the journal articles.

ABBREVIATIONS USED IN THE BOOK

cm	centimeter
dL	deciliter
ft	foot/feet
g	gram
kg	kilogram
km	kilometer
L	liter
lb	pound
m	meter
m^2	square meter
mg	milligram
mL	milliliter
mm	millimeter
mm Hg	millimeters of mercury
nm	nanometer
oz	ounce

qt	quart
bpm	beats per minute
cal	calories
hr	hour
kph	kilometers per hour
min	minute
mph	miles per hour
psi	pounds per square inch
$C_3H_6O_3$	lactate
$C_6H_{12}O_6$	glucose
CO	carbon monoxide
CO_2	carbon dioxide
Fe^{2+}	iron
H^+	hydrogen ion
Hb	hemoglobin
H_2CO_3	carbonic acid
HCO_3^-	bicarbonate
H_2O	water
Na^+	sodium
N_2	nitrogen
O_2	oxygen
$PaCO_2$	arterial partial pressure of carbon dioxide
PaO_2	arterial partial pressure of oxygen
PCO_2	partial pressure of carbon dioxide
PO_2	partial pressure of oxygen
SaO_2	arterial oxygen saturation (%)
$\dot{V}O_{2max}$	maximal oxygen uptake

The Altitude Challenge

Humans visit high altitudes for many reasons. Sometimes altitude is just an obstacle—Hannibal didn't cross the Alps because he wanted to go sightseeing. Sometimes it's just a job—miners in the Andes, astronomers in Hawaii, high-altitude porters in Nepal. But the most common reason that most of us travel to high altitude in this day and age is recreation.

Hikers, trekkers, and climbers are visiting high places in numbers never before seen. In 1957 there were only four climbers in the area around the world's second-highest peak (K2) in northern Pakistan, but in 2004 more than 700 Italian trekkers visited K2 Base Camp, and there were hundreds of other trekkers, climbers, porters, and workers on these glaciers at 5,000 m (16,400 ft) above sea level. In 1930 only about 20 people had climbed Mount Kilimanjaro; now that peak is attempted by about 20,000 climbers each year. From 2000 to 2004 more than 6,000 climbers registered to climb Denali (aka Mount McKinley), and from 1999 to 2003 more than 56,000 registered to climb Mount Rainier. Clearly, the number of people traveling to altitude is increasing.

Motivations aside, travelers to altitude all share the same goal: keeping mind and body healthy in an environment that is increasingly more hostile the higher one ascends. Today's travelers have the advantage of knowing how the body changes in response to altitude (the process of acclimatization) and how to recognize and treat the various forms of altitude illness. You could fill a backpack with the books that have been written about altitude illness and high-altitude medicine, and you should have one or two of these.

Fortunately, most of us traveling high don't succumb to serious altitude illness. The success of our endeavor depends instead on a combination of preparation, attention to detail, and overall decision making, as well as luck with the weather. Your trip can be ruined by failing to put on sunscreen or by attempting to summit before you're acclimatized. Little decision, big decision, same result. Even if you're on a guided trek or climb, your leader can't make all of the little decisions for you, so a personal understanding of life at altitude is still crucial. And there's this sobering fact: The highest fatality rates among trekkers are found in guided groups trying to stick to a predetermined schedule. So trekkers need to take direct ownership of their well-being.

HUMAN RESPONSES TO ALTITUDE

The effects of altitude are far better understood today than they were even 10 years ago, but we still have a long way to go. There are several reasons for this. First, doing research on altitude issues is difficult. To determine what causes a particular response, it's necessary to hold everything constant except for one possible cause. For example, exposure to altitude leads to an increase in the rate of breathing. But what actually causes the rate to increase? It could be a decrease in oxygen availability, but it could also be a decrease in carbon dioxide availability. It could even be a simple response to lowered atmospheric pressure and have nothing to do with oxygen or carbon dioxide. So the scientist needs to do several experiments in which two of these factors don't change and one does change. This means that many experiments can only be done under artificial conditions in the lab-

oratory. Gathering data at altitude is difficult—there's no lab on the summit of Everest to allow scientists to accurately collect data.

Second, exposure to high altitude generally includes exposure to cold, heat, exercise, and dehydration in various combinations. All of these have an affect on your body's response to altitude. It's possible to get around these confounding factors by measuring lots of people (say, hundreds or thousands). This is logistically impossible in all but a few circumstances.

Third, the money just isn't available to support all aspects of altitude research. The military and space agencies have supported some altitude research, and some altitude research is used to help understand

A trekker lounges beneath Wedge Peak in eastern Nepal.

A couple of semantic issues. First, what's the difference between *altitude* and *elevation*? *Webster's Unabridged Third New International Dictionary* defines *altitude* as "the vertical elevation of an object above a given level (as a foundation, the ground, or sea level)," and *elevation* is "the height above sea level." In this book, I use the two terms interchangeably to indicate the height above sea level, whether on the ground or in the air.

The terms *acclimation, acclimatization,* and *adaptation* are all used and defined in various ways in scientific and daily use. Here are the ways I have used these terms in this book:

  Acclimatization: The various temporary, reversible changes in an individual that help compensate for higher altitude.

  Adaptation: The genetically based changes that occur in populations that result in increased reproductive success in particular environments.

  Acclimation: I did not use this term.[eul]

As individuals, we can acclimatize to, but not adapt to, high altitude. However, your ability to acclimatize may be influenced by your genetic makeup.

other diseases. But for the large part, altitude research has been conducted by a cadre of dedicated scientists who have managed to finagle funding to do the work summarized in this book.

YOU ARE A UNIQUE INDIVIDUAL

Even if we understood every aspect of human responses to altitude, there would still be a wild card: you. You are a unique set of genes that have experienced a unique environment. As endurance athlete Kevin Setnes says, you are "an experiment of one." Why did one person on your trek get altitude illness but not anyone else? Why did you get altitude illness on this trip even though you've gone higher many times in the past? Why does your partner take two weeks to acclimatize, while you take three weeks?

My golden rule of altitude is this: *You may respond to altitude differently than your companions respond, and you may respond differently than you did in the past.*

Throughout this book, remember your uniqueness. The basic concepts in each chapter will apply to you, but maybe not exactly as stated. I have tried to present a range of experiences, but, again, you may not fit some of these alternatives.

HOW HIGH IS "HIGH ALTITUDE"?

This book covers all altitudes that you can reach on foot, with 2,500 m (~8,000 ft) as a lower cutoff point (though the effects of altitude can sometimes be felt as low as 1,500 m) and 8,848 m (29,029 ft—the summit of Mount Everest) as the highest elevation. This altitude range has been broken into a number of functional categories:

- Less than 2,500 m (8,000 ft). Relatively few altitude issues arise below this level.

- 2,500 to 4,500 m (8,200 to 14,800 ft). This covers the mountains of the United States and Canada (except for the giant peaks in northwestern Canada and Alaska), most of the mountains of Europe, and most of the high habitations of South America and Asia.

- 4,500 to 5,500 m (14,800 to 18,000 ft). This includes the base camps of high peaks in Asia and the very highest human habitations.

- 5,500 to 7,800 m (18,000 to 25,600 ft). The highest peaks on most continents and the altitude of many "trekking peaks" in Asia.

- 7,800 to 8,848 m (25,600 to 29,029 ft). The world's highest peaks. This is referred to as the "Death Zone," a reference to the short period of time humans can survive there without supplemental O_2. There are 14 official peaks that are over 8,000 m tall; all are in Pakistan, Nepal, or China.

- 8,500 to 8,848 m (27,900 to 29,029 ft). This encompasses only the summits of Lhotse, Kangchenjunga, K2, and Everest. Many people may be physiologically incapable of summiting these peaks without supplemental oxygen.

PEAKS AND ELEVATIONS MENTIONED IN THIS BOOK

Peak	Elevation	Location
Aconcagua	(6,962 m/22,841 ft),	Argentina
Annapurna	(8,091 m/26,545 ft),	Nepal
Broad Peak	(8,047 m/26,400 ft),	Gilgit Baltistan, Pakistan/China
Cho Oyo (Oyu)	(8,201 m/26,906 ft),	Nepal/Tibet
Denali (aka McKinley)	(6,193.6 m/20,320 ft),	Alaska
Dhaulagiri	(8,167 m/26,794 ft),	Nepal
Droites, Les	(4,000 m/13,123 ft),	France
Elbert	(4,401 m/14,440 ft),	Colorado
Elbrus	(5,642 m/15,554 ft),	Russia
Everest (aka Chomolungma/ Qomolangma and Sagamartha)	(8,848 m/29,029 ft),	Nepal/Tibet
Fuji	(3,776 m/12,388 ft),	Japan
Gasherbrum I (aka Hidden Peak or K5)	(8,080 m/26,509 ft),	Pakistan/China
Gasherbrum II	(8,035 m/26,362 ft),	Pakistan/China
Gasherbrum IV	(7,925 m/26,001 ft),	Baltistan and Northern Areas, Pakistan/China

Grand Teton	(4,197 m/13,770 ft),	Wyoming
Haramosh (aka Peak 58)	(7,397 m/24,270 ft),	Pakistan
Hunter (aka Begguya)	(4,442 m/14,573 ft),	Alaska
Ixtacihuatl	(5,286 m, 17,338 ft),	Mexico
Jannu (aka Limbu Phoktanglungma)	(1,035 m/3,396 ft),	Nepal
K2 (aka Qogir)	(8,611 m/28,251 ft),	Gilgit Baltistan, Pakistan/China
Kangchenjunga (aka Sewalungma)	(8,586 m/28,169 ft),	India/Nepal
Karakoram	(8,612 m/28,255 ft),	Pakistan/India/China
Kilimanjaro	(5,895 m/19,341 ft),	Tanzania
Lenin	(7,134 m/23,406 ft),	Tajikistan/Kyrgyzstan
Lhotse (aka Lhozê)	(8,516 m/27,940 ft),	Nepal/Tibet
Makalu (aka Makaru)	(8,462 m/27,762 ft),	Nepal/Tibet
Moran	(3,842 m/12,605 ft),	Wyoming
Nanda Devi	(7,816 m/25,643 ft),	India
Nanga Parbat	(8,125 m/26,657 ft),	Kashmir
Popocatépetl (aka El Popo, Don Goyo)	(4,200/13,776 ft),	Mexico
Pamir Mountains, highest point Ismail Simani	(7,495 m/24,590 ft),	Tajikistan/Kyrgyzstan/ Afghanistan/Pakistan
Rainier	(4,392 m/14,410 ft),	Washington
Sneffels	(4,312 m/14,150 ft),	Colorado
Troll Wall (Trollveggen)	(1,100 m/3,609 ft),	part of massif Trolltindene (Troll Peaks), Norway
Uli Biaho	(6,109 m/20,043 ft),	Pakistan

A climber ascends fixed ropes at 16,000 ft on the West Buttress of Denali.

CHAPTER TWO

The Air, the Body, and Oxygen

Your body is a fickle beast. It doesn't work as well when you give it too little or too much water, if its core temperature is too high or too low, or if you have too much or too little sodium in your blood. Luckily, the body has the ability to sense these imbalances and to return to its preferred state. This phenomenon is known as **homeostasis**. Most systems are interconnected, so changing one characteristic often affects others. For example, a lack of oxygen leads to faster and deeper breathing. This in turn lowers carbon dioxide levels in the blood, changing its acidity. This puts the system back in balance for oxygen yet out of balance for carbon dioxide concentration and blood acidity.

In the broadest sense, this entire book is about maintaining homeostasis in the face of the stresses imposed by altitude, or, more correctly, trying to maintain homeostasis. The further an organism slips from its optimal condition, the more its performance will suffer. At some point, stresses can lead to imbalances so severe that recovery is simply not possible—just ask anybody who has frozen to death.

Why is it important to understand the science behind homeostasis? Simple: To optimize your performance at altitude. If you want to follow the old-school recommendations for altitude travel that have been around for decades, you'll find they get you only so far. But if you want to perform your best at altitude, you're going to need to have a clear understanding of the difficulties your body experiences and the ways in which your body might respond. Since you're not likely to be traveling alone, you need to figure out ways to match your teammates' performance to your performance. Actually, the body is pretty interesting; it sometimes responds properly, sometimes improperly, and occasionally when it acts poorly it still succeeds.

I'll start with some basics of atmospheric science, then discuss the importance of individual differences, and finally dive into the main question: How does the body improve its ability to harvest oxygen when oxygen is scarce?

ALTITUDE AND ATMOSPHERIC PRESSURE

Altitude is an indirect measure of the atmospheric pressure, the factor that actually has a direct effect on your body. The atmospheric pressure at any particular place is influenced by several factors that can have a noticeable effect on the amount of oxygen in the air where you happen to be trekking or climbing. This means that your brain may be thinking, "I'm at 16,000 feet," while your body is experiencing the equivalent of 18,000 feet. And it's what your body experiences that counts. Throughout this book, I'll use the words *altitude* and *atmospheric/barometric pressure* interchangeably.

Standard atmospheric pressure at sea level is 760 mm Hg (millimeters of mercury),[*] and it decreases to somewhere around 253 mm Hg at the summit of Everest (8,848 m).[368] Why does pressure decrease as altitude increases? Less gas is piled up above. Atmospheric pressure is measured with a barometer; in weather reports, this value is referred to as the barometric pressure (in the United States, it's reported in inches, not millimeters, of mercury).

The following rules apply to altitudes of interest to trekkers and climbers (up to about 9,000 m):

- The barometric pressure is higher at the equator than at the poles. At the same altitude, equatorial peaks (e.g., Kilimanjaro) will have higher partial pressures of oxygen than polar peaks (e.g., Denali), all else being equal.

FUNDAMENTAL CONCEPTS OF GAS BEHAVIOR

The atmosphere is composed of a mixture of gases and is 78% nitrogen and 21% oxygen regardless of barometric pressure.

Gases in a mixture behave independently of each other. The pressure exerted by any particular gas in a mixture is the partial pressure of that gas.

The amount of a gas dissolved in a liquid is determined by the partial pressure of the gas and the solubility of the gas in the liquid.

Gases will diffuse from a region of higher partial pressure to a region of lower partial pressure.

If you need to brush up on these topics, go to Appendix A for a more detailed course in gas behavior.

---

[*] This is a somewhat arcane but common unit, so I'll use it throughout the book. Blood pressure is measured in these units as well.

- Barometric pressure is higher in the summer than in the winter at all latitudes. West et al.[367] predict that summer pressures on the summit of Everest will average 254 mm Hg, while winter pressures will average 243 mm Hg.
- The effects of season on barometric pressure are stronger at high latitudes than at low latitudes.
- Weather (specifically, areas of higher or lower pressure) will affect barometric pressure. Climbers will usually attempt a summit during a period of high pressure (good weather), but low pressure could raise the apparent altitude by 300 m/1,000 feet. Intense low-pressure systems spin in from the Gulf of Alaska and hit the high peaks, changing a 14,000-ft camp to an equivalent elevation of 17,000 ft.

BIOLOGICAL DIFFERENCES

Remember my golden rule of altitude: *Your response to altitude will be different than your companions' responses to altitude.* Understanding why you are unique and how this uniqueness affects your ability to perform is crucial if you are to develop reasonable goals for travel at altitude and to prepare your mind and body to meet those goals. Some aspects of this discussion are straightforward, while others are quite tricky.

FUNDAMENTAL CONCEPTS OF BIOLOGY

While biology lacks the simple, fundamental theories we see in other sciences, such as Newton's laws in physics, there are some concepts that are general enough, and useful enough, to keep in mind throughout this book:

Organisms are composed of a series of compartments, separated by membranes that limit the movement of substances, such as oxygen and glucose, between compartments.

These compartments are often arranged as a series of boxes within boxes within boxes. The cell is the fundamental compartment or "box." Cells can be of different types (muscle cells, nerve cells).

The business of life (obtaining energy, responding to a stimulus, reproduction, etc.) is all done by moving substances from one compartment to another.

The business of life does not violate any chemical or physical laws.

Chemical reactions in the cells are regulated by special proteins called **enzymes,** which speed up reaction rates thousands to millions of times faster than they would occur naturally.

Every characteristic of an organism is a result of the interaction between the genetic makeup of that organism and the environment that it has experienced.

Evolution is a change in the genetic makeup of a population (of a species) that occurs over time. Individuals cannot change their genetic makeup in response to, say, altitude stress.

Not all characteristics we see are adaptive; in other words, not all characteristics improve the ability of an organism to survive and reproduce.

The observed or measured value for any characteristic for any individual is called the **phenotype.** Your height, weight, 100 m dash time, body fat percentage, and IQ are all examples of phenotypes. If it can be described, it's a phenotype. Just like the word *color* is a generic term that can represent any specific hue, the term *phenotype* serves as a shorthand for any characteristic that we can measure. Throughout this discussion I'll use height as an example of a phenotype.

Look around at a group of people. There are some short folks, some tall folks, and a lot of people of intermediate height (phenotype). Don't you look twice at the person who's 6 ft 6 inches or 4 ft 5 inches? Those individuals are relatively rare, while a person who's 5 ft 8 inches tall wouldn't attract attention due to the commonness of that phenotype. Let's take a random group of 100 people and measure their heights. If we count the number of individuals of a given height (say, 5 ft 1 inch), we can plot that information on a graph (an example using fat burning capacity is shown in Fig. 2) and also calculate the average phenotype (average height). This bell-shaped distribution is common for complex characteristics like height.

For this discussion, we're not interested in the height (or the fat burning capacity) of any particular individual. Instead, we're interested in the differences among individuals—

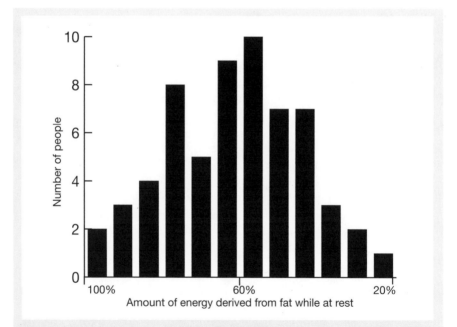

Fig. 2. An example of phenotypic variation. Individuals differ greatly in the amount of fat they burn while at rest. While the average person obtains about 60% of his energy from fat, some individuals obtain virtually all of their energy from fat (left side) or almost none of their energy from fat (right side). Data from Goedecke et al. (2000).

the **phenotypic variation.** Why aren't we all the same height? Why can't we all run the same speed? Why are some people patient and others impatient? Any phenotype is the consequence of an individual's genetic makeup **(genotype)** and the **environment** that the individual has experienced. The environment is all the nongenetic influences that the individual has experienced from the moment of conception onward. Just as a cake can't be separated into its original ingredients (sugar, flour, etc.), it's technically not possible to determine how much genotype and environment each contribute to the phenotype of any particular person; we can't say, for example, that your 6 ft height comes from 5 ft of genes and another 1 ft of environment. Scientists are identifying more and more individual genes that affect specific characteristics,[273] so someday it may be possible to identify all of the genes that contribute to a particular genotype.

However, we can calculate the percentage of the phenotypic variation we see that is caused by genetic differences among individuals. This is known as the **heritability** and ranges from 0% (the phenotypic differences are all caused by the environment) to 100% (the phenotypic differences are all caused by genetic differences). Here are some examples of traits in which phenotypic differences are under more or less genetic control.[*]

- **Strong   Genetic   Control**
  Traits that vary primarily due to genetic differences among individuals include neuromuscular coordination,[234] response to training,[145] reaction time,[194] some addictive behaviors,[204] and a number of size/shape characteristics, such as height. Your parents' genetic contributions decided these for you, and there's not much you can do about it. As the saying goes, "If you want to be a superstar, choose the right parents."

- **Moderate   Genetic   Control**
  Traits that are affected equally by genetic and environmental differences include predisposition toward recreational exercise,[75] muscle strength and endurance,[54, 8] lean body mass,[8] body fat distribution,[54] and female orgasmic ability.[104]

- **Weak   Genetic   Control**
  Differences in body mass index, body fat percentage, submaximal exercise capacity, and maximal aerobic power are much more strongly influenced by environmental factors than by genetic differences.[55] The take-home message is that for traits that vary among individuals, some are under weak genetic control and some are under strong genetic control.

A final topic that deserves consideration is genotype–environment interaction. I'll use a

---

[*] Be careful with language. A characteristic can be under genetic control but have a heritability of zero. That's because a characteristic that doesn't vary (e.g., eye number) is entirely under genetic control. But there are no differences to account for, and that's what heritability measures: the percentages of phenotypic differences due to genetic differences. If you're an expert, I've used both broad- and narrow-sense heritabilities here.

Hiking at 12,000 ft requires altitude know-how.

rather silly example concerning plants. Take a cactus and a water lily and put them both in the desert. Which will grow better? Now take an identical cactus and water lily and put them in a swamp. Which will grow better? Overall, which plant shows superior growth? The answer is, it depends on the environment. The particular genetic makeup of an individual will determine how it responds in a particular environment. This happens in humans, and the variation among individuals in their hypoxic ventilatory response (HVR) is a great example (see upcoming Fig. 5).

You and your teammates may respond quite differently to the same environmental stress— cold, heat, or altitude, for example.

This also means that when we talk of reaching our "genetic potential" for a performance trait such as running speed, we mean the maximum (running speed) capable of being produced by that genotype in the best environment for that genotype. At altitude, we know that our maximum physical performance will be limited by hypoxia. In that case, we could talk about reaching our personal genetic potential at 6,000 or 8,000 m. I'll explore this more thoroughly in Chapter 3.

As you examine your own abilities and compare yourself with others, remember that genetic differences and nonreversible environmental effects may limit your abilities, and your performance in one environment may not be possible in another environment. The key is to understand your own abilities and limitations, then scale your ambitions to match; failure to do so can be deadly at altitude.

THE QUEST FOR OXYGEN

Obtaining oxygen is not the only issue for the body at altitude, but it's certainly the main one. The process of acclimatization (Chapter 4) leads to changes that allow for more efficient transport of oxygen to the tissues. These changes often affect other systems, which then must be readjusted to allow for normal body function. The rest of this chapter provides the scientific background needed to understand the changes in the body that occur at altitude, the causes of altitude illnesses, and the ways in which the body can't cope with altitude.

Delivery of oxygen to tissues, such as muscles, consists of two phases: delivery of oxygen to the blood (**respiration**) and transport of oxygen to the tissues (**circulation**). I'll first review the basic biology of these two systems, then consider the transportation of oxygen while at rest, during exercise, and at altitude.

BIOLOGY BASICS

In this discussion, I'll assume that you have a clear understanding of these processes:

   The movement of substances from one compartment to another by diffusion, active transport, facilitated diffusion, and convection

   The assembly and disassembly of molecules by enzymes arranged in biochemical pathways

If you don't, see Appendix A. It's especially critical to have a clear understanding of diffusion, so brush up now.

Respiratory System

The **lungs** serve as our most intimate connection with the atmosphere. The first animals colonized land, in part to take advantage of the higher oxygen levels found in the atmosphere. The lungs not only serve to take in oxygen when we inhale but also to eliminate carbon dioxide when we exhale. An unintended consequence of exhalation is the loss of water vapor from the lungs; as we shall see, this is an important consideration at altitude.

The simplest lung would be a bag, like a balloon, with blood vessels covering its surface. Some amphibians have lungs like this. It turns out that this is very inefficient because there is a limited amount of membrane through which gases can diffuse (see Fig. A5 in Appendix A). Let's belabor this important point. Suppose we envision this bag as a cube, with each side being 10 inches long (or 10 cm, or 10 cubits). Each side is 10 × 10 inches, and there are six sides to our cube, so the **The center of an object will be closer to the surface if the object has a relatively high surface area for its volume.** total surface area is 6 × 10 × 10 = 600 square inches. The volume of gas in this cube is 10 × 10 × 10 = 1,000 cubic inches of gas. For each cubic inch of gas, there is 600/1,000 = 0.6 square inch of surface area for diffusion.

Just as water naturally flows downhill, oxygen must diffuse from the air to the tissues. Phole, Nepal.

Now let's take this same 1,000 cubic inch box and slice it into eight smaller cubes. Each cube will have sides that are 5 inches square, a volume of 125 cubic inches, and a surface area of 150 square inches. But we have eight cubes, so the total volume is still 1,000 cubic inches, and the total surface area is 1,200 square inches. Now we have 1.2 square inches of surface for every cubic inch of gas. Carry this even further and subdivide our original cube into 1,000 cubes, each 1 inch square. Now we will have 6,000 square inches of surface area for our volume of 1,000 cubic inches of gas, or 6 square inches of membrane per cubic inch of gas. This will increase the rate of diffusion dramatically. The exact same principle means that sliced bread will dry out more quickly than an unsliced loaf (Fig. 3).

Our lungs are not one big inefficient bag but are subdivided into about 300 million small bags, greatly increasing the surface area available for the diffusion of oxygen and carbon dioxide. These small bags are called **alveoli** and are a single layer of thin cells covered in **capillaries** (blood vessels). While visualizing alveoli as a bunch of grapes isn't quite accurate, it's close enough for our purposes. The alveoli are connected to tubes called **bronchioles,** which are connected to the larger **bronchi,** which are connected to the **trachea** and the throat.

Fig. 3. An unsliced loaf of bread has a small surface area. Slicing the bread doesn't increase the volume of bread, but it does dramatically increase the surface area. The cut loaf will dry out much more quickly because water will rapidly diffuse from the increased surface area. This same principle accounts for the subdivision of the lung into many tiny bags.

DON'T TRY THIS AT HOME

If we skinned a typical person and measured the surface area of skin, it would be about 2 m². The surface area of the lungs of a person will be somewhere between 50 m² and 100 m². That high surface area will allow diffusion to occur very rapidly.

Mechanics of Ventilation

The lungs themselves lack muscles, so they can't inflate or deflate on their own. Instead, the lungs are inflated by the same process you use to drink through a straw (Fig. 4). Before you start sucking on the straw, the level of the liquid in the straw is the same as the level of liquid in the cup. That's because the atmosphere is pressing down equally on all parts of the liquid's surface, including the inside of the straw. When you suck on the straw, you're not "pulling" the liquid up, but lowering the air pressure in the straw; the air pressure on the liquid in the cup is strong enough to push the liquid up the straw.

Fig. 4. Sucking on the straw (A) lowers the air pressure in the straw. The higher pressure on the surface of the liquid (B) pushes liquid up the straw (C).

The same thing happens in the lungs. The lungs are completely encased in an airtight lining (the **pleural lining**) and surrounded by the ribs and **diaphragm**. The ribs are connected to each other by the **internal** and **external intercostal muscles** (that's what you eat when you buy barbecued ribs). This arrangement creates three distinct spaces: the external atmosphere, the lung, and the pleural cavity. While the atmosphere and lung spaces are connected, the pleural space is completely isolated and is always at a lower pressure than the other two spaces. As a result, air pressure inside the lungs is constantly pushing them into the walls of the pleural space. Blow up a balloon inside a box; it's the same thing.

Take a deep breath and hold it. Notice that your chest rises and expands due to the contraction of the external intercostal muscles (along with some other muscles). Less obvious is the contraction of your diaphragm—put your hand on your stomach to get a better feel for this. Your belly rises as a result of the downward movement of the diaphragm. These two actions make your pleural space bigger and reduce the air pressure inside it. Because the lung air space has a higher pressure than the pleural space, the lungs expand to fill up the newly available space. This lowers the air pressure in the lungs, and air flows into the lungs from the atmosphere. Go back to the balloon inside the box. If we could make the box bigger, the balloon would expand (just like your lungs do). OK, now you can exhale.

Exhalation is generally a passive process; just relax the muscles, and the pleural space gets smaller. When breathing hard and fast, the internal intercostal muscles will help lower the rib cage more rapidly. During inhalation, the diaphragm is responsible for about two-thirds of the total air intake.

The Control of Breathing at Low Altitude

The volume of air taken into your lungs in one minute is called **minute ventilation**. This will be determined by the number of inspirations (= respiration rate) and the depth (= volume) of those inspirations. Surprisingly, minute ventilation is determined mostly by the amount of carbon dioxide in the body, not the amount of oxygen.[*] Respiration is controlled primarily by the **central chemoreceptors** in the brain, which respond to carbon dioxide levels in the **cerebrospinal fluid** (CSF) that bathes the brain. Actually, they respond to the blood pH, because as carbon dioxide concentrations go up, pH goes down (which means acidity increases).

Carbon dioxide, not oxygen, controls the rate of breathing at low elevations.

The pH of the blood turns out to be very important to normal functions in the body. Normal blood pH is 7.4 (slightly alkaline), and it is strongly influenced by blood carbon dioxide concentration. Don't believe it? Hyperventilate by breathing rapidly until you're lightheaded/dizzy. You've just caused **respiratory alkalosis** by increasing the pH of your blood and the CSF. The effects last only a few seconds after you allow your body to regain control. Holding your breath leads to **respiratory acidosis** and a drop in pH. When you exercise, lactic acid and other acids build up in the bloodstream to cause **metabolic acidosis**.

Hyperventilation lowers carbon dioxide levels in the blood, raising the pH.

A QUICK WORD ABOUT pH

The pH scale measures acidity. It ranges from 0 to 14.0; a pH of 7.0 is neutral. Lower values represent more acidic substances; the higher the number, the more alkaline (or basic) the substance. Chemically, an acid adds protons (H^+) to the solution, while a base adds hydroxyl groups (OH^-). Here are the pH values of some common substances:

pH	Substance
0	Pure hydrochloric acid
1	Stomach acid
2	Lemon juice
3	Beer, cola
6	Urine
8	Seawater
11	Household ammonia
13	Oven cleaner
14	Pure sodium hydroxide

Decreasing the pH by one unit (e.g., from 5.0 to 4.0) increases the acidity by a factor of 10, so a pH 2.0 solution is 1,000 times more acidic than a solution that's pH 5.0. Just remember that a small change in pH mean a large change in acidity.

---

[*] In aquatic vertebrates, respiration is controlled by oxygen levels in the water.

Oxygen is sensed by receptors known as the **carotid body** and the **aortic body** (found in arteries in the neck and chest); collectively, these are called the **peripheral chemoreceptors.** If oxygen concentrations fall too low, these bodies send signals to increase minute ventilation. They are also thought to sense carbon dioxide levels and pH to some extent.

Consider a person sitting quietly at low altitude. Minute ventilation will be low, with roughly 350 mL (about one-third of a quart) of fresh air entering the alveoli on each breath. Ventilation will be controlled by the central chemoreceptors monitoring the levels of carbon dioxide in the CSF. The blood will be saturated with oxygen, and the peripheral chemoreceptors will be inactive.

If this person begins to exercise (e.g., an easy jog or bike ride), breathing increases. Why it increases is a good question; neither blood carbon dioxide levels nor blood acidity can explain it. Oxygen concentrations don't usually drop enough to engage the peripheral chemoreceptors in most people (but see discussion of exercise-induced arterial hypoxemia later in this chapter). Breathing is likely influenced by stretch receptors in the muscles and other sensory input. This may allow the brain to tell the respiratory system, "Hey! We're exercising, so breathe more!"

The Control of Breathing at High Altitude

As long as the blood is nearly saturated with oxygen, breathing is controlled by carbon dioxide concentrations in the blood and cerebrospinal fluid.[*] At high altitude, especially with exercise, arterial oxygen levels drop low enough to trigger the peripheral chemoreceptors. They signal the brain to increase ventilation, which raises oxygen levels (which is good) but cause too much carbon dioxide to be exhaled (which is bad). This then triggers the central chemoreceptors, which attempt to slow down breathing. Apparently, low oxygen overrides low carbon dioxide since minute ventilation remains high.

Breathing hard at 6,300 m is the normal state of affairs.

If you go into a laboratory and breathe air with progressively less oxygen in it, your minute ventilation will probably increase (Fig. 5). This is the **hypoxic ventilatory response** (HVR), an important short-term response to acute hypoxia. There is much variation among lowlanders in their HVRs. Highland natives, such as Tibetans, show very little HVR, presumably because natural selection has led to other adaptations at the tissue level that eliminate the need for such a response.[360]

---

[*] The central chemoreceptors are directly stimulated by changes in acidity, which is primarily controlled by CO_2.

Hypoxia creates a conflict in the body. Either oxygen levels are too low (due to hypoventilation), or carbon dioxide levels are too low (due to hyperventilation). Since oxygen will win this battle, the body must deal with the lack of carbon dioxide in some way. Some research suggests that the central chemoreceptor resets itself to a lower carbon dioxide trigger point (summarized by Ward et al.[360]), much like you lower the thermostat to keep the furnace from turning on. However, other research indicates that this doesn't happen and that other mechanisms control breathing after acclimatization (summarized by Smith et al.[324]).

At altitude, low oxygen levels stimulate breathing and cause the loss of carbon dioxide from the blood.

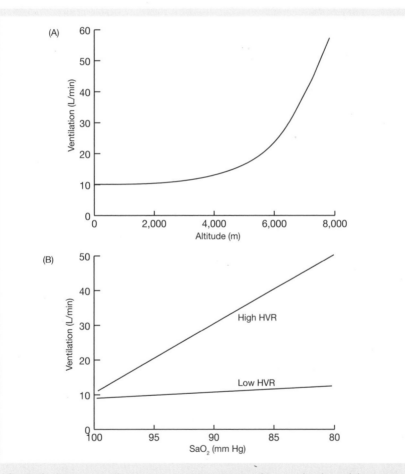

Fig. 5. The hypoxic ventilatory response (HVR). (A) Breathing sea-level air while at rest leads to low respiration. If we reduce the amount of oxygen in the air to simulate higher altitudes, most people increase respiration, although there is little change in respiration below 3,000 m. (B) Some individuals have a low HVR, and some have a high HVR. This is an example of genotype–environment interaction. SaO_2 is arterial oxygen saturation.

Cardiovascular System

The word *cardiovascular* refers to the heart and blood vessels. The **cardiovascular system** circulates blood throughout the body, delivering oxygen, nutrients, hormones, water, and electrolytes to the tissues and transporting any excess substances and wastes to the various organs that deal with those materials. In addition, blood is a major supplier of heat to the skin and extremities. The cardiovascular system is controlled by a complex set of neural and hormonal pathways that maintain homeostasis.[144]

The general plan of the circulatory system is simple (Fig. 6). Blood is pumped away from the heart in **arteries** and returns to the heart in **veins**. Materials enter or leave the

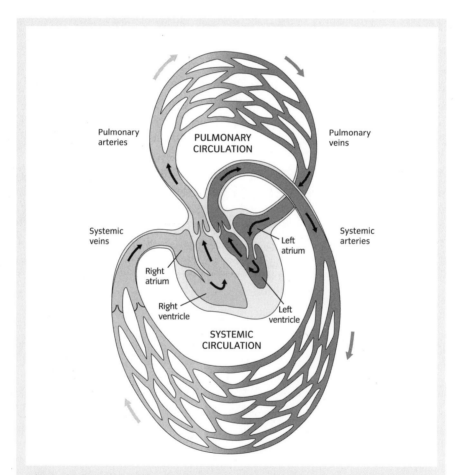

Pulmonary arteries

PULMONARY CIRCULATION

Pulmonary veins

Systemic veins

Systemic arteries

Left atrium

Right atrium

Right ventricle

Left ventricle

SYSTEMIC CIRCULATION

Fig. 6. The flow of blood through the heart, lungs, and body. The right side of the heart pumps blood through the lungs, while the left side pumps blood through the rest of the body. Blood going into the lungs is pumped at a much lower pressure, which prevents damage to the thin capillaries and alveoli.

blood in tiny vessels called **capillaries.** The arteries are elastic and can increase in diameter if blood pressure increases. As a result, the arteries reduce the fluctuations in blood pressure that would otherwise occur as the heart alternately contracts and relaxes. Most, but not all, arteries carry oxygenated blood, as explained below.

Arteries branch and become smaller and smaller as they approach their destinations. The actual site of exchange between blood and tissues is the capillary. A typical capillary is about 1 mm long and barely big enough for a red blood cell to squeeze through. Capillary walls are only one cell thick, and materials can pass through this vessel wall quite easily. Each cell in the body is, at most, about three cells away from a capillary. The flow of blood through a capillary bed is controlled by the muscles in the smaller arteries; these can be completely closed if necessary.

Veins are responsible for returning blood to the heart. Vein walls are thinner than artery walls and generally are not elastic. If you think about it, lifting blood from the feet back up to the heart requires a fair amount of force. This lift is not generated by the pushing of the blood from the heart; the capillary beds absorb most of the pressure. Instead, contracting skeletal muscles squeeze the veins, and one-way valves in the veins force the blood to move only toward the **Muscle contractions are needed to help move blood toward the heart.** heart. A failure of these valves leads to varicose veins as a result of blood pooling in the limbs and stretching the veins. Sitting for a long time (e.g., on a plane flight) can lead to blood and other fluids pooling in the lower legs as well.

There is another, quasi-independent set of vessels in the body called the **lymphatic system.** Think of this as a storm sewer. Tiny lymphatic capillaries penetrate most tissues and pick up any fluid, proteins, fat, hormones, and other junk found outside the cells. These lymphatic capillaries then join to form larger and larger lymphatic vessels. All of the lymphatic fluid eventually is dumped into the bloodstream. Lymph does not circulate; it goes from the tissues to the bloodstream on a one-way trip.

The Structure and Function of the Heart

The heart beats nonstop from birth to death. At an average resting rate of 70 beats per minute, your heart will beat 100,800 times per day and 2.5 trillion times in 70 years. There are four chambers in a mammal's heart: the left and right **atria** and the **left** and **right ventricles** (Fig. 6). The atria serve to fill the ventricles, which are the main pumping chambers. Of course, there are all sorts of valves and nerves and such, but these can safely be ignored here (assuming yours work OK).

The heart is really two separate pumps. The right side of the heart pumps blood from the body to the lungs, and the left side of the heart pumps blood from the lungs to the body. This allows the body to have different blood pressures in these two circuits (more later). Since the left ventricle is responsible for moving more blood at a higher pressure, the muscular walls are thicker and stronger on that side of the heart.

Like all other muscles, the heart needs to be supplied with oxygen. If you think about it, the heart is the most important muscle in the body, so it has a rich network of arteries that ensure a good oxygen supply. When these coronary arteries are blocked, chest pain (angina) or myocardial infarction (heart attack) can result.

The Flow of Blood through the Body

It is useful to think of two separate pathways of blood flow: Right heart to lungs to left heart is the pulmonary circulation, in which blood is oxygenated and carbon dioxide is eliminated, and left heart to body to right heart is the whole-body circulation, in which oxygenated blood is delivered and carbon dioxide is taken from tissues (Fig. 6).

Altitude significantly affects the pulmonary circulation but not the whole-body circulation; we'll return to this later. In rare cases, people have variants to the normal structure of the pulmonary arteries.[172, 311] These folks may be predisposed toward high-altitude pulmonary edema (HAPE; see Chapter 5).

Altitude, heat, cold, digestion, and exercise can affect patterns of blood flow within the body.

Other factors will affect patterns of circulation at any altitude. Heat and cold can challenge the body's temperature controls, leading to changes in the amount of blood sent to the limbs. Digestion also changes blood flow patterns to shunt more blood to the digestive organs.

Blood Pressure, Heart Rate, and Cardiac Output

Blood pressure is always presented as two numbers: 120 over 70, or 120/70, for example. These refer to the pressure in the circulatory system when the ventricles are contracting (**systolic**, larger number) and relaxing (**diastolic**, smaller number). If your blood pressure is 120/80 or lower, you are considered to have normal blood pressure.[245] There are tons of reasons why your blood pressure could be higher than this, so see your doctor if this is the case for you.

Blood pressure varies depending on your position—lying down (lowest), kneeling, sitting, standing (highest). If you lie down, your heart doesn't have to pump blood against gravity, so pressure can be lower. If you stand up too quickly, you may feel lightheaded or dizzy because of the blood pressure drop that occurs when you stand up. The sensors that control blood pressure aren't reacting quickly enough, leading to a lack of blood to the brain and the resulting head rush.

Heart rate or pulse rate is a measure of how fast your heart is beating. When you are resting, it is easy to measure by feeling the beat in your wrist or neck (use your fingers, not thumb). When the heart rate is high (at altitude or when exercising), this method is inaccurate; there's more in Chapter 12 on ways to accurately measure heart rate. In general, a lower heart rate is better and indicative of better training (or better genetics).

The amount of blood leaving the heart per minute (**cardiac output**) is determined by the heart rate multiplied by the amount of blood pumped each beat (**stroke volume**). Two individuals can have the same cardiac output but very different heart rates. The person with the higher heart rate has a heart that can't pump as much blood during each contraction.

Blood

Blood is water with lots of stuff in it: salts, red blood cells, white blood cells, platelets, dissolved gases, nutrients, hormones, and waste products, to name a few. We will focus on the two parts that are most important at altitude. **Plasma** is the fluid (water and dissolved substances) that circulates throughout the body. Floating within the plasma are the red blood cells **(erythrocytes),** which are the key players in the transport of oxygen and carbon dioxide through the body. The shapes of these cells maximize the surface area available for diffusion (Fig. 7).

Adults have about 4.7 to 5.0 L (~5 qt) of blood at sea level, so each time you donate a pint of blood, you have lost about 10% of your blood volume. Of this 5 L, red blood cells occupy about 42% to 45% of the volume, and plasma takes up the remainder. If we assume that there are roughly 5 billion red blood cells in each milliliter of blood (about 10 drops), that means there are about 25 trillion red blood cells in your body. Women have slightly fewer red blood cells than men, on average.

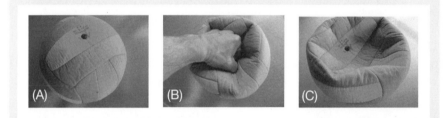

Fig. 7. If we take a round ball (A) and punch in both sides (B), we get the donutlike shape of a red blood cell (C). This decreases the volume without changing the surface area, so materials will diffuse in and out more quickly.

Transport of Oxygen and Carbon Dioxide

The science of oxygen transport is of central importance to the biology of high altitude, so let me be clear on how I'll approach it. In this section I'll talk about the basic physiology of oxygen and carbon dioxide loading, transport, and unloading. Later we'll look at oxygen delivery in a more general way during both exercise and hypoxia. It's actually most useful to start by talking about carbon dioxide transport.

Carbon Dioxide Transport

Carbon dioxide is a waste product of cellular activity, and all excess carbon dioxide must be eliminated from the body. Concentrations are highest in tissues, intermediate in blood, and lowest in the atmosphere, and all actual movement of carbon dioxide is by diffusion. Carbon dioxide dissolves easily in water (unlike oxygen).

When carbon dioxide is dissolved in water (H_2O), they can combine to form **carbonic acid** (H_2CO_3). This molecule then naturally falls apart into **bicarbonate** (HCO_3^-) and a hydrogen ion (H^+). This hydrogen ion makes the solution more acidic (lowers the pH). This whole set of reactions occurs very slowly in nature:

$$CO_2 + H_2O \rightleftharpoons H_2CO_3 \rightleftharpoons HCO_3^-$$

If we examine a cell lying next to a capillary (Fig. 8), the cell will be producing carbon dioxide, which naturally diffuses into the blood plasma. Some of this carbon dioxide will remain in the plasma, and some will enter the red blood cells. In the red blood cells there is an enzyme called **carbonic anhydrase**. Recall that enzymes speed up chemical reactions, and carbonic anhydrase speeds up the conversion of carbon dioxide to carbonic acid so that the reaction is complete by the time the blood exits the capillary. Carbon dioxide also binds with hemoglobin to form a molecule called a **carbamino compound** ($HbCO_2$ in Fig. 8).

Chemical reactions within the red blood cells modify carbon dioxide for transport by the blood.

After the carbon dioxide enters the blood from the tissues, these reactions all occur; in the veins about 10% of the carbon dioxide travels as carbon dioxide, 30% travels as carbamino compounds, and about 60% is transported as bicarbonate.

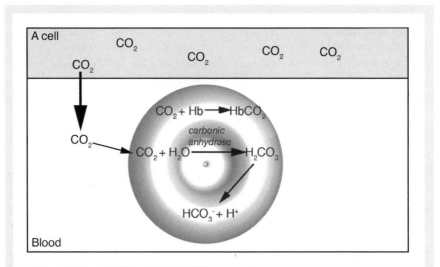

Fig. 8. CO_2 is produced by respiration in body cells. This diffuses into the plasma, where some of it then enters the red blood cells. The enzyme carbonic anhydrase chemically modifies the CO_2 into carbonic acid (H_2CO_3), which then breaks down into bicarbonate (HCO_3^-) and a hydrogen ion (H^+), which lowers the pH of the blood. These reactions are reversed in the lungs to unload CO_2. Hb is hemoglobin; $HbCO_2$ is carbamino compound (see text).

Once the blood reaches the lungs, the reactions in Fig. 8 are reversed to convert bicarbonate and carbamino compounds back to carbon dioxide, which rapidly diffuses into the alveoli and is then eliminated by exhalation. It's important to realize that all of carbon dioxide doesn't leave the blood; the partial pressure of carbon dioxide only drops from 46 to 40 mm Hg after carbon dioxide is lost in the lungs. This remaining carbon dioxide is crucial for regulating the acidity of the blood and tissues.

Oxygen Transport

Red blood cells contain **hemoglobin,** a protein made up of four subunits that each contain an atom of iron (Fe^{2+}). Hemoglobin is the central player in the transport of oxygen in humans and other vertebrates. Other types of critters have different compounds that carry oxygen. For example, mollusks (e.g., snails) and arthropods (e.g., lobsters) contain hemocyanin, which contains copper instead of iron and is blue when oxygenated. Each of the 25 trillion red blood cells in a normal person contains 200 million to 300 million hemoglobin molecules.

Since oxygen isn't very soluble in water, only 1.5% of the oxygen carried in the blood is dissolved in the plasma; the remaining 98.5% is bound to hemoglobin. Hemoglobin therefore allows the blood to carry much more oxygen than the plasma could carry alone. Each hemoglobin molecule can transport four molecules of oxygen.

Oxygen doesn't dissolve well in water, so hemoglobin dramatically increases the amount of oxygen carried in the blood.

Hemoglobin has some features that make it very efficient at rapidly loading oxygen in the lungs and rapidly unloading it in the capillaries. The most important feature is that the shape of the hemoglobin molecule changes when oxygen binds to it. If no oxygen molecules are attached, the binding sites are partially blocked and are difficult for oxygen to enter (Fig. 9). However, some do manage to attach; this changes the shape of the molecule, relaxing it and making it easier for oxygen to bind. In the same way, once an oxygen molecule is released from a hemoglobin molecule, the other oxygen molecules are more likely to be released.[*] Think of it this way: If a nightclub is popular and has a line to get in, more people are attracted, and the line gets longer. If you walk into a night spot that's mostly empty, you're more likely to leave too.

A DEADLY COMPETITOR

It turns out that another substance, carbon monoxide (CO), also binds to the same sites on the hemoglobin molecule as does oxygen. Unfortunately, carbon monoxide binds 200 times more strongly to hemoglobin than does oxygen—a fatal attraction. If carbon monoxide levels are high, there are no empty sites available to bind with oxygen, so oxygen is not transported to the cells. The result is death from lack of oxygen. This is why you should have carbon monoxide detectors in your house and why you should never cook in a sealed tent or snow cave (more in Chapter 7).

---

[*] There is still uncertainty as to whether hemoglobin changes shape gradually as O_2 molecules attach or changes completely after the first O_2 molecule binds.[40]

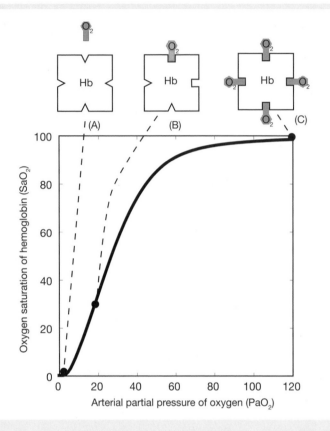

Fig. 9. (A) When the partial pressure of O_2 in the blood (PaO_2) is low, the shape of the hemoglobin molecule makes it very difficult for oxygen to bind to it, so the percentage of hemoglobin-binding sites occupied by O_2 (SaO_2) is near zero. (B) As PaO_2 increases, some O_2 binds to hemoglobin, changing the shape of the molecule and making it easier for more O_2 to bind to it (the molecule has only partially changed shape in this example). (C) As PaO_2 reaches typical sea-level values, almost every site is occupied by O_2. Hb is hemoglobin.

The primary factor that determines how many oxygen molecules will bind to hemoglobin is the partial pressure of oxygen in surrounding plasma; we'll call this PaO_2 (the *a* stands for arterial; Appendix A provides background on partial pressures). The higher the PaO_2, the more likely oxygen will be bound by hemoglobin. This relationship is shown graphically by the oxygen dissociation curve (Fig. 9). This relationship is crucial to the body's response to altitude, so let's dive in deeper.

> **Every time an oxygen molecule attaches to hemoglobin, it makes it easier for the next oxygen molecule to attach; each time an oxygen molecule leaves hemoglobin, it makes it easier for the next oxygen molecule to leave.**

As you move from left to right on the graph in Fig. 9, PaO_2 is increasing. The vertical axis represents SaO_2, or the arterial oxygen saturation of hemoglobin. If none of the hemoglobin molecules are carrying any oxygen, then $SaO_2 = 0\%$. If all of hemoglobin molecules are carrying four oxygen molecules, then $SaO_2 = 100\%$.

Start at the lower left-hand corner of the graph and move right, increasing the amount of oxygen (PaO_2). Note that, initially, SaO_2 increases very slowly. This is because the hemoglobin molecules are in a shape that partially blocks the oxygen binding sites. After most of the hemoglobin molecules have bound with one oxygen molecule ($SaO_2 = 25\%$), there is a rapid increase in the SaO_2 for a small increase in PaO_2. As PaO_2 continues to rise, the curve flattens out (at this point there are relatively few unoccupied binding sites available for oxygen), and the hemoglobin is mostly saturated.

Now consider what actually happens when oxygen enters the bloodstream in the lungs and when oxygen is delivered to the tissues (Fig. 10). Recall that the alveoli in the lungs are covered with capillaries and that oxygen will diffuse from a region of greater partial pressure (the air in the alveoli) to an area of lesser partial pressure (the blood). This leads to a PaO_2 of about 105 mm Hg at sea level. Since oxygen is abundant, it immediately attaches to hemoglobin, resulting in an SaO_2 of nearly 100%.

At low elevations, the hemoglobin is carrying nearly a full load of oxygen when it leaves the lungs.

Because no oxygen is lost until the blood reaches the tissues, the hemoglobin will stay saturated in the bloodstream. The capillary wall is in direct contact with oxygen-poor cells of some tissue. Carbon dioxide will dissolve into the blood, changing the pH. The higher levels of carbon dioxide, lower pH, and slightly higher temperatures in the tissues all affect the affinity of hemoglobin for oxygen. These changes make hemoglobin release more oxygen than would be otherwise expected. The oxygen released into the plasma will immediately diffuse into the oxygen-starved tissues. It's apparent that not all of the oxygen is delivered to tissues, so the partial pressure of oxygen in the veins (PO_2) is typically around 40 mm Hg or higher unless the person is exercising.

Not all of the oxygen in the blood is delivered to the tissues; some stays attached to hemoglobin.

PaO_2 doesn't tell us how much oxygen is actually being carried in a given amount of blood. Because almost all oxygen is bound to hemoglobin, the amount of hemoglobin is the main determinant of the oxygen-carrying capability of the blood. I'll talk about this in more detail shortly, but for now note that a typical person at sea level has about 19 mL of oxygen in each 100 mL of blood.

The Oxygen Cascade

If you've ever worked an old-style hand water pump, you know that it takes energy to move water uphill, against gravity. Water moves downhill (by gravity) with no additional energy input needed. A river will flow more quickly along a steeper gradient, creating a waterfall, rapids, or cascade. Keep this idea in mind as we discuss the flow of oxygen from the atmosphere to the cells of the body. Once again, a clear understanding of diffusion (Appendix A) is required here.

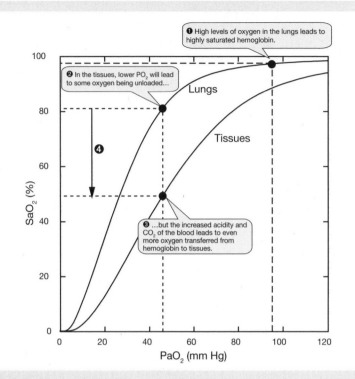

Fig. 10. **❶** As O_2 diffuses from the lungs into the blood plasma, the blood pH is 7.4, and CO_2 is scarce. This positions the O_2 dissociation curve as shown and leads to high SaO_2. **❷** In the tissues, some O_2 would be unloaded from the hemoglobin, but **❸** the increase in CO_2 and decrease in pH make hemoglobin more likely to release O_2, shifting the curve to the right. This means an additional amount of O_2 is unloaded **❹**.

Oxygen will naturally diffuse from areas of higher partial pressure to areas of lower partial pressure. The only place oxygen is actually used is inside compartments (mitochondria) found in the cells of the body; the problem is getting the oxygen to the mitochondria. At sea level, the partial pressure of oxygen in the atmosphere is as follows:

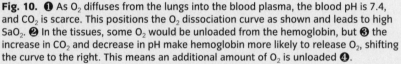

21% (atmospheric O_2 concentration) × 760 mm Hg (sea level air pressure) = 160 mm Hg

In the utopian world of Dr. Pangloss,* blood would carry oxygen at a partial pressure of 160 mm Hg. Because partial pressures of oxygen in the cells are very low, the partial pressure gradient would be very steep, and large amounts of oxygen would diffuse into

---

* From Voltaire's character in *Candide*. Dr. Pangloss was an expert in "metaphysico-theologo-cosmolonigology." Pangloss believed that "things cannot be other than they are, for since everything is made for a purpose, it follows that everything is made for the best purpose." In this case, we're interested in what would happen in the best of all possible worlds, oxygen-wise.

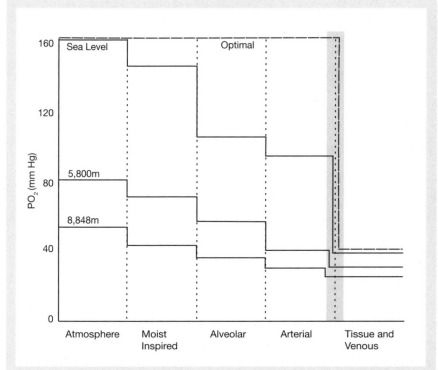

Fig. 11. The oxygen cascade. The partial pressure of oxygen decreases as we move from atmosphere to tissue. Diffusion is fastest when the difference between arterial PO_2 and tissue PO_2 (gray) is greatest. In a perfect world (top line), arterial oxygen levels would be very high and lots of oxygen would be available for diffusion into the tissues. At sea level, the cascade is still steep enough to lead to adequate tissue oxygen. At higher elevations, acclimatization helps maintain tissue oxygen levels. The lines are displaced slightly for clarity.

the cell very quickly (Fig. 11). The oxygen cascade is more of a waterfall in this scenario.

This doesn't happen in the real world. It takes several steps to transfer oxygen to the cells, and each of these steps results in the loss of some oxygen. Since the body's response to altitude is to minimize these losses, an understanding of the factors that turn the potential "oxygen waterfall" into a sluggish stream is critical.

The Oxygen Cascade at Sea Level and at Rest

This is the baseline situation, against which we compare the effects of altitude and exercise. Follow along in Fig. 11 and Fig. 12.

1. As air is inhaled, water vapor is added, and the temperature of the air is raised to 37°C or 98.6°F (body temperature). The partial pressure of water vapor in this now-saturated air is about 47 mm Hg. Since the gas mixture in the throat and lungs is not closed off

to the atmosphere, the total pressure can't increase above 760 mm Hg. This means that water molecules will displace a fraction of all the other molecules in the mixture of gases; nearly 10 mm Hg of oxygen is displaced by the water vapor (21% of 47 mm Hg). So at the end of the first step, PO_2 has fallen to 150 mm Hg.

2. The moist inspired air now enters the alveoli. If this air was not at 100% humidity and body temperature, the delicate lung tissue would be damaged. Keep in mind that the alveoli still contain some air with low oxygen levels and high carbon dioxide levels. At the end of your next exhalation, pause for just a moment without breathing, then force out the remaining air. That air would normally mix with the air from your next breath. This mixture of fresh and stale air has a PO_2 of roughly 100 mm Hg.

3. The next step is diffusion into the blood and binding with hemoglobin. Under perfect conditions, this drop of 5 to 10 mm Hg would be smaller, but blood flow through the lungs (perfusion) is often slightly mismatched with the amount of air entering the lungs (ventilation). I'll talk about this issue more in a moment during the discussion of exercise.

4. Blood then flows to the tissues, where PO_2 is low. Oxygen then diffuses into the tissues, where it is used in the aerobic respiration pathway to release energy. Myoglobin (a hemoglobin-like molecule) may be used in muscle tissues to help transfer oxygen within the cell. The blood never loses all of the oxygen it carries; the venous PO_2 is roughly 40 mm Hg, or 25% of the PO_2 of the atmosphere.

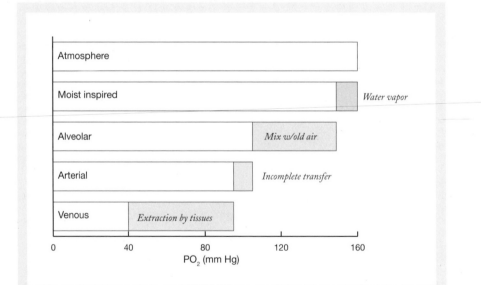

Fig. 12. At each step in the O_2 cascade, there is some O_2 that isn't transferred to the next step (light gray bar). This example is for resting individuals at sea level. See text for more details.

The Oxygen Cascade at Altitude

I'll keep the same numbering as above for each of the steps and use values estimated for an atmospheric pressure of 380 mm Hg, half of sea-level pressure and equivalent to an elevation of 5,800 m. This results in an atmospheric PO_2 of 80 mm Hg. Let's consider what happens in an acclimatized, resting person (Fig. 11).

1. Atmosphere to moist inspired: As before, a loss of about 10 mm Hg due to the addition of water vapor, so the moistened warm air has a PO_2 of 70 mm Hg.

2. Moist inspired to alveoli: You're breathing deeper and faster, which increases the amount of oxygen delivered to the alveoli. Rather than a drop of 50 mm Hg seen at sea level, alveolar PO_2 drops about 15 to 20 mm Hg to 55 mm Hg.

3. Alveoli to arteries: Little difference from the drop in the resting individual, resulting in an arterial PO_2 of about 50 mm Hg.

4. Arteries to tissues: There is a smaller difference between arterial PO_2 and tissue PO_2, so there will be less of a diffusion gradient, and oxygen will enter tissues more slowly.

An acclimatized, resting individual at 5,800 m has only half the oxygen available at sea level but maintains a tissue PO_2 only 20% lower than at sea level. Even at the summit of Everest, tissue PO_2 values remain **At altitude, the body becomes more efficient at transferring the available oxygen to cells.** nearly the same (Fig. 11). It's important to remember that the amount of oxygen delivered and the PO_2 delivered are two different things; this difference will be examined shortly.

The Effect of Exercise at Low and High Altitudes

Exercise increases the need for oxygen, and at any altitude the body will increase oxygen uptake by increasing minute ventilation, heart rate, and cardiac output. Although the science isn't completely clear yet, it appears that oxygen delivery to the blood is limited in different ways during exercise at sea level and high elevations.

These limitations involve three processes that occur in the lungs: ventilation (inhalation and exhalation), diffusion of oxygen from the alveoli to the hemoglobin, and **perfusion**. Perfusion is the flow of blood through the capillaries surrounding the alveoli (Fig. 13A). For oxygen to reach the tissues, it needs to enter the lungs, diffuse across the membranes into the blood, and attach to a hemoglobin molecule.

The process is analogous to an assembly line (Fig. 13B).* The bloodstream functions like a conveyor belt, with the hemoglobin moving along within the red blood cells (perfusion). Oxygen needs to be supplied to the blood, represented here by the Diffusion Robot. As oxygen enters the blood and is attached to hemoglobin, the "parts bin" needs to be resupplied with more oxygen (ventilation).

If the blood moves too slowly, the Diffusion Robot will need to slow down, and oxygen transport will be perfusion-limited. If the Diffusion Robot works too slowly, not all the hemo-

---

* I'm going to ignore shunts and other intrapulmonary issues for this discussion.

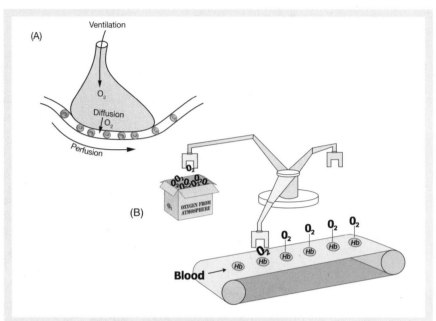

Fig. 13A. A schematic diagram of an alveolus and capillary. Oxygen enters the lung via ventilation, while blood is pushed through the capillary via perfusion. Oxygen is transferred to the blood via diffusion. **Fig. 13B.** The Diffusion Robot is on an assembly line. The conveyor belt is moving along and has hemoglobin (Hb) on it, and the Diffusion Robot attaches oxygen to the hemoglobin. To get the maximum number of Hb-O_2 units, enough oxygen must be delivered to the Diffusion Robot. If the Diffusion Robot can't keep up with the conveyor, Hb won't have oxygen attached. If the conveyor is too slow, fewer Hb-O_2 units will be formed. Any of the three steps: oxygen supply, diffusion, or hemoglobin delivery (perfusion) can limit the amount of oxygen transported in the blood.

globin will be saturated with oxygen; this is called diffusion limitation. Finally, if the lungs can't deliver enough oxygen for diffusion, the system is ventilation-limited. This might be better named "supply limitation," as both low atmospheric oxygen levels and inadequate ventilation could lead to low oxygen levels in the alveoli.

> **Oxygen levels in the blood will be reduced if oxygen delivery to the alveoli, oxygen diffusion into the bloodstream, and the movement of blood though the capillaries are not evenly matched.**

Recall that SaO_2 is a measure of the percentage of the binding sites on the hemoglobin molecules that are occupied by oxygen. A normal value for SaO_2 is 98% at rest and at sea level. If SaO_2 drops more than 2% to 3%, then one or more of the three limiting factors—perfusion, diffusion, and/or ventilation—are preventing the hemoglobin from becoming saturated before it leaves the alveolar capillary.

A healthy, sea-level individual at rest has adequate diffusion and a good balance between ventilation and perfusion, leading to very high blood oxygen saturation. A person with a weak heart can't pump enough blood to the lungs and may be perfusion-limited. A person with lung disease may have inadequate ventilation, preventing complete blood oxygen saturation.

What happens when the healthy person exercises at sea level? The heart beats faster and stronger, leading to a higher rate of blood flow through the lungs. At the same time, ventilation increases, providing more oxygen for diffusion into the blood. In most people, ventilation, perfusion, and diffusion remain matched, so that SaO_2 doesn't vary much with exercise intensity.

Some individuals do see a drop in their SaO_2 as they approach their maximal exercise levels at sea level. This is known as exercise-induced arterial hypoxemia (EIAH; *hypoxemia* means low blood oxygen content). One or more of the factors above must be limiting oxygen delivery to the blood. While it is still unclear which mechanisms are involved, it seems that ventilatory limitations are responsible for part of the hypoxemia, and some form of diffusion limitation may account for the rest. The blood may be moving too fast through the capillaries to allow diffusion to be completed. EIAH was originally thought to occur mostly in elite athletes who had excellent cardiac output, but it now appears that it can be found in non-elite athletes as well.[96, 156]

At altitude, the transfer of oxygen from the lungs to the blood can't keep pace with oxygen delivery or blood flow, which limits blood oxygen saturation.

At altitude, diffusion limitation appears to become far more crucial in limiting saturation. The science is beyond the scope of this book, but it has to do with the fact that the body is working along the steeper section of the oxygen dissociation curve (Fig. 9).[356] The higher the altitude, the more severe the diffusion limitation.

Increasing Oxygen Delivery to the Tissues at Altitude

A primary goal of the acclimatization process is to reduce the difference between atmospheric PO_2 and arterial PO_2. There are a number of ways to do this; in real life they all happen in all of us, though the degree of adjustment varies a lot between people. Table 1 summarizes the issues discussed in the paragraphs below.

Oxygen delivery to the tissues consists of two phases: delivery of oxygen to the blood (respiration) and transport of oxygen to the tissues (circulation). There are two ways to increase respiratory delivery of oxygen to the blood. The simplest way is to increase the oxygen concentration of the atmosphere by using bottled oxygen. This raises the PO_2 of the atmosphere and restores some (but not all) of the lost atmospheric oxygen. The downside of this approach is that it is completely artificial, expensive, and has ethical drawbacks (see discussion in Chapter 10). Here are the natural ways:

Hyperventilation. The first natural response that you notice upon arrival at altitude is increased ventilation—both increased respiration rate and depth of breathing. The net result of hyperventilation is to increase the amount of oxygen entering the lungs at any

Table 1

WAYS OF INCREASING OXYGEN DELIVERY TO THE TISSUES

Goal	Method	Comments
1. Increase oxygen delivery to the alveoli	a. Increase atmospheric PO_2 with bottled oxygen	Expensive, ethically dubious except for medical purposes
	b. Increase minute ventilation (depth and rate of breathing)	Energetically expensive
2. Improve diffusion of oxygen into the blood	Decrease perfusion by decreasing pulmonary vasoconstriction	No drawback; can be accomplished with drugs
3. Increase hemoglobin concentration	a. Reduce plasma volume	Increases viscosity of the blood
	b. Produce more red blood cells	A very slow response; increases viscosity of the blood
4. Increase hemoglobin saturation (SaO_2)	Biochemical changes in hemoglobin–oxygen binding (shift the hemoglobin curve to the left)	Some argue that shifting the curve the other way would be advantageous as well
5. Increase the amount of blood arriving at the tissues	Increase cardiac output (heart rate and stroke volume)	Occurs on acute exposure to altitude but not after acclimatization

point in time. Using values presented by Hultgren,[172] we can examine the effects of hyperventilation. Recall that minute ventilation is the amount of air taken in by the lungs in one minute. At sea level, a typical respiration rate might be 12 breaths per minute, and minute ventilation might be 9 L per minute. At 7,300 m, a typical respiration rate would be 27 breaths per minute, and minute ventilation would be 23 L per minute.

The air is much thinner at 7,300 m, so while the volume of air inhaled is 2.5 times greater, the number of air molecules inhaled isn't 2.5 times greater; it's actually lower than at sea level. However, the increased respiratory intake is a major step toward offsetting the reduced oxygen content of the atmosphere.

Breathing deeper and faster increases oxygen delivery but requires a lot of energy.

There's a downside to hyperventilation: It requires additional muscular energy to breathe deeper and faster. At sea level, ventilation requires about 5.5% of the oxygen taken up during maximal exercise ($\dot{V}O_2$max), while at 5,000 m, over 26% of the oxygen taken up during maximal exercise is needed for the work of respiratory muscles.[82] As a result, the net amount of oxygen available for skeletal muscle movement may be further limited.

Pulmonary hypertension. A counterproductive change that occurs at altitude is an increase in the pressure in the pulmonary arteries **(pulmonary hypertension)**, caused by constriction of the arteries due to hypoxia. Different people show strikingly different degrees of pulmonary hypertension.

Pulmonary hypertension makes sense at sea level, given that the normal lung has areas that are well ventilated and areas that are hypoxic.[240] At the end of your next inhalation, hold your breath for a moment and then continue to inhale. This extra inhalation provides oxygen to areas of the lung that would otherwise be hypoxic. Blood entering the hypoxic areas in the lung can't pick up any oxygen, and vasoconstriction detours blood around these areas. The whole lung is hypoxic at altitude, so this mechanism leads to restricted blood flow throughout the lungs.

Pulmonary hypertension doesn't improve oxygen uptake. Lower pulmonary pressures would lead to more blood in the capillaries surrounding the alveoli, allowing more oxygen to be loaded during blood transit. Higher pulmonary artery pressures are most likely important in high-altitude pulmonary edema (HAPE; see discussion in Chapter 5). Many high-altitude populations show low levels of pulmonary hypertension, presumably the result of natural selection. [274]

Hemoglobin levels. Once oxygen enters the blood, the amount that's delivered to the tissues is determined by several factors. Let's start with the amount of hemoglobin in the blood. Women average 14 g of hemoglobin per 0.1 liter of blood (14 g/100 mL), whereas men average 16 g/100 mL. A person acclimatized to altitudes greater than 5,500 m will have a hemoglobin content of approximately 19 g/100 mL, increasing the number of binding sites available to carry oxygen by 20%.

The total amount of oxygen in a given amount of blood (say, 100 mL) will be directly determined by the number of binding sites multiplied by the percentage of those sites that are bound to oxygen. At sea level, assume 15 g of hemoglobin per 100 mL of blood and a PaO_2 of 94 mm Hg. At 5,500 m, assume a hemoglobin concentration of 19 g/100 mL and a PaO_2 of 40 mm Hg.

Increasing hemoglobin content can compensate for lower oxygen levels at altitude.

We must remember the relationship between PO_2 and the saturation of hemoglobin—the oxygen dissociation curve. Fig. 14 summarizes the effects of increased hemoglobin on blood oxygen content. At sea level, a PaO_2 of 94 mm Hg leads to a hemoglobin saturation (SaO_2) of 97%. At a PaO_2 of 40 mm Hg, SaO_2 will be 76%. Given these saturations, the total amount of oxygen contained in both samples of blood is roughly 19.4 mL O_2/100 mL blood.*

---

* The complete calculation is CaO_2 = Hb (g/dL) x 1.34 mL O_2/g Hb x SaO_2 + PaO_2 x (0.003 mL O_2/mm Hg/dL), where CaO_2 = arterial O_2 content, PaO_2 = arterial O_2 partial pressure. The calculations in the text ignore plasma O_2.

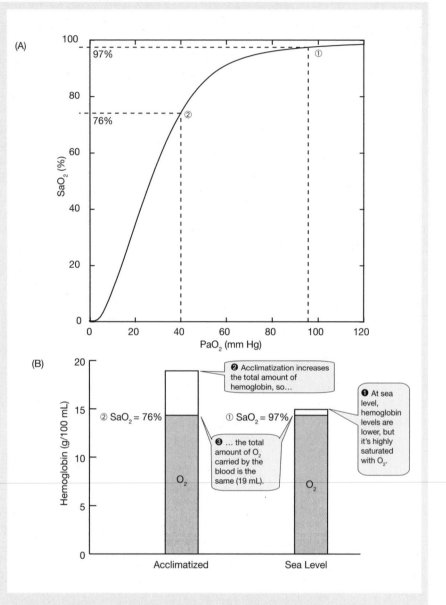

Fig. 14. The total amount of O_2 in the blood will be determined by the amount of hemoglobin in the blood and the saturation (SaO_2) of that hemoglobin. (A) At sea level **❶**, a person will have a higher saturation than at altitude **❷**. (B) At altitude (e.g., 5,500 m), an acclimatized person will have over 25% more hemoglobin than at sea level. Therefore, the total O_2 content of both blood samples is the same (about 19 mL). Adapted from Ward et al.[360]

There are two ways to increase the amount of hemoglobin in a given volume of blood. The less obvious way, and the one that occurs most quickly upon arrival at altitude, is a loss of plasma volume. If you take 120 mL of blood and remove 20 mL of plasma, you now have 100 mL of blood with all of the hemoglobin still in it. This loss of fluid happens within a day or two of arrival at altitude, and plasma volume remains low for many weeks. Note that this won't increase the total amount of oxygen carried in the body.

The other way is to manufacture more red blood cells. Red cell production is stimulated by the hormone **erythropoietin** (EPO), which is made in the kidneys. Higher elevations lead to a rapid increase in EPO (within hours). It takes at least 7 to 10 days for red blood cells to mature, so the hemoglobin response is relatively slow; this is likely one of the main factors preventing rapid acclimatization. This response leads to hemoglobin concentrations of about 19 g/100 mL after about six weeks. Spending time at altitudes above about 5,500 m does not appear to cause a further increase in hemoglobin levels.[381]

The body produces more hemoglobin at altitude, but too much hemoglobin will cause other problems.

While it may seem like "the more, the merrier" is the rule for hemoglobin, there is a downside. Too many red blood cells slow down the movement of blood by increasing the viscosity (thickness) of the blood. Just like too many cars cause a traffic jam, too many red blood cells will retard blood flow, slowing the delivery of oxygen. The optimal makeup of the blood may be about 50% red cells and 50% plasma.[360, 140]

The oxygen dissociation curve. When we examined hemoglobin concentrations (Fig. 14), we assumed that the same relationship (curve) holds at both sea level and high altitude. This is unlikely. Fig. 15 shows two different curves, a sea-level curve and a high-altitude curve. The high-altitude curve is shifted to the left of the sea-level curve. The best way to compare these curves is to determine the SaO_2 for the two different hemoglobin samples at a given PaO_2. For example, on the summit of Everest, PaO_2 has been estimated to be about 30 mm Hg).[372] Normal hemoglobin would be 56% saturated, but the left-shifted hemoglobin has an SaO_2 of 79%. We can conclude that the hemoglobin represented by the high-altitude curve has a higher affinity for oxygen.

What might cause the affinity of hemoglobin for oxygen to change? There are four factors that can increase the affinity of hemoglobin for oxygen: temperature, carbon dioxide concentration, acidity, and the concentration of a compound called DPG. If we lower one or more of these, the curve will shift to the left, and hemoglobin will more easily bind with oxygen. In reality, the temperature of the hemoglobin doesn't really vary much, so that's not important in acclimatization.

Chemical changes can make it easier or more difficult for the hemoglobin molecule to bind with oxygen.

Carbon dioxide and acidity are tightly connected; as carbon dioxide concentrations decrease, the blood becomes less acidic, and the pH rises. Hyperventilation lowers carbon dioxide levels in the blood and causes a rise in pH (respiratory alkalosis), shifting the curve to

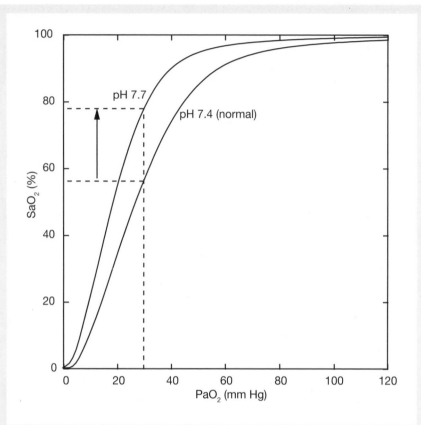

Fig. 15. Shifting the O_2 dissociation curve can have a large impact on hemoglobin satura-tion. At a PaO_2 of 30 mm Hg, the saturation of hemoglobin would be about 58%. Shifting the curve left causes the hemoglobin to accept O_2 more readily, leading to a saturation of about 78% in this example.

the left. At extreme elevations, blood pH can increase from the normal value of 7.4 to 7.7. Given the importance of pH to normal body function, this is a rather remarkable shift. The

At altitude, hemoglobin binds with oxygen more easily than it does at sea level.

high-altitude curve in Fig. 14 is based on a pH of 7.7 and a PCO_2 of 7.5 mm Hg (normal values are 7.4 and 40, respectively).

The compound DPG (more technically, 2,3-diphosphoglycerate) is formed in red blood cells when

they are exposed to a higher than normal pH. The amount of this compound increases with elevation,[381] and it will shift the dissociation curve to the right. The effects of pH tend to overwhelm the effects of DPG, so the net shift of the curve is to the left.[*]

The biological consequence of this leftward shift is more efficient loading of oxygen in the lungs. The biochemical changes in the affinity of hemoglobin for oxygen are likely a major reason we can ascend to great heights.

KEY CONCEPTS

1. The atmospheric pressure decreases as altitude increases, but this relationship can change with latitude and season of the year.

2. The movement of individual gases such as oxygen in a mixture of gases follows physical and chemical laws.

3. Individuals differ from one another because they are genetically different and because they have been exposed to a different environmental history.

4. Breathing is controlled primarily by carbon dioxide levels at low altitude and oxygen levels at higher altitude.

5. Oxygen must diffuse into the blood, bind to hemoglobin for transport to tissues, and diffuse into the tissues. Some oxygen is lost at each step in the transport process.

6. Changes in breathing rate, heart rate, and the amount of hemoglobin allow the body become more effective at transporting the available oxygen to the tissues.

---

[*] There may be an adaptive role for DPG in coronary circulation.[140] Shifting the curve to the right would enhance O_2 unloading in the tissues (including the heart), allowing lowered coronary blood flow.

Climbers approaching Camp II (6,400 m) on Gasherbrum II, Pakistan.

The Biology of Exercise

Trekking and climbing require exercise. Unless you're riding in a cable car or working as an astronomer at a high-altitude observatory, chances are that you will be using your own legs and lungs throughout your time at altitude. While your ability to acclimatize is not correlated with either strength or endurance, these two factors will determine what you're physically capable of doing while at altitude. Performance at altitude is thus determined by both fitness and acclimatization.

In this chapter, I'll start with some basics of muscles and skeleton, then move to the concepts of exercise physiology. Finally, I'll lay out the relationships between fatigue, will, and performance. That last section is particularly important because I'll refer to those ideas throughout the book.

SKELETAL SYSTEM

The skeleton serves as a structural foundation for the body. It anchors the various organs against the pull of gravity, protects many organs (such as the brain) and provides anchorage for the muscles, allowing movement. The bones are also the site of red blood cell production. There are about 206 bones in the human body, give or take a few in different individuals.

Which parts of your skeleton could you live without? The head, spine, and pelvis are pretty indispensable for just staying alive. This axial skeleton has shoulder and pelvic girdles to which the arms and legs (organs of action, as the yoga folks say) are attached. Bones are connected to each other in a number of different ways, and these joints allow for movement.

Muscles contract and relax to cause movement. We are specifically talking about skeletal muscle here. Smooth muscle, which is found in the organs (e.g., intestines) and cardiac muscle (heart), also contracts, but these muscles don't move bones and are structurally different as well. Skeletal muscle can be controlled by conscious thought, while smooth and cardiac muscle generally cannot.[*]

The next time you're chewing on a chicken leg, take a moment to study your dinner. Muscles are usually attached to bone by tendons, with one or more tendons at each end of the muscle. Remove the skin of the chicken leg and pick out a nice bit of meat—that's the muscle. Carefully chew your way down to one end of muscle, and you'll encounter a rubbery inedible structure—that's the tendon. Try and pull the tendon off the bone; unless the chicken is very overcooked, it won't come off. Some muscles attach directly to the bone or via a fibrous sheath rather than a tendon.

Skeletal muscle is made of long, thin muscle cells (called muscle fibers). A group of muscle fibers is connected to a single nerve (motor neuron) and forms a functional unit known as a motor unit. The fibers of a motor unit are not located next to each other; they are scattered throughout the muscle. When the motor neuron sends a nerve impulse, all muscle fibers in the motor unit contract.

Bones are joined to bone by ligaments. Grab an intact chicken leg and thigh. Cut through all of the muscles on both sides of a joint with your knife. The bones are still being held together by the ligaments. If you twist and pull the two bones, the ligaments will snap, and the bones will separate. Many people have heard the same sickening sound when their own knee or shoulder was injured.

As with bones, we generally ignore tendons and ligaments except when injury occurs. Muscles do contribute to success at altitude and deserve more careful consideration.

MUSCLES

Types of Muscle Fibers

There are several types of muscle fibers, each of which has different characteristics. Each person has a different mix of these fiber types, which contributes to differences in muscular performance. All motor units are composed of one fiber type. The major fiber types are:

- *Slow oxidative fibers* (also called Type I or slow-twitch fibers) contract relatively slowly, have lots of myoglobin, and fatigue relatively slowly. These fibers are small and are found in motor units with relatively few fibers. Myoglobin is a molecule that's similar to hemoglobin and serves as an oxygen carrier within the cell. It produces a red or dark color in the muscle (dark meat in our chicken).

A fiber can either fatigue slowly or contract quickly, but not both.

- *Fast oxidative fibers* (Type IIa, fast-twitch fibers) contract quickly, fatigue more quickly

---

[*] Conscious control of various automatic functions is possible with training, though most of us have other things to do with our time..

than slow-twitch fibers, and are somewhat larger in fiber size and motor unit size. They also contain myoglobin.

- *Fast glycolytic fibers* (Type IIb, fast-twitch fibers) contract quickly, fatigue quickly, and are the largest of the muscle fibers and form the largest motor units. They contain little or no myoglobin and are supplied by fewer capillaries than the other two types. There are other muscle fiber types, but these are the most common.

Muscle Control and Strength

Muscle control is essential to coordinated movement and fine-scale movements. If all of your arm muscle fibers contracted completely each time you picked up a glass, your milk would go flying all over the place. Control is realized in two ways. First, some motor units have fewer fibers and will exert less force when the nerve stimulates contraction. The muscles of the eyes and fingers have motor units with fewer muscle fibers, allowing fine-scale control.

Second, the number of motor units contracting varies depending on the muscular force needed (Fig. 16). Suppose somebody is piling books in your hands. The first book requires little muscular effort, so only a few slow-twitch motor units contract. Keep adding books, and the Type IIa fast-twitch motor units will start to engage. Finally, the Type IIb motor units engage to develop full strength in the muscle. Speed-wise, sprinting at full speed engages all muscle fiber types, while slower running relies on Type I, slow-twitch fibers. Full speed can only be maintained for a short time due to the rapid fatigue of the fast-twitch fibers.

Elite athletes in different sports appear to have different proportions of slow-twitch and fast-twitch fibers. These differences are mostly genetic, although there may be some conversion of muscle fiber types through training. In addition, there appear to be genetic differences in the shapes of muscles; people with skinny calves may be unable to develop a more bulbous calf muscle, even with training. These genetic differences are responsible for much of the variation in strength and endurance seen among equally trained individuals (more on this later in the chapter).

Arrangement of Muscles, Muscle Actions, and Types of Contractions

In the simplest arrangement, muscles occur in pairs. Each muscle is attached to two bones, and the contraction of one muscle causes the joint betwen the bones to bend (flexion). Contraction of the other muscle causes the joint to straighten out (extension). In reality, there are usually many muscles that help with flexion and extension of the major joints. Limbs and portions of limbs can move side to side (abduct or adduct) or rotate. A highly mobile joint like the shoulder can move in many planes while the arm is rotated in different ways—all of this must be controlled by coordinated movement of many muscles.

The action that occurs while a muscle is contracting has important consequences for both exercise physiology and training. Pick up something slightly heavy (say, 5 kg/10 lb) and hold it in your hand, elbow bent at 90 degrees. Are your muscles contracting? Yes. Is

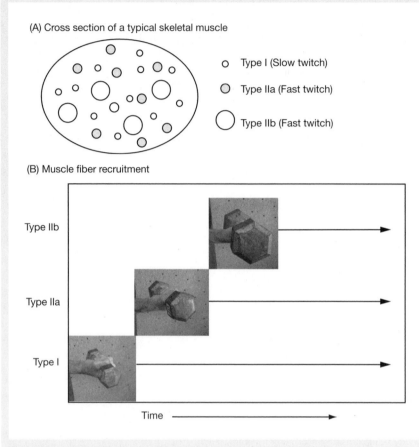

(A) Cross section of a typical skeletal muscle

o Type I (Slow twitch)

○ Type IIa (Fast twitch)

◯ Type IIb (Fast twitch)

(B) Muscle fiber recruitment

Type IIb

Type IIa

Type I

Time

Fig. 16A. The different muscle fiber types are scattered throughout the muscle.
Fig. 16B. A light load will engages the Type I motor units. As the load increases through time, the Type IIa and then the Type IIb motor units will engage, increasing the force generated by the muscle.

there any movement of the object? No. This is an isometric contraction. The muscles are contracting, but the muscle is not getting longer. *Isometric* means "same length," so the muscles aren't changing length.

Now bend your elbow and bring the object up to your shoulder as in a biceps curl (Fig. 17). The biceps is contracting and getting shorter at the same time. This is a concentric contraction and is the type of contraction that your muscles do best. Most of your weight-room training is through concentric contractions.

Pick the object back up and do a biceps curl as above. Now slooowly lower the object. Your biceps is contracting but is getting longer (Fig. 17; an eccentric contraction). If your biceps wasn't contracting, the weight would fall quickly until your elbow was completely

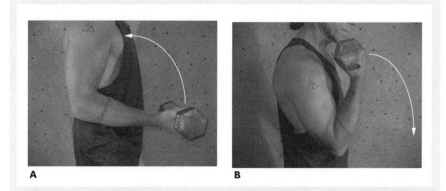

Fig. 17A. When the weight is held without movement, the muscles are undergoing an isometric contraction. If the arm is flexed and the weight brought upward, the biceps is contracting concentrically (it shortens under load). **Fig. 17B.** If the weight is lowered down slowly, the biceps is contracting eccentrically (it lengthens under load). This eccentric contraction determines how slowly you lower the forearm.

extended. The biceps' contractions help to maintain control of the object as you lower it.

Most coordinated movements are a combination of all three types of contractions. In practical terms, muscles really aren't meant to do lots of eccentric work, but hiking and climbing (especially downhill) involves a lot of eccentric work.

Altitude causes some changes in muscles;[157, 158] I'll summarize the important points in the chapter on acclimatization (Chapter 5).

CONCEPTS OF EXERCISE PHYSIOLOGY

If I could explain the true secrets of exercise success, I'd be rich enough to have myself carried to the top of Mount Everest. Here's my best attempt. This chapter will provide the scientific background, while Chapter 12 covers actual training techniques. Keep in mind that there are some deep philosophical differences among exercise scientists and coaches, and that there's a lot of money involved at both the professional and consumer level. Go warily as you explore this area; there's a lot of questionable information and advice in print and on the Web.

Limits to Performance

I'm going to use the term *performance* throughout to describe any physical activity. At altitude, this could mean a day hike, carrying a pack to the next camp, or climbing technical rock and ice. It's important to think about performance in a relative way; as an example, I'll use a simple measure of physical performance, such as the ability to run 400 m, a lap around a track. Follow along closely in Fig. 18.

Performance will be limited by a sequence of effects:

1. *Species limits.* No human will ever run 400 m in 2 seconds, 4 seconds, or even 10 seconds (the current world record is 43.18 seconds). Following this logic, there is some maximum performance that the human species can attain as a consequence of our physiology and biomechanics, which are determined by our evolutionary history.[102] Other species are faster; a human won't ever be able to run a mile as fast as a horse or a cheetah.

2. *Genetic limits.* All humans can't run the same speed. Why? Your theoretical best performance is determined by your genetic makeup. This assumes you perform in the best environment for your particular set of genes; this ideal environment will differ for each of us. Some of us are luckier than others in the genetics department; as the basketball coach said, "You can't coach tall."

3. *Environmental effects.* Even if you have the genetic potential to become a superstar, you might never be able to perform well because of the environment in which you developed. If your mom was chain-smoking cigarettes and washing them down with whiskey while you were in the womb, chances are that your development was compromised and that you will never reach your genetic potential. The same holds true for the environmental factors that shaped your body after birth. Some effects of the environment are reversible, some are not. None of us develop perfectly or experience a perfect environment, so our genetic potential simply can't be reached. After accounting for the environment, we have a performance phenotype that is attainable in real life.

4. *Training effects.* To reach your potential, you will need to train your body to maximize your physical capabilities. An untrained or improperly trained person will have a lower performance; since nobody knows what perfect training is, assume that you are not perfectly trained. The result of training (or the lack of it) is to bring you to a performance level that you could actually attain on a given day. Later I'll point out that the ability to train a characteristic is under genetic control.

   Your performance is limited by a cascade of effects, some of which you can influence.

5. *Current environment and mental state.* Your performance at any particular moment will be determined by two final factors: your mental state at the time and the current environmental conditions. Each of us has a different optimal environment; some people perform better in warm weather, some in cold weather. If the environment isn't optimal, your performance will suffer. The mental aspects of performance are complex but can have a major impact on your actual performance that day.

Factors That Determine Performance

While the effects described above explain the reasons why performance is reduced, they don't explain which bodily attributes contribute to differences in performance among individuals. There are a number of explanations floating around in the literature to explain limits to performance (Table 2).

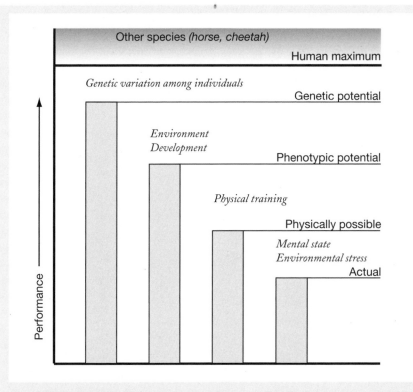

Fig. 18. The general factors that control performance. Use this figure as you read along in the text.

Table 2

Major Explanations for Differences in Performance among Individuals

1. Inadequate oxygen supply to skeletal muscles (the conventional wisdom)
2. Inadequate oxygen supply to critical organs (heart/brain/diaphragm)
3. Muscle fatigue or damage not related to oxygen delivery
4. Exertional discomfort
5. Central command fatigue
6. Biomechanics/economy of movement

Think of the problem this way: What would we change to improve performance? Movement requires energy, and energy release requires both fuel and oxygen. So either oxygen supply or fuel supply could limit performance. If you go to the weight room, the guy who can lift more than you isn't relying on more fuel or oxygen, he's relying on stronger muscular contractions. Or maybe his muscular contractions are as strong as yours, but he is more mechanically efficient than you are. Finally, superior performance may depend on the brain's ability to command the muscle fibers to completely and repeatedly contract. Let's take a closer look at each of these possibilities from the viewpoint of endurance performance (exercise that lasts for more than 30 minutes).

Maximum Oxygen Uptake and Muscle Limitation

For decades, it has been an accepted fact of exercise physiology that an inadequate oxygen supply to the muscles is *the* factor that limits exercise performance. Here is the standard explanation, which you may already know. As you begin to exercise, your body will respond by increasing ventilation, heart rate, stroke volume, and therefore cardiac output. As you continue to increase your level of effort, you breathe harder and harder, and your cardiac output increases even more. At some point, the amount of oxygen used in the muscles becomes greater than the amount supplied by the blood. As a result, your muscles will start to use anaerobic metabolism, and lactic acid is produced (see the discussion of fuel supplies for the cells in Chapter 7). This leads to fatigue, and the burning sensation you feel in your muscles is due to lactic acid buildup. When you rest, oxygen concentrations go back up, lactate is removed, and you recover.

Unfortunately, parts of this conventional wisdom are just plain wrong, so we need to develop a new model. I'll return to lactic acid a bit later; at this point I want to deal with the general concept of maximal oxygen uptake, otherwise known as $\dot{V}O_2$max. It is possible to duplicate the exercise experiment above and monitor the amount of oxygen taken in by a person as exercise level increases. As muscle power output increases, oxygen uptake increases (Fig. 19). At some point oxygen uptake does level off, even if workload increases. This is the maximum rate of oxygen uptake, $\dot{V}O_2$max, and is usually expressed as milliliters of oxygen per kilogram body weight per minute (mLO_2/kg/min).

The highest $\dot{V}O_2$max values (mid 80s) are found in elite triathletes, cross-country skiers, and marathoners. Pound for pound, women have a lower $\dot{V}O_2$max than men, roughly 10% to 12% lower at the elite level. This is likely a result of differences in muscle mass between the sexes. Studies to date have shown that $\dot{V}O_2$max decreases 5% to 10% per decade, with the lower value applying to those who continue training. My guess is that we really haven't tested the inevitability of this decline with age using enough well-trained, non-elite athletes.

At sea level, work rate (performance) increases as the amount of oxygen uptake increases (Fig. 19). The erroneous conclusion from this is that people with higher $\dot{V}O_2$max have higher work outputs, and higher work output means they can run/climb/cycle faster. But the relationship between work output and oxygen uptake differs between individuals, so the best performer may not be the person with the highest $\dot{V}O_2$max.[249]

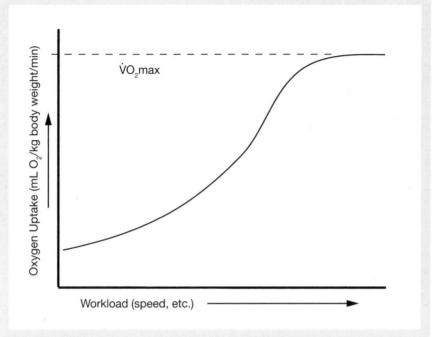

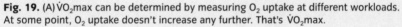

Fig. 19. (A) $\dot{V}O_2$max can be determined by measuring O_2 uptake at different workloads. At some point, O_2 uptake doesn't increase any further. That's $\dot{V}O_2$max.

The relationship between work rate and oxygen uptake is the same at sea level and at altitude for any one individual.[270] Your performance at a given level of oxygen consumption doesn't change; the maximum amount of oxygen you can take in does decrease at altitude. At 2,500 m, your $\dot{V}O_2$max has decreased to about 90% of sea-level values. At 6,000 m, it's about 50% of sea level, and on the summit of Everest it would be about 20% of sea level. This provides enough oxygen to stay alive and walk slowly, but that's about all.

Do elite high-altitude climbers have high $\dot{V}O_2$max? Oelz et al.[257] studied the physiology of six climbers who had ascended at least one 8,500 m peak and one 8,000 to 8,500 m peak without supplemental oxygen. They ranged in age from 34 to 50 years and weighed between 60 and 81 kg

$\dot{V}O_2$max doesn't explain why elite climbers are elite climbers.

(132 to 178 lb). Their $\dot{V}O_2$max was measured in two ways: running up a 10% grade and walking up a 35% grade. The lowest $\dot{V}O_2$max was recorded by Reinhold Messner during the walk, with a value of 47 mL/kg/min. The only climber tested who approached elite status was Peter Habeler, with a $\dot{V}O_2$max of 66 mL/kg/min. As a result of these and other tests, Oelz et al.[257] concluded that these elite climbers were not physiologically unique.

Oxygen Supply to Other Organs

Maybe it's not the oxygen supply to the skeletal muscles, but the oxygen supply to the heart (and possibly the brain and diaphragm) that is the critical limiting factor. As exercise level increases, at some point one of these organs may experience oxygen stress. Since the brain, heart, and diaphragm (unlike skeletal muscles) are absolutely critical to life, the brain acts to limit further increases in performance to preserve the oxygen supply to these crucial organs. Lundby et al.[211] found that during exercise at altitude, blood flow to the legs is lower in acclimated individuals, supporting the idea that the blood is being diverted to other organs. Lower $\dot{V}O_2$max at altitude may be due to diversion of blood to nonmuscular organs.[74] At altitude, a combination of high workload and lack of oxygen supply to the diaphragm may cause a reduction in the force generated by the diaphragm,[141] suggesting the possibility of performance limitation.

Muscle Fatigue

It could be that muscle is fatigued in some way not related to oxygen delivery. It's clear that functioning muscles don't completely run out of energy because a contracted muscle requires ATP to relax, while a relaxed muscle doesn't need ATP to contract.* At death, ATP is no longer produced, and the muscles lock up in rigor mortis (death rigor) because they can't relax. Living muscles don't lock up in rigor at maximal exercise, so ATP is not limiting (don't confuse rigor with cramp). That being said, ATP production may be limited by the biochemical interplay between glycolysis and aerobic respiration, thus limiting sustainable muscle activity.[86] There are genetic differences in the ratios of the different muscle fiber types;[190] sprinters have far fewer Type I (slow-twitch) fibers than do endurance athletes.[249] If your muscles are designed for sprinting and you engage in endurance exercise, you may fatigue more easily.

The Brain

Exertional discomfort and central command fatigue are both centered in the brain. Go out and run or cycle at full speed. At some point your body is crying out in pain—that's exertional discomfort—and when you can't take anymore, you stop. This is likely caused by your brain interpreting the various signals from your body and protecting itself against real damage.

Central command fatigue is a lack of recruitment of muscle motor units by the brain. The reason for this is not clear, but it is demonstrated regularly in weight rooms by coaches and fellow lifters who urge you on to complete that one last lift. Central command fatigue has been demonstrated at altitude in acclimatized subjects,[126] where verbal encouragement led to increased work output. The idea of the brain as a central controller of exercise is becoming more widely accepted and is now discussed in some introductory

---

* As part of the relaxation process, the energy in ATP is used to ready the muscle for the next contraction, much like cocking a gun readies it to fire.

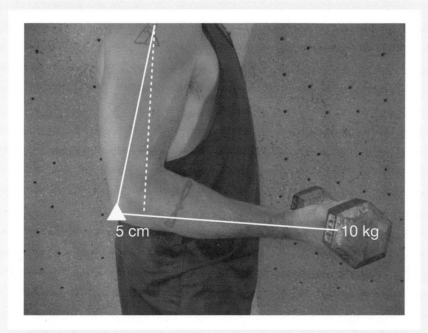

Fig. 20. The biomechanics of the arm will determine how much force is needed to lift the weight. See text for details.

texts (e.g. Vander et al.[353]). Evidence supporting the central command fatigue theory has been summarized by Noakes et al.[252]

Biomechanics and Economy of Movement

Movement is caused by muscle contractions. These contractions apply force to levers, which then lead to movement of the body part. Without going into the physics of levers too much, keep in mind that the amount of force needed to cause movement depends on the spatial arrangement of the lever. The forearm can serve as an example (Fig. 20). In this case, the elbow is the fulcrum of the lever—the portion of the arm that doesn't move. The resistance includes the arm and any additional load that needs to be moved. The force applied by the muscle is generated at the muscle attachment point.

The amount of muscle force that needs to be generated can be calculated if we know the values shown in Fig. 20. If the muscle is attached 5 cm from the elbow, it will require 70 kg of force to lift 10 kg of the combined mass of the arm and load. If we move the attachment point just 0.5 cm (about 0.2 inch) toward the hand, the force required to move the same load decreases to 63.6 kg, or about 9% less than the original force. Or suppose somebody has a forearm that is 5 cm shorter. The force needed is now 60 kg, or 14% less.

While this is a very simplistic example, the point is that the relative lengths of bones and the location of muscle attachments must be important in determining how much energy you use to move any particular limb segment. These characteristics are influenced by genetics and prenatal development and are untrainable. Those with unfavorable biomechanics can only strengthen their muscles to compensate for the extra force needed.

Economy of movement can be improved through training. Whether it's running or climbing, you can always tell the best performers by the ease with which they move. Just as fiscal economy can be defined as getting the most stuff for the least amount of money, economy of movement can be thought of as getting the most movement from the least amount of energy. By reducing the amount of energy and oxygen needed to perform a particular activity, you should be able to perform faster/harder/longer, regardless of the actual factors that limit performance. Noakes[249] postulates that individuals with higher $\dot{V}O_2$max also have more efficient muscles, allowing better performance at a given rate of oxygen uptake. Himalayan porters are more efficient than Westerners when carrying loads due to superior skill in balancing and shifting the weight of the load.[232]

Lactic Acid and Performance

Ah, lactic acid. Let's try and rehabilitate this unjustly despised molecule. Lactic acid is produced when muscle oxygen concentrations are too low, preventing aerobic respiration from taking place (see discussion on energy expenditure in Chapter 7). The accumulation of this lactic acid supposedly changed the pH of the muscle (which you'll recall is called metabolic acidosis). This concept is ingrained in textbooks, the Web, magazines, and popular thought.

To quote Robergs et al. (p. 502),[288] this idea "is not supported by fundamental biochemistry, has no research base of support, and remains a negative trait of all clinical, basic, and applied science fields and professions that still accept this construct." Evidence to date shows that metabolic acidosis does occur, but not because of lactic acid accumulation. Lactate actually helps prevent metabolic acidosis and serves as an alternate energy source, since it is a carbohydrate ($C_3H_6O_3$). When muscle energy stores are low, glycogen (starch) can be broken down in other tissues and transported as lactate to the exercising muscles, where it is used as fuel.[131]

Blood lactate concentrations may be an indicator of metabolic stress, but lactate doesn't cause the stress. The dogma of exercise physiology through the 1990s insisted that both $\dot{V}O_2$max and lactate levels (e.g., lactate or anaerobic threshold) were keys to understanding fitness and for training. While they are generally correlated with certain performance indicators, they are not the causes of performance differences. Metabolic acidosis may reduce performance by causing central fatigue in the brain.[73] The technical difficulties of understanding the biochemistry of functioning human muscles are impressive, and since we still don't understand the true limits to performance, we use what we can. But don't use lactic acid buildup in your muscles as your excuse anymore!

If you "feel the burn," you're not feeling lactic acid.

There is an intriguing relationship between blood lactate levels and altitude. In exercising, acclimatized individuals, lactate levels drop with altitude. Given the old theories about lactate, this didn't make sense; low oxygen should lead to higher lactate levels. The origins and significance of this lactate paradox are still unclear.[268]

So, What Really Limits Performance?

The old-school answer was $\dot{V}O_2max$. The new-school answer is that nobody is really sure. Noakes[249] and others propose that $\dot{V}O_2max$ is the consequence of other factors that limit performance and not the cause of limited performance.* Lindstedt and Conley[208] concluded that $\dot{V}O_2max$ is just one of many factors that contribute to human aerobic performance (distance running, cycling, hill-climbing speed). Using the ideas in Fig. 18, we see that the relationship between $\dot{V}O_2max$ and performance changes, depending on the people we are looking at:

- If you randomly grab a bunch of people off the street, the differences in their $\dot{V}O_2max$ values are a good predictor of aerobic performance.
- If you take a random group of individuals with similar $\dot{V}O_2max$ values, the differences in performance will be due primarily to differences in the level of training.
- Well-trained individuals with similar $\dot{V}O_2max$ values will differ in performance primarily due to mental issues, such as exertional fatigue and mental command fatigue.

I think the problem is that we want to find *the* limit to performance. There is no such thing. Instead, all of the factors listed in Table 2 will figure into the brain's decision to cease exercise. oxygen limitation is clearly an issue at altitude, and $\dot{V}O_2max$ decreases with altitude. Roach and Kayser[285] stress the importance of the brain in determining maximal work output at altitude. They also cite evidence to suggest that brain hypoxia or respiratory muscle fatigue may contribute to performance limitation. Finally, they conclude that high $\dot{V}O_2max$ isn't necessary for success at altitude and that the effects of training are less pronounced at high altitude. Those elite climbers didn't have amazing physical characteristics to succeed,[257] but they certainly had the will to succeed. Let's turn to that important topic now.

Performance is limited by multiple factors, but central command fatigue is likely very important.

---

* More on this controversy can be found in Noakes et al.[251] and the other papers associated with it as well as Noakes[249].

FATIGUE, WILL, AND PERFORMANCE[*]

Every person who travels to altitude will have to confront fatigue at some point during the trip. On some journeys fatigue is your constant foe, an enemy who must be overcome if you want to survive. While the relationship between performance, motivation, and fatigue has long been recognized,[46, 301] fatigue and its cousins are barely mentioned in any medically related high-altitude text. The best coverage of the topic is found in Noakes[249] and Twight and Martin.[351]

Webster's Third New International Dictionary provides these definitions:

Fatigue: weariness from labor or exertion; exhaustion of strength; exhaustion from causes other than physical or mental exertion (such as an illness)

Lassitude: weariness or debility; being listless or indifferent

Lethargy: abnormal drowsiness; being lazy or indifferent

Will: the power of controlling one's own actions or emotions

Motivation: drive or incentive

Passion: depth or vehemence of feeling for something

Fatigue is of central importance at altitude. In its simplest form, muscle damage may cause fatigue.[109] As stated earlier, lactate doesn't cause fatigue but may instead inhibit nervous system drive to activate muscles.[73] At altitude, the heart isn't beating very fast (relative to sea level), and the large muscles are not fatigued in the traditional sense.[183] The traditional definition of fatigue is the inability to sustain a desired force during a muscle contraction. Noakes[249] has spearheaded the argument that fatigue is not just a measure of muscle function but also an emotion or sensation that emanates from the brain. These two definitions are termed *peripheral fatigue* (muscles) and *central fatigue* (brain). It has been theorized that peripheral fatigue may dominate at sea level, while at altitude fatigue of the brain may be most important.[183, 3] Altitude can lead to some puzzling cases of severe lassitude that defy categorization (an instructive example is provided by West).[369]

From a practical perspective, it's important to consider fatigue of the body and fatigue of the mind. We all have felt exhausted at the end of a day that included no physical exercise. This fatigue seems just as real to our brain as the fatigue brought on by physical exercise. The difference is that the mental fatigue shouldn't impair our ability to go out and exercise that evening, while exercising earlier in the day would likely impair further exercise. In reality, mental fatigue does impair exercise; hence the statement "exercise begins and ends in the brain."[285]

Let's consider more carefully the factors that cause bodily fatigue and mental fatigue. Fig. 21 lays out a road map of how these factors interact. I make no attempt to include all

---

[*] This section was stimulated by some ideas from alpinist Scott Backes and a presentation by Tim Noakes.

OTHER ASPECTS OF PERFORMANCE

I hope it's easy to see that technical rock or ice climbing requires a higher degree of skill than hiking up a well-groomed trail. A small decline in the quality of performance of a technical climber can have serious consequences. There is a vast literature out there that addresses the mental factors that contribute to higher-quality performance. I like to think that the concepts of performance anxiety, optimal arousal, visualization, relaxation, and so on relate to the quality of the performance. My discussion of fatigue and performance relates more to the quantity of performance: how many hours you can walk, how much weight you can carry, how many vertical feet you can climb.

Most altitude travelers face the latter fatigue-related performance problem. Fewer face the need for technical precision as well. If you're into technical climbing at altitude, the ability to maintain your cool is just as important there as at sea level. All of the aspects of fatigue that I talk about here also apply. The successful high-altitude technical climber is a master of performance in all of its dimensions. See resources such as Hörst[163], Ilg[173], and Ilgner[174] for further discussions of that aspect of performance.

factors that might be involved, so feel free to pencil in all the other issues that you can think of. I will divide the factors that influence mind and body into three general categories: environmental stresses, physiological stresses that result from a disruption of normal body function, and psychological stresses.

Direct Environmental Stresses

While hypoxia is the main environmental stress of interest, it is clear that heat, cold, and dehydration can have significant effects on the various organs of the body. These organs then send information about their status to the brain for processing. It's important to realize that the body doesn't experience these stresses independently; they interact in sometimes unpredictable ways. In other words, instead of 4, 2 + 2 might equal –3, 5, or 24, so heat + hypoxia + dehydration might generate some unpredictable reactions. For example, dehydration impairs performance at moderate temperatures but not at cold temperatures.[80] In addition, the brain can be affected directly by the environmental stresses, for example, by low oxygen levels or dehydration.

Physiological Stresses

Exercise stresses the body, especially when taken to excess. We'll be discussing exercise throughout this book, so I'll just note it here. Some folks (myself included) are hit by jet lag rather hard. We all have an internal biological clock that needs to be reset as we move across time zones.[361] If you fly halfway around the world, it can take nearly a week to complete this clock shift. Even if you don't cross many time zones, travel can cause fatigue,

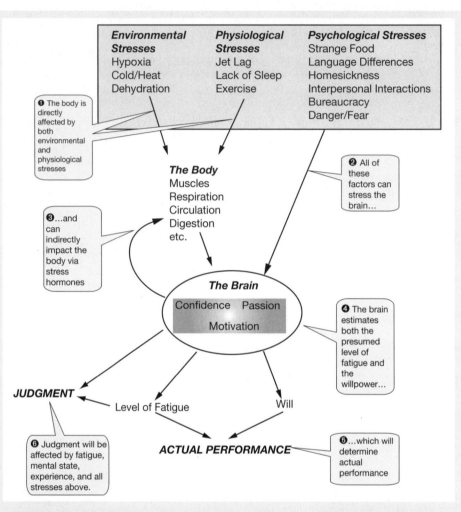

Fig. 21. The brain generates the sensation of fatigue based on inputs from the body and other sources. The brain also generates the willpower needed to perform in the face of fatigue. At altitude, fatigue and mental changes can lead to changes in decision-making ability.

which luckily resolves more quickly than jet lag.[361] Even without jet lag, your sleep may be disturbed, and sleep loss (obviously) is a major contributor to fatigue.

Indirect Psychological Stresses

The body and brain are indirectly affected by a host of other stresses, examples of which are listed in Fig. 21. The formal study of indirect stresses on athletes has only just begun.[146] The indirect stresses will be low on a day hike in the mountains and very high on a technical ascent of one of the world's highest peaks. However, even on longer trips to moderate

Backpacking through grizzly country can make for a stressful trip.

altitudes, these indirect stresses can be considerable. Here are a few comments on some of these factors, most of which are covered in more detail in later chapters.

Food. This can be a major source of stress for some travelers. This is almost entirely a psychological problem that you can mitigate prior to travel through practice:

> *In the past I'd at least gone as far as to condition my digestive system by spending plenty of time in some of Britain's worst curry houses.* (Fowler 2005, p. 80)

If you're going to Canada, practice eating your french fries with gravy.

Language differences. It can be mentally exhausting to deal with teammates or locals if you can't talk to each other. Russian climber Anatoli Boukreev climbed with German partners on K2:

> *Because of nuances in languages, it was easy for us to misunderstand one another in subtle ways.... The effort we each had to make to understand one another created a fatigue of sorts.* (Boukreev 2001, p. 74)

Interpersonal interactions. Even if you speak the same language, you may be thrown together with one or more people who are just plain irritating (even at sea level). At higher elevations these difficulties are magnified and can consume an incredible amount of energy (see discussion in Chapter 9).

Bureaucracy. Most expedition accounts spend a seemingly inordinate amount of time describing all of the hassles involved in just getting all of their gear into the country and to the base of the mountain. And for good reason, because these can be the most stressful times of a trip. The rank-and-file trekker or climber generally won't feel this pain, but leaders can expend a lot of energy on these matters, leading to serious stress (often a burden of leadership).

Danger. Even the simplest hike in the mountains can turn dangerous due to a lightning storm or a grizzly bear encounter. The constant danger experienced on some big mountains results in a cumulative fatigue that only the need to survive can overcome.

Fear. Fear of unknown altitudes, fear of potential dangers, fear of a new culture, fear of a poor performance: All are more common in the inexperienced traveler.

Uncertainty. More typical athletic activities have clear end points that allow the participant to pace his effort appropriately. For example, a runner in a 10 km race knows that he can run faster than in a 20 km race. When the duration of exercise is uncertain, the perception of exertion increases at the same level of effort.[17] This corresponds more closely to activity at altitude, where unknown issues lurk around every corner, making proper pacing quite difficult.

Boredom/inactivity. An alpine climb, a hike, or even an extended trek seldom leads to serious boredom, but any relatively difficult peak at the higher elevations may require weeks of sitting around, waiting for weather suitable for climbing.

> [To succeed, one needs] the stoic, mind-numbing patience that's an integral part of the Himalayan game. (Viesturs 2006)

Homesickness. This underrated aspect has probably wrecked more trips than any other indirect stress. Strange people, strange languages, strange food, and a general lack of normalcy all contribute to homesickness. The telephone and Internet can help minimize homesickness (given enough money and/or online access), but many inexperienced travelers fail to honestly assess their susceptibility to this malady.

One could easily argue that these last three—uncertainty, boredom, and homesickness—lead less to fatigue than to loss of will (see below).

Most (if not all) of the stresses in these three groups cause the body to release stress hormones, such as epinephrine and cortisol. These hormones then can have both positive and negative effects on the body (Fig. 21), and in some cases the stress response can be more damaging than the stress itself.[306]

Returning to Fig. 21, the brain, in its infinite wisdom, integrates all of this information together and analyzes it. The sensation of fatigue is your brain's estimate of your body's ability to perform at that moment. This estimate of fatigue is the sum of your true bodily (neuromuscular) fatigue and your mental fatigue. I'll define mental fatigue as that fraction of your total fatigue that isn't due to a physical inability to perform. This mental fatigue skews your estimate of your ability to perform downward—after a hard day at the office, you feel tired (mental fatigue), but your body is perfectly capable of a good performance because your muscles and other organs aren't actually tired. As we'll see in a moment, overcoming this mental fatigue while still listening to your bodily fatigue is the key to optimal performance.

Will and Motivation

Even if your body has the physical capability to perform at a certain level in a particular environment, you won't necessarily perform that well. This is where will, motivation, and your general mental outlook come in. What I'm calling your general mental outlook is the filter through which you view the world. This determines if a glass is half empty or half full. A more real-world example: I had just finished the first 26 hours of a 100-mile trail race. As I left an aid station, a spectator cheered me on by yelling, "You're running with the angels!" My thought was, "Lady, I'm running from the devil!" It really doesn't matter what your outlook is, as long as your filter doesn't lead to excessive negativity.

Before we get to will, let's examine **motivation**. What drives you to do what you do? External motivators might be peer pressure, business obligations, a spouse, or fame—anything from the outside. Internal motivation is just that; it comes from inside (though psychologists will argue that internal motivations have their roots in external factors). A person who is passionate about something has high levels of internal motivation. *Obsessive, driven, monomaniac, single-minded,* and *selfish* are words often used to describe people with excessively high internal motivation. See Coffey[85] for a summary of the motivations of high-altitude climbers.

Now to **will**. Will is the mental fortitude that makes you do what you don't want to do. Will is what makes you pick up your pack and start walking even though it's hot and you're dehydrated. Will is what gets you to unzip your sleeping bag in subzero temperatures and start the stove. Will is what gets you up that 5.11 finger crack even though it hurts like hell. The relationship between fatigue, will (motivation), and performance has been recognized for quite some time.[301]

A climber exhibits lassitude on Ixtacihuatl (5,286 m), Mexico. Popocatépetl is the background peak.

Lassitude (lethargy) is a vague concept that may apply to both will and mental fatigue. I think of lassitude as "negative will." The word *laziness* is sometimes used as a synonym for lassitude or lethargy, which I think is inappropriate. Laziness is by choice; lassitude is decreed from without. The best example is glacier lassitude. There is likely nothing in the world more able to evaporate will than trying to carry a load up a hot, sunny glacier. Even the strongest climbers wilt under the glacial sun.

How does **passion** fit into this? It's possible that a person could perform to his maximal ability without being overly passionate about the activity, but it's unlikely:

> The best antidote for high-altitude lassitude is an all-consuming passion to climb. (Clinch 1982, p. 7)

Excessive levels of passion can lead to fear of failure, overarousal, and reduced performance. But insufficient passion means you really don't care that much about your goal, and when the going gets tough, you'll likely flame out. At the same time, passion can be carried too far and turned into obsession. The history of climbing is replete with examples of obsession getting in the way of sound judgment (Chapter 11).

Your brain determines your level of fatigue and generates willpower; the interaction between those two will determine your level of performance (refer back to Fig. 21). Fig. 22 is an attempt to describe the interplay between these two competing forces. Your brain will estimate your total fatigue, which is a combination of your true bodily fatigue and your perceived mental fatigue. There's really no way to separate these two forms of fatigue; your brain just reports a single fatigue level. To optimize your performance, you need to overcome the mental fatigue but not the true bodily fatigue. So you have to estimate your level of mental fatigue as best you can.

Faced with the need to perform while fatigued, a variety of responses are possible. A person with very low willpower will roll over, go back to sleep, and not even try to perform (an excellent list of excuses is provided by Patey[263]). A person with inadequate willpower will perform, but not up to his physical capabilities. A person with excessive willpower will attempt a performance that the body can't safely complete. You've probably seen these people on TV, collapsing near the end of an Ironman triathlon or marathon. Why do they collapse within sight of the finish line? Willpower keeps them going until they see the finish line, the brain says "I've done it," and the body immediately ceases to function properly. This is known as John Henryism, in reference to the folkloric figure who fell over dead after winning a drilling duel with a machine.[306]

These levels of performance are sometimes necessary. In a survival situation, the will must force the body to perform, regardless of damage, in order to survive. In extreme situations, will may be the difference between life and death:

> I can scarcely go on. No despair, no happiness, no anxiety. I have not lost the mastery of my feelings, there are actually no more feelings. I consist only of will. (Messner 1989, p. 244)

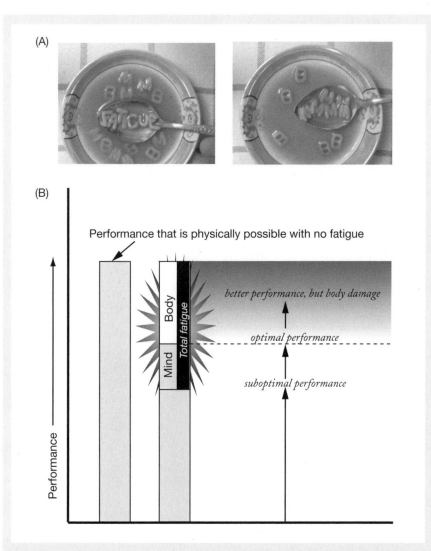

(A)

(B)

Performance that is physically possible with no fatigue

better performance, but body damage

optimal performance

suboptimal performance

Body

Mind

Total fatigue

Performance

Fig. 22. The fatigue you experience at any one time is a combination of true bodily fatigue and mental fatigue, represented by the Bs and Ms in the left bowl in (A). Both types of fatigue can influence your potential performance. In reality, it's not possible to remove the effects of mental fatigue from our overall estimate of fatigue (right bowl).

The relationship between fatigue, will, and performance is shown in (B). First, go back to Fig. 18 and note the maximum performance that's physically possible on any given day. That assumes no fatigue and is represented by the left bar in (B). Fatigue is a mixture of true bodily fatigue and mental fatigue, and is represented by the right bar. Each type of fatigue results in a decrease in your potential performance. The optimal sustainable performance overcomes the mental fatigue. Lack of willpower to fight the mental portion of fatigue leads to a suboptimal performance. If your willpower forces your performance above the optimal level, you will perform better, but bodily damage will occur. The more extreme the performance, the more bodily damage.

The optimal performance under normal circumstances will be one that fully exploits the capabilities of the body by overcoming mental fatigue while not exceeding the body's capabilities at that time (Fig. 22). As with all other characteristics, the accuracy of our "fatigue-o-meter" will vary from person to person.

At this point, examine Fig. 21 one more time. Note that judgment (decision making) is another process that will be affected by stress, fatigue, and emotional outlook. For example, even though you're physically tired (fatigue), you're still ready to hike to the summit (will), but there's a storm moving in, so you decide to delay your ascent (judgment). There are numerous psychological factors affecting judgment, such as passion, experience, and motivation, but it's important to remember that both fatigue and hypoxia may directly affect judgment. I'll cover these issues more thoroughly in Chapter 11; at this point, the key is to realize what your goal actually is at high altitude:

> Getting to the summit is only half of any climb. Getting back down is every-thing—the finish line is at the bottom, not at the top. (Breashears 1999, p. 250)

If you run a 10 km race and overestimate your ability to perform, the worst that can happen is you won't finish the race. At altitude, poor judgment and/or excessive will can lead to serious injury or death. The higher you go, the thinner the margin between proper and improper judgment.

Environmental stresses will reduce your potential performance on any given day. Indirect stresses contribute to overall fatigue as well. Success at altitude may require you to manage these stresses in a proactive way to reduce your overall level of fatigue. Most of us need to cultivate our will, because any activity at altitude requires this mental drive. Frank Smythe summarizes the goal:

> Nowhere else is the power of the mind over the body demonstrated to a greater extent than at high altitudes. It is not sufficient for the mind deliber-ately to force the body into action, it must humour it, even delude it into think-ing that it is not working as hard as it really is. (Smythe 1930/2000, p. 287)

We normally think of training as a way to get stronger. But training is also a way for our mind to better understand the true capabilities of the body.[249] Your "fatigue-o-meter" is usually conservative and forces your body to cease exercise before it's really necessary. Elite athletes are able to perform closer to their potential maximum in part because the mind is not limiting the body's performance. You can train your body to feel less fatigue, you can train your will, and you can train yourself to tolerate more suffering. But not too much, or you may damage yourself beyond repair.

KEY CONCEPTS

1. The skeleton and muscles allow the body to move in a coordinated fashion.

2. Muscle strength can vary due to the types of fibers in the muscle and the type of contraction.

3. Athletic performance is limited by genetic factors, environmental history, level of training, and mental factors.

4. The biological cause of differences in performance among individuals is still debatable. The importance of the brain in controlling performance is now generally recognized. $\dot{V}O_2$max is clearly important when comparing large groups of people.

5. A complex set of factors will interact to determine levels of fatigue. Fatigue is a combination of true neuromuscular fatigue and mental fatigue that arises from a number of sources.

6. Performance will be determined by the strength of willpower relative to fatigue.

7. Fatigue and altitude will also affect judgment and decision making.

Trail runners approach Virginius Pass (Colorado) in preparation for the Hardrock 100.

Acclimatization

In 1978 Peter Habeler and Reinhold Messner became the first to climb Mount Everest (8,848 m) without the use of supplemental oxygen. While training for their attempt, both climbers were able to ascend 860 m in 30 minutes during training at low altitude (Fig. 23). Yet if either of these supremely fit individuals were immediately transported to the summit of Everest, they would be immobilized, then lose consciousness, and finally die in a relatively short period of time. It was only after six weeks of living at altitudes of 5,000 to 7,000 m that these climbers were able to ascend to the summit at a rate of 100 m/hr.

This example demonstrates that your body changes in response to altitude; we call this process **acclimatization**. You can be exposed to high altitude either very abruptly **(acute hypoxia)** or over a longer period of time **(chronic hypoxia)**. You experience mild acute hypoxia when you take a plane flight because the cabins are pressurized to altitudes of 5,000 to 8,000 ft. Driving over a high mountain pass would be a similar experience. If your airplane depressurized, you would be exposed to severe acute hypoxia until you started breathing oxygen from the masks. I'm not going to specifically address acute hypoxia in this book.

A longer camping trip, backpacking trip, trek, or expedition at high altitude would expose your body to chronic hypoxia. Several days spent in Leadville, Colorado (10,000 ft), would qualify, as would a couple of months at K2 Base Camp (5,100 m). A third form of exposure to altitude is intermittent hypoxia. Here we have individuals who are experiencing hypoxia on a regular basis (daily-weekly); these visits may occur through technology (breathing low-oxygen air) or the old-fashioned way (hiking up a nearby peak every two to three days).

This section covers the typical pattern of acclimatization seen during continuous exposure to moderately high altitude (e.g., up to 4,500 m or 14,800 ft). Let's examine a theoretical timeline of a two- to six-week-long trip taken by a person living at low altitude (Fig. 24). This lucky person can visit altitude prior to the trip, allowing him to preacclimatize for his primary adventure. But it takes our trekker several days at low altitude to travel to his des-

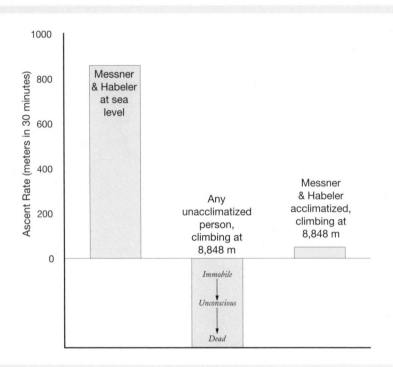

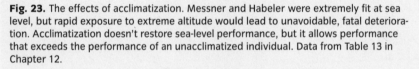

Fig. 23. The effects of acclimatization. Messner and Habeler were extremely fit at sea level, but rapid exposure to extreme altitude would lead to unavoidable, fatal deterioration. Acclimatization doesn't restore sea-level performance, but it allows performance that exceeds the performance of an unacclimatized individual. Data from Table 13 in Chapter 12.

tination, causing him to deacclimatize. Finally, the actual trek/climb begins. As he ascends, he continues to acclimatize to higher altitude (up to a point). On this trip a high point (a summit or pass) is reached, and upon descent, deacclimatization will begin. At some time after descent, all acclimatization will be lost.

It's important to remember that acclimatization does not restore your performance or homeostasis to sea-level values.[370] Also remember that being acclimatized to 4,000 m doesn't mean you are acclimatized to 5,000 m.

One more thing. The medical research literature sometimes equates incomplete or unsuccessful acclimatization with altitude illness. While altitude illness is certainly proof of lack of acclimatization, imperfect acclimatization can result in a decreased performance at altitude without an accompanying illness. Imperfect acclimatization is a continuum that can lead to consequences as minor as slightly reduced performance or as severe as altitude illness that leads to death.

FACTORS AFFECTING ACCLIMATIZATION

Table 3 summarizes the factors that may influence your level of acclimatization at a single point in time. My comments refer to trips to altitudes of 5,000 m or less for up to two to three months (more extreme altitudes are discussed later in this chapter and in Chapter 10). Here's a brief explanation of the factors mentioned in Table 3:

- *Time at altitude:* The longer your stay at altitude, the better you will be acclimatized.
- *Ascent profile:* There are too many variables here to make any predictions, but slower is usually safer.
- *Home altitude:* Unless you're living at 8,000 ft (2,400 m) or higher, the effects of home altitude will be minimal.
- *Preacclimatization:* This would include sleeping in a hypoxia tent or hypoxic training. The more you do, the faster you'll complete acclimatization.
- *Sex:* There are no known major differences in the ability of men and women to acclimatize.
- *Age:* Little is known about how quickly or completely children acclimatize, but rates of altitude illness are similar in children and adults. Young adults may acclimatize more slowly than somewhat older adults, but this may be due to inexperience and/or impatience. Adults older than 60 may acclimatize more slowly than younger individuals, but there is essentially no research to support this.
- *Experience:* There's a lot of anecdotal evidence to suggest that experienced individuals acclimatize more quickly. It is unclear whether this is due to a "physiological memory" that allows the body to speed up the process or due to the brain's ability to optimize exercise pacing, sleep, food intake, and other factors for better acclimatization. The

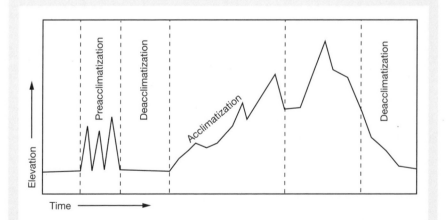

Fig. 24. A hypothetical ascent profile showing the possible stages of the acclimatization process. Not all stages will be part of every trip to altitude.

experienced person also lacks the uncertainty and apprehension experienced when traveling to a particular altitude for the first time (refer back to Fig. 21).

- *Other medical conditions:* During an attempt on Popocatépetl (5,452 m), one of our party was going very slowly and jeopardizing the group's chance of success that day. She finally told us that she had lost half of her lung capacity due to disease. She eventually turned back while we went to the top. A myriad of conditions (congenital and acquired) can affect acclimatization, and there is almost no way to predict exactly how acclimatization will be disturbed by your condition. *Remember that I assume a normal, healthy individual throughout this book.*

- *Uniqueness of response:* Some experienced and successful climbers recognize that they acclimatize more slowly than others;[351, 57] you need to determine how you respond. Hypoxia triggers rapid responses in some people and very little response in others.[79] For example, individuals differ dramatically in their production of erythropoietin (EPO), which stimulates red blood cell production[128] and total red blood cell volume[79] after exposure to altitude.

If that isn't enough, each of us can respond differently to altitude on each trip. Forster[118] examined the altitude sickness scores for 18 men who repeated the same ascent from sea level to 4,200 m on two separate occasions. On their second visit, four men had fewer symptoms, six men had more symptoms, two showed the same symptoms, and five showed no symptoms on either trip.

Some individuals simply are unable to acclimatize to even moderate altitudes (8,000 ft) due to genetics, congenital defects, or as a result of prior illness. You should consult a doctor if you have questions about your personal health history and altitude. There are no tests available to assess the altitude tolerance of an otherwise healthy individual.[22]

Table 3

Factors Influencing Your Level of Acclimatization, Categorized by Their Relative Importance

Major Impact	Minor Impact	Uncertain or Variable Impact
Your genetic makeup	Sex	Experience at altitude
Time spent at altitude on this trip	Age	Other medical conditions
Preacclimatization		
Home altitude		
Ascent profile		

CHANGES THAT OCCUR DURING ACCLIMATIZATION

The major changes that occur during acclimatization are shown in Fig. 25. Because changes start occurring within a minute of exposure to hypoxia and can continue for years, the time scale in Fig. 25 needs to be noted carefully. Also keep in mind that we're not interested in all changes that occur as a result of hypoxia, but only those that help the body attempt to regain homeostasis. Let's approach this topic from the perspective of a person who ascends via vehicle to 3,000 m (10,000 ft) and remains at that altitude.

As soon as cells experience hypoxia, changes begin to occur. You can't feel these changes, but they are responsible for the eventual improvement in homeostasis at altitude. In particular, a molecule known as hypoxia-inducing factor 1 alpha (HIF-1α) normally is degraded by oxygen almost immediately after it is produced. In the absence of oxygen, HIF-1α doesn't degrade and instead changes the production of dozens of different enzymes and other regulatory elements inside the cells.

One of the first changes you'll actually notice is an increase in heart rate, which can occur almost immediately. Cardiac output (the total amount of blood pumped per minute) increases for a couple of days, then returns to normal (or to slightly below normal). The heart rate increases, but the stroke volume (amount pumped each beat) actually decreases after a few days and stays lower than normal. Plasma volume is lost during this time as well. This leads to an increase in the hemoglobin concentration, so each milliliter of blood can carry more oxygen.

Increased ventilation (both the rate and depth of breathing) begins almost immediately as well. This increases oxygen uptake, but oxygen saturation is still below normal, so the oxygen sensors continue to call for hyperventilation. However, hyperventilation also causes too much carbon dioxide to be exhaled, causing the pH of the blood to rise. This inhibits hyperventilation. But low oxygen wins the battle, and ventilation continues to increase slowly for about a week before leveling off.

This shift in pH is a disturbance that the body would normally correct very quickly. Your kidneys excrete bicarbonate, which lowers the pH of the blood back to normal. This homeostatic process is by all accounts very slow,[360] and a normal pH may not be reached for several weeks.

The total amount of hemoglobin in the blood (and thus the total oxygen carrying capacity) will only increase with the production of new red blood cells. EPO begins to increase within a couple of hours of exposure to altitude[128] and returns to normal levels after about three weeks at altitude. Red blood cells take at least seven days to form and mature, so any advantage is not going to appear immediately. Red cell mass continues to increase for several months and is accompanied by a rebound in plasma volume.

Muscle capillary density increases over time as a result of the decreasing diameter of muscle fibers. This makes some sense as an acclimatory response, as there's a shorter distance for oxygen to travel to the muscle cell. However, blood flow to the leg muscles is reduced at altitude,[212] suggesting no need for a better oxygen transport mechanism in the tissues.

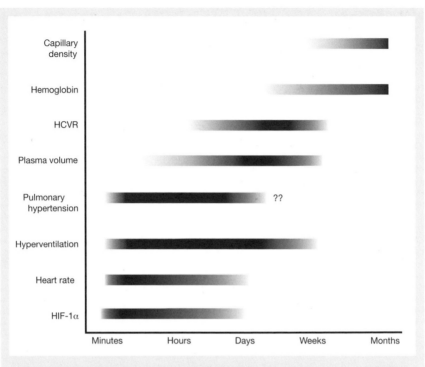

Fig. 25. Major changes that occur during acclimatization. Note the time scale carefully. The time course of changes in pulmonary hypertension is not clear at this time. HIF-1α is hypoxia-inducing factor 1 alpha; HCVR is hypercapnic ventilatory response.

How do you know when you're acclimatized? In practice, normal sleep,[57] a normal appetite,[67] and a normal heart rate[193] have all been used as signs that acclimatization is adequate. Your own ascent rate is probably the best overall indicator of acclimatization; example rates are found in Table 13 in Chapter 12.

Acclimatization versus Deterioration above 5,500 m

While acclimatization will improve performance at altitude, the body begins to deteriorate once you go above about 5,500 m (18,000 ft). This high-altitude deterioration is cumulative and only reversible upon descent. This is why almost all expedition base camps are below 5,500 m. Symptoms of high-altitude deterioration are weight loss (including muscle wasting), lack of appetite, lethargy, and loss of will.[359] High-altitude deterioration was a significant problem during the war in Kashmir, where Indian and Pakistani soldiers were stationed for long periods at 6,000 m and higher. The armies now limit the exposure of soldiers to these high altitudes to a much shorter time period.

The higher you go, the faster the deterioration occurs. The highest standard camps on the biggest peaks are at 7,800 to 8,000 m (Kangchenjunga, K2, and Everest South Col) and 8,300 m (Everest North Ridge). The standard procedure is to spend no more than 48 hours at that elevation (including the summit attempt). With supplemental oxygen, that time can be extended. On K2 in 1986, seven climbers spent five nights without supplemental oxygen at 7,900 m in a storm; only two survived. In contrast, a couple of months can be spent at 6,000 m before deterioration forces most people to descend and recuperate.

How Quickly Do You Deacclimatize after Return to Lower Altitudes?

Frankly, nobody knows. Deacclimatization (of ventilatory characteristics, at least) may involve different mechanisms than acclimatization.[37] Ward,[360] citing anecdotal evidence, suggests that acclimatization falls off rapidly over a two- to three-week period. Hultgren[172] cites studies that concluded that the chance of high-altitude pulmonary edema (HAPE) upon reascent to altitude increases after a descent of as little as five days. Beidleman[37] found that acclimatization in a number of characteristics, such as saturated oxygen (SaO_2), was retained for at least eight days after descent. Excess red blood cells degrade rapidly after descent to low altitude,[206] though one report states that it might take six weeks for red blood cell count to return to normal after several weeks of acclimatization.[360] Beidleman[37] summarized other studies that suggest different aspects of acclimatization can be lost in as little as 4 days and as many as 45 days after descent to low altitude.

Similarly, there is speculation and anecdotal information (but little scientific data) to suggest that repeated trips to altitude over the years result in long-term, residual acclimatization.[45, 172] My suspicion is that this is more of a psychological acclimatization than a physical one. Experienced, elite high-altitude climbers are physiologically no different than normal folks.[257] Experience removes the fear of the unknown and brings a better appreciation of the nuances of altitude. Think of it as developing an economy of travel that minimizes the stresses of altitude.

AGE AND SEX

As with most medical research, neither women nor children are adequately represented in studies of the effects of altitude on the body. Adult males make the majority of visits to altitude (especially extreme altitudes). Increasing attention is being paid to the effects of both age and sex on all of the factors dealt with in this book, so new findings may change the recommendations presented here.

Sex

Women and men generally react similarly to hypoxia. For example, there are no differences between men and women in respiratory gas exchange,[259] load carriage,[305] or thermoregulation.[343] Given this overall conclusion, here are some examples of differences between the sexes. Women show a slower rate of respiratory muscle fatigue than men,[133] which agrees with other studies showing that women (matched for strength with men) fatigue more slowly. Women are more likely to develop hyponatremia (low sodium) than men.[329] While women are more likely to sustain injury on wilderness trips,[352, 302] sex has no impact on summit success or survival on Mount Everest.[171]

Women use less carbohydrate and more fat at altitude,[62] but utilization rates don't differ between the sexes at rest or during exercise at sea level.[149, 132] Women may use their arms differently while walking uphill[181] and use their legs differently during single-leg squats.[379] This may be a consequence of differences in the relative eccentric strengths of quadriceps and hamstrings in women and men.[241] Men and women may respond differently to stress.[306]

The Medical Commission of the Union Internationale des Associations d'Alpinisme/ International Mountaineering and Climbing Federation (UIAA), an international climbing group, has published medical recommendations for women traveling to altitude.[176] The commission notes that, compared to men, women have a lower incidence of HAPE, the same incidence of acute mountain sickness (AMS), and a higher incidence of swelling in hands and feet (peripheral edema) and that there are no data about the incidence of high-altitude cerebral edema (HACE). Menstrual cycles may be disrupted at altitude and may be eliminated by the use of oral contraceptives—a good idea, according to at least one female climber[384] and the practice of about a third of high-altitude climbers. Keep in mind that oral contraceptives increase your risk of deep-vein thrombosis,[167] which can occur on long plane flights and while tent-bound. There are numerous issues for pregnant women at altitude; consult Jean et al.[176] and discuss the issues with your doctor.

Jean et al.[176] make several suggestions for women traveling to altitude, which I summarize here:

- Have a clothing system that allows convenient urination and defecation.
- Have a workable system for urination in a tent: large ziplock bags, a widemouthed bottle, or a specialized device for urination.
- Shaving genital hair can aid with hygiene during menstruation during long expeditions.
- Have treatments available for urinary or vaginal infections.

Wolf[384] adds a couple of suggestions. Tampons can be hard to find in less-developed countries, and packing lists generally don't include brassieres (take at least two or three).

Women may face more psychological and social issues than physical problems when visiting some cultures. Become familiar with the cultures you're visiting (and the cultures of your traveling companions) so that there will be no surprises.

Older Travelers

Age is assumed to mean an obligatory decline in physical ability. While some declines may be inevitable, continued exercise can prevent the loss of much of your fitness and indeed is a key feature of continued success at altitude.[69] My observation is that the recovery

Giant groundsels greet the trekker at 4,000 m on Kilimanjaro.

period after strenuous exercise becomes longer with age, so adequate recuperation is important. Age does not seem to affect one's risk of altitude illness[360] and may even decrease the risk of acute mountain sickness.[123] On Everest, summit success is lower for climbers over 40 years old, and the risk of death is higher for climbers over 60 years old.[171] The older you are, the more likely that you will have other medical conditions that will affect your health and performance at altitude; a consultation with your physician may be appropriate for any wilderness travel if your health indicates.

Age confers a number of benefits for high-altitude travel. The impatience of youth has diminished, allowing you to "go with the flow" as needed, reducing stress levels. Experience (which often comes with age) allows you to conserve energy, while the inexperienced burn up unnecessary calories. You'll notice that I haven't mentioned any particular ages. That's because there are old 40-year-olds and young 40-year-olds; you know about what your effective age is based on your health and level of long-term physical activity. Many of the highest peaks have been climbed by individuals over 60 years old, and exceptional levels of fitness are not necessarily required.[186]

Children

The best summary on children at altitude is by Pollard et al.[266] However, this paper is concerned primarily with altitude illness and doesn't deal much with other issues. These authors conclude the following:

- The incidence of altitude illness seems to be about the same in children and adults.
- There is no established maximum altitude for children; however, ascents above 3,000 m (10,000 ft) should be considered carefully for young children (< 3 years). The body's response to hypoxia may be age-dependent.[389]
- The effect of long-term altitude exposure on growth and development is not known.
- Infants and young children (< 8 years) can't adequately describe their symptoms to you.
- Infants are more susceptible to cold than older children.

In general, children are more susceptible than adults to cold temperatures.[248]

If you plan to travel with children to a nonwilderness altitude destination (ski area, day hikes), keep the kids well-hydrated and watch for unusual behaviors. Ask verbal children to describe their symptoms and use the Children's Lake Louise Scoring System for AMS (Appendix C) to monitor preverbal children. Another example of a score sheet modified for children can be found in Southard et al.[328] Don't hesitate to descend or seek treatment.

If your travel will take you to the wilderness or to remote areas in less-developed countries, obtain a copy of Pollard et al.[266] and Yaron et al.[388] and discuss them with your doctor. If you have an infant, see Niermeyer.[247] It is especially important to discuss proper dosages of medications. And keep in mind that millions of children live at altitude without any serious problems. Be careful, be prepared, but don't be hypersensitive.

ACCLIMATIZATION STRATEGIES

There are many possible strategies that will allow for proper acclimatization. The strategy that will work for you will depend on your goal, your body, and the weather. While there is no single correct way to acclimatize, there are many ways to go wrong. After considering preacclimatization, I'll make some comments according to the type of activity and the style of travel.

Preacclimatization

In the past 10 years an industry has bloomed around the desire to sleep, train, and live "at altitude" without really being at altitude. This industry has arisen not to help the altitude traveler, but to help the competitive athlete. As you ponder the benefits of preacclimatization, remember that athletes and travelers have two very different goals. The goal of the athlete is to gain a competitive edge during competition at low altitude. The goal of the traveler is to shorten the acclimatization period required to attain a goal at altitude, due to a lack of time or other logistical issue. However, both assume that altitude exposure will lead to changes that lead to increased oxygen uptake, so all studies are at least partially applicable to high-altitude travelers.

Prior to your primary trip to altitude, there are a number of options available to help you preacclimatize. Your need for preacclimatization will be unique, so the solution will be unique as well. The possible options are as follows:

- No preacclimatization
- Experience short periods of hypoxia during the day (at rest or with exercise; live low, train high)
- Use of a hypoxia tent for sleeping (live high, train low)
- Occasional short trips to higher altitude (e.g., weekends)
- Pretrip excursion for preacclimatization (live high, train high)

The middle three options can be labeled intermittent hypoxia because periods of hypoxia are interspersed with periods of normoxia. There is currently a lot of research being done on intermittent hypoxia, and there is still a lot of uncertainty about what strategies actually work. Much of the research is being kept under wraps by both industry and national sports organizations[267, 299] because of the potential competitive advantages gained from altitude training by athletes.

Because there are an infinite number of ways to achieve intermittent hypoxia, it's very difficult to summarize the effects of different strategies and compare studies. Almost all of these studies are concerned with improving low-altitude athletic performance in the shortest time and with the least effort. From the perspective of the altitude traveler, these studies are interesting because they more clearly define the minimum altitude/hypoxia exposure and duration of exposure needed to induce acclimatization.

If we look at changes in athletic performance, the maximum gain seen from any of these strategies will be about a 1% increase in speed.[139] While that can make the difference between a gold medal and no medal at the Olympics, it's unlikely you will notice that performance difference during your trip to altitude. Instead, the acclimatization will allow you to perform well at higher altitudes more quickly.

There are three different classes of intermittent hypoxia that can be used to preacclimatize. Let's look at some of the evidence for each.

Hypoxia during sleep. This is often called "sleep high, train low," and the most accessible approach is to use an altitude (hypoxia) tent at night. The theory is that the body gains acclimatization by sleeping in hypoxia, while training at low altitude allows for more effective muscular and cardiovascular conditioning. Although there has been considerable study of this technique, there is still disagreement over the mechanisms leading to improved performance, and even whether it improves performance at all.[139, 205, 250] Some researchers suggest that the minimum exposure needed to raise red cell mass and hemoglobin content of the blood is 12 hours per day for at least three weeks at 2,000 m or higher.[299]

I've never used a hypoxia tent and so can't comment on the experience. An important issue is the quality of sleep while using the device. Sleep quality in a hypoxia tent varies significantly among individuals,[265] so it would be prudent to try before you buy. The smaller ones are the size of a mountain tent, but it is possible to buy larger tents that allow you to enclose your bed. The truly wealthy can have their bedrooms sealed and turned into a hypoxia chamber. The amount of oxygen in the air is manipulated, allowing you to set the "altitude" used for sleeping. If you think about using the smaller tents, don't forget that you can't just pop out to use the toilet. There are several companies that offer these hypoxia tents, and rentals are available.

A climber takes an acclimatization hike above Ghunsa, Nepal.

Daytime hypoxia. Short bouts of hypoxia (a few minutes to a few hours) over a period of days or weeks might be useful for preacclimatization. The hypoxia can be experienced while resting or while exercising and might be logistically easier to handle than sleeping in a hypoxia tent.

The results of the research are confusing, to say the least. A natural group of test subjects is airline pilots, who spend many hours a week at altitudes between 5,000 and 8,000 ft. These folks don't show any change in red blood cell volume or hemoglobin levels, though there might be other acclimatory changes.[172] A review of earlier research[267] showed that short bouts of hypoxia with exercise can lead to ventilatory acclimatization.

Red blood cell production increases under intermittent hypoxia while at rest (2 hours per day for 5 days at 3,800 m), but the increase is greater during chronic hypoxia.[125] At a molecular level, short-term hypoxia with exercise leads to an increase in the production of a number of enzymes in skeletal muscle and also increased time to exhaustion in an exercise test.[396] Exposure to 4 hours per day for 21 days at 4,300 m increased respiration rates and reduced the severity of AMS symptoms, regardless of the amount of exercise done during hypoxia.[35] Lots of research, lots of different results. Of course, different individuals will have different responses, further complicating the picture.[206]

Short trips to altitude. If you're lucky enough to live near a high-altitude destination, it's possible to take day trips (equivalent to daytime hypoxia; see discussion above) or spend a weekend up high. Bircher et al.[45] found that climbers who had more recently traveled to 3,000 m were less likely to contract AMS or HAPE at 4,559 m. They also found that the number of days spent above 3,000 m significantly influenced the chance of AMS and HAPE. Significant cardiovascular acclimatization is retained for 8 days after return to sea level following 16 days at 4,330 m.[37]

Like many other climbers, Anatoli Boukreev used short trips as part of his training strategy:

> To maintain a basic level of adjustment to altitude and to keep up endurance, my routine training includes rapid ascents on 3,000-to-4,000-meter-high peaks all year. (Boukreev 2001, p. 63)

Mark Twight[351] and others have used short trips to altitude for preacclimatization prior to quick ascents in Alaska.

Practical Advice

Preacclimatization requires time and/or money. Mechanical means (hypoxia tents) are expensive but convenient; spending time at altitude may be cheap but takes time. Those who live close to high altitude (e.g., in Denver) will have options that a person living in Iowa won't have. So your approach will have to fit your circumstances.

There are three issues that need to be considered: your goal trip (duration, maximum altitude, and ascent profile), the length of the deacclimatization period prior to reascent during your goal trip, and the preacclimatization options available to you. If you have to spend too long between the end of your preacclimatization and the return to altitude, your efforts will all be in vain. I wish I could give you a hard-and-fast rule here, but (1) everybody's different and (2) there has been almost no good research in the area. If your preacclimatization is strong (say, two to three weeks in an altitude tent at 3,500 m), then you probably have 7 to 10 days at low altitude before you will lose enough acclimatization to make the whole process useless.

For weekend trips it is certainly not worth the effort to preacclimatize; the same is true of almost any trip you might take to the Rockies or Alps. Your time and money would be better spent training, which won't help you acclimatize but will help you perform better than you would if you were weaker.

If I was near a high-altitude location (e.g., 8,000+ ft) and was planning a trip to Kilimanjaro, Aconcagua (or other South American mountain), the Mexican volcanoes, Elbrus, or

Denali, I would spend several days and nights immediately prior to departure at altitudes over 8,000 ft, then get back up to that altitude as soon as possible after arrival at my destination (three days' deacclimatization at the most). Frankly, these trips to 6,000 to 7,000 m peaks are the greatest challenge from the standpoint of acclimatization. The trips are too short (5 to 15 days) to allow full acclimatization, and the surrounding countryside is often too low to allow you to acclimatize while doing other things.

If preacclimatization at real altitude isn't convenient and you're reading this book, you probably don't need to preacclimatize using an altitude tent or other short exposures to hypoxia. Scheduling a realistic itinerary with some spare time is your best strategy. For trekkers, it's relatively cheap to add a couple of days to the walk. Schedule these either early in the trek (and above 2,500 m) or after difficult days, allowing your body to recover.

I'm extremely hesitant to encourage anyone who has not climbed to 8,000 m before to use preacclimatization to shorten the time spent on an expedition to one of these peaks. While acclimatization is important, it is not the only factor that will influence your performance at altitude (refer back to Fig. 18).

Specific Situations

Regardless of your travel plan, accept the fact that it *must* be flexible. Most altitude experiences involve travel in the mountains, and mountains have unpredictable weather. The weather has a nasty habit of getting in the way of a finely tuned plan. Deal with it by being flexible. Even more important is to accept the fact that your body (or a teammate's) may simply be unable to deal with your planned ascent profile. I hope that I've convinced you that we are all different from each other; failure to acclimatize in a given time isn't a weakness, it's just a fact of life for some people. In all of the examples below, I'll assume that you are ascending from low altitude, without prior acclimatization.

Day Hikes/Climbs

These trips do not involve overnight stays at high altitude and probably account for the vast majority of all altitude experiences in North America and Europe. Since exposure to altitude is limited to a few hours, most people don't acclimatize completely unless they make multiple trips up high and sleep high as well.

If you are working toward a goal that will require acclimatization, such as a high-speed alpine climb, then you'll need to sleep above 2,500 m/8,000 ft for as many nights as possible prior to your attempt. Sleeping at lower elevations will limit your acclimatization even if you are traveling high during the day. Although technical climbers may find it more fun to do low-altitude day climbs, they will be better off loading up the packs and bagging some easy peaks while sleeping at a high camp for a few nights.

Acetazolamide (Diamox) is often handy on these short trips, but it's important to learn the proper dose for your body, as the side effects can be distracting. If you really must do a high-speed ascent with no prior acclimatization, it's OK to start taking acetazolamide a couple of days prior to the start of your ascent, then continue taking it while at altitude.

Personally, I don't take it unless I develop a headache that won't respond to ibuprofen. The only time prophylactic use of dexamethasone is warranted is for rescuers or others who absolutely must ascend to very high elevations on short notice.[312] These drugs are discussed in more detail in Chapter 5.

Overnight Backpacking Trips

A multiday trip in the Sierras or Rockies will seldom require preacclimatization. The best strategy is to adapt a conservative approach to both altitude gained and distance walked the first one to four days to minimize the potential for altitude illness and general discomfort. An itinerary that takes you rapidly from low altitude to 10,000 to 12,000 ft for several days and nights has the potential to cause problems.

Trekking

Trekking is similar to a backpacking trip, though it's usually at higher altitude and you're carrying a lighter pack. The good news is that the ascent profile on any standard trekking route should be reasonable; the bad news is that everyone is different, and you might still have trouble with altitude. Unlike a self-led backpacking trip, a trek is usually led by somebody else, involves members you don't know, and has a staff that will have some indirect (but important) influence over decisions.

A novice trekker will be traveling to altitudes never before experienced, in a culture never before experienced, eating strange food, and conversing in a polyglot of languages. The new and higher altitudes increase the chance of altitude illness, and the social system can impede proper treatment.

Before signing on the dotted line, ask some important questions. How many guides will be on your trek? How experienced are your guides in recognizing and treating altitude illness? What medications are carried on the trek? How old are these drugs? If a person needs to leave the trek due to altitude illness, will the escort have the skills and supplies to diagnose and treat further illness? Is there a satellite phone (or cell phone where appropriate) with the group? Will helicopter rescue be available if necessary? Is there a chance that the entire trek could be canceled due to health problems of a member or guide?

Much depends on the skill of your head guide. If you're reading this, it's safe to assume that you are willing to take some personal responsibility for your own health. I would carry a personal first-aid kit with the drugs to treat altitude illness and instructions on how and when to use them. It's very important, however, to keep your group leader clearly informed as to your health. If your leader asks, "How are you this morning?" you don't say, "Fine." You say, "I slept OK, but my pee was dark yellow and I have a headache, so I took 125 mg of acetazolamide and drank a liter of water."

If somebody does get sick, it may be necessary for the group to change its itinerary. This is equivalent to a climbing team aborting the climb to aid a teammate. It happens, but rarely, so you might have to put on your happy face and help out with the rescue. Your best defense is a good trip cancellation insurance policy.

If you get sick, it's important to be comfortable with the diagnosis and the treatments. If you're not, you need to speak up and demand satisfaction. The most dangerous aspect of a trek is the tension between staying on schedule and allowing a sick person to recover. A person with HAPE or HACE should never continue to ascend. There is one exception to this— sometimes a short ascent (to the top of a pass, for example) will then allow a rapid descent to better care. The sick person should not be left with a nontrained person while the trained guide continues ahead with the main group. If necessary, demand the satellite phone or cell phone and call home, or call the trekking agency office to demand proper care.

Climbing Expeditions

Climbing expeditions have an ascent of one or more peaks or climbing routes as their goal. Any associated trekking is usually just a way to get to and from the peak. There are many possible styles that an expedition may adopt:

Expedition style. Multiple camps are established over time by carrying loads progressively up the mountain. Acclimatization takes place by the continual ascent and descent over time and the gradual increase in the maximum elevation reached.

Capsule style. Only one camp is established, and this camp is gradually moved up the hill as the route is established. This style is more common on technical terrain, where carrying many loads is difficult and campsites are rare. Supplies may be ferried up the hill and cached, but only one set of tents, sleeping bags, and other camp gear is available.

Pure alpine style. Again, there is only one camp, but the ascent is continuous; you camp where you stop at the end of the day. On the highest peaks this is sometimes called superalpine style to indicate the increased scale and difficulty of continuous ascents of the highest peaks. The epitome of superalpine style might be the audacious ascent of Everest in 1986 by Jean Troillet and Erhard Loretan. They spent five weeks at 5,800 m, took a couple of side trips to 6,500 m, then set out on a 43-hour round trip to the top of Everest via the North Face. Some[164] have confused alpine style with a reckless "rush" up a peak before one is acclimatized. True practitioners of this style are careful to acclimatize properly prior to their ascent (see below).

There are hybrid strategies as well. Perhaps you establish fixed camps on the lower part of the route, then go capsule-style to the top of your route. Caches can be left all along the way, blurring the distinction between capsule and expedition style. Strictly speaking, pure alpine style doesn't allow the climber to set foot on the peak prior to the attempt on the summit, but there are tricks that are played to finesse this requirement.[115]

Your acclimatization strategy will depend on a number of factors: the altitude of the peak, the length of the climbing route, the technical difficulty, the ability and experience of the climbers, and the length and altitude of the approach. Given the obvious differences between a hike up a high-altitude volcano such as Aconcagua and a desperate technical ascent of the South Face of Lhotse, it should be clear that a single acclimatization strategy doesn't exist for climbers.

There is a venerable rule that you should gain no more than 300 m (1,000 ft) between campsites, and that every two or three days the sleeping altitude should remain the same for a second night. This amount of altitude gain will prevent altitude sickness in most people.[360] In the real world this rule is commonly ignored; Kilimanjaro (5,895 m) is commonly climbed in five days (with an elevation gain of over 4,000 m), Aconcagua (6,962 m) is usually climbed in a week, and in 2006 I met two Argentineans who climbed Gasherbrum II (8,035 m) 10 days after arriving at Base Camp. These faster rates of ascent are clearly possible and are seductive due to the cost savings involved in a shorter trip, but they can also lead to the failure to accomplish your goals (including staying alive).

There is value to a longer approach to Base Camp. Driving to Base Camp (on Cho Oyu, for example) leads to a fast ascent with no exercise. After arrival, impatience and inactivity lead to the desire for a quick further ascent and set the stage for altitude illness. If you drive to 4,000 m or above, count on taking a couple of days at Base Camp prior to any further ascent. If you walk from a lower elevation, you should still take a day after arriving at Base Camp. There's always plenty to do to get camp organized.

Ascents of lower (< 7,000 m), easier peaks are often undertaken as more or less continuous ascents. On Kilimanjaro you will usually climb up each day (with a possible rest day) until you reach the summit. On Aconcagua or Denali you will often carry a load to the next camp, then descend to sleep. The next day you'll climb up and sleep at the higher camp, capsule style. A rest (acclimatization) day or two may be interspersed in the ascent.

On higher peaks this constant upward advance has been found to be counterproductive due to the rapid deterioration that sets in at higher altitudes. Recall that deterioration sets in at about 5,500 m and accelerates rapidly above 7,000 m; only a few days can be spent at 8,000 m. As a result, the current tactic is to make short forays of two to four days to higher altitude, then retreat to Base Camp for rest. After three or four of these short trips to progressively higher altitude, the typical climber is acclimatized enough to reach the summit.

An example of this strategy is provided by Scott and MacIntyre.[316] For a technical route on an 8,000 m peak, they suggest two presummit acclimatization forays. The first would be for two or three nights with a maximum sleeping altitude of 6,400 m and involve a climb of 300+ m above the highest camp. After a rest at Base Camp, a second trip would take several days and reach a sleeping altitude of 7,000 m and involve a couple additional nights at 6,000 to 6,500 m. Again, a climb above 7,000 m will be beneficial. This is very similar to the routine used by guided ascents of Everest and as proposed by Boukreev.[57] If one is climbing pure alpine style, these acclimatization forays need to be somewhere other than your proposed route to remain ethically pure.

The very highest peaks (> 8,500 m) pose special problems. Is it necessary to do a further acclimatization trip to 8,000 m? The consensus, at least for ascents with supplemental oxygen, appears to be no. Venables[354] summarizes a number of expeditions that successfully climbed Everest without supplemental oxygen. The highest altitudes reached during acclimatization were 6,500 to 7,400 m. However, I would take an additional excursion to

Trekking in bad weather isn't unusual, so prepare yourself mentally beforehand.

7,400 m (to sleep) and if possible climb another 300 to 400 m higher before descending to Base Camp for a rest prior to the summit attempt. Boukreev proposed a similar strategy to his partners on an ascent of K2. His partners disagreed (and later died).

Boukreev[57] states that the altitude of the highest camp and the highest altitude for acclimatization are calculated by determining the height one can gain and lose in 10 hours. Subtract that height from the summit altitude; that determines the height of the final camp. This allows about six to seven hours for ascent and three to four hours for descent. Frankly, few can move as fast as Boukreev, so the number of hours spent on summit day will be longer, in the range of 14 to 18 hours. This, of course, exposes you to more danger, but an unrealistic notion of your abilities is even more dangerous.

Any time you ascend to a camp (other than on the summit attempt) you should ascend a bit higher on that day to aid acclimatization and, if possible, carry some gear up toward the next camp. Even 100 to 200 m will aid acclimatization. The day after the arrival at a new sleep altitude is often a rest day, so there is a lot of mental inertia to overcome if you plan this further ascent on that rest day.[57]

Drugs as Aids to Acclimatization and Performance

Whether it's bottled oxygen or a pill, people have been trying to find a magic bullet to "cure" hypoxia for ages. A pill is preferred because it's lighter and cheaper. Prior to the first ascent of Makalu, the French experimented with hormones to speed acclimatization, but these not used on the mountain.[120] Ergogenic aids (these increase performance) will allow the body to do more than it might otherwise. Sleep is a problem at altitude, and sleeping pills have been used over the years.

Herman Buhl took Pervitin (a methamphetamine) during his epic solo first ascent of Nanga Parbat. He speculated as to its effect:

> Doubtfully, I swallowed two tablets and waited for them to take effect; nothing seemed to happen and I felt no benefit. Or was it that they had already done their work and that without them I would never have been able to get up again? You never know with tablets! (Buhl 1956, p. 277)

Tom Hornbein gave Dexedrine (an amphetamine) to Lute Jurstad and Barry Bishop during their descent of Everest in 1963.[159] While these drugs may still be used, they have severe side effects, including loss of judgment and other behavioral modifications.[43] I see no need to take these types of medications with me.

Nutritional supplements may help lessen fatigue at low altitudes, but there is no single substance that appears to be effective.[224] At high altitudes, eating simple or complex carbohydrates (sugars and starches) may improve brain function.[272] In particular, branched chain amino acids (BCAA) may help prevent muscle loss during longer trips to high altitude.[309]

Sleeping pills and other downers used to be taken regularly by top high-altitude climbers. Bonington[52] took 100 Valium, 1,000 Tuinal, and 1,000 Seconal (various sedatives) on the first ascent of the South Face of Annapurna. Messner took Mogadon (nitrazepam, a sleeping pill) and Habeler took Valium during their first oxygen-free ascent of Everest.[142] During the first ascent of Everest, George Lowe took a sleeping pill on the Lhotse Face; the next morning he could hear everything, but his body refused to function.[256] For her second bivouac at 8,300 m on K2, Wanda Rutkiewicz[300] took two and a half Mogadon sleeping pills and had difficulty keeping her balance on descent the next day. Most sleeping pills also depress respiration. For those reasons most sleeping pills are dangerous at altitude and are really not necessary; some modern sleeping meds might not be as harmful.[43, 246]

I'm not going to cover the vast (if uncertain) realm of ergogenic (performance-enhancing) aids; see Twight and Martin[351] for that topic. There is one issue that involves both response to hypoxia and performance: the increase in pulmonary artery pressure that occurs during hypoxia (Chapter 3). If this pulmonary hypertension could be reduced, perhaps oxygen saturation (and performance) would increase.

Jean Troillet used nifedipine during his 43-hour round trip of Everest in 1986.[354] This drug is a potent vasodilator and is used as a field treatment for HAPE (Chapter 5). It's tricky to use and certainly not a good choice for an ergogenic aid. But a newer class of drugs, which includes sildenafil (Viagra) and tadalafil (Cialis), only dilates blood vessels in certain areas—including your lungs.

Sildenafil lowers pulmonary artery pressures and increases maximum workload at altitude.[130] It improved cycling performance in a 6 km time trial at simulated altitude of

3,874 m, increasing SaO_2 and decreasing times by 15%.[166] No improvements were seen in performance at sea level, and individuals were split evenly between responders (who improved their times by 39%) and nonresponders (who averaged only a 1% improvement).

I anticipate much more research and casual use of these drugs over the next few years. There are few side effects, and the potential benefits could be significant. We then only need to worry about the ethics of drug-assisted ascents. Where do we draw the line?

KEY CONCEPTS

1. Acclimatization to altitude involves a series of changes in the way the body functions to allow for more efficient use of the oxygen available in the thinner air of altitude.
2. Some changes occur very quickly, some very slowly.
3. Different people acclimatize at different rates.
4. A number of factors influence how quickly you acclimatize; in general, the longer you spend at altitude, the better you are acclimatized.
5. At altitudes higher than about 5,500 m, the body will begin to deteriorate; the higher you go, the faster the deterioration.
6. Men and women acclimatize equally well. Children who are too young to verbalize symptoms of altitude illness need to be watched carefully.
7. Preacclimatization using hypoxia exposures at low altitudes is unlikely to be cost-effective for most travelers.
8. The acclimatization strategy used will depend on the type of activity, maximum altitude to be reached, and style of ascent (in the case of climbers).

Altitude Illness

This book is *not* a stand-alone resource for the diagnosis and treatment of altitude illness. There are various books out there that are written by medical professionals who are qualified to dispense medical advice. A fine, very compact book that I carry with me is by Bezruchka.[43] My goal here is to outline the various types of altitude illness, present some practical issues involved, and provide some ideas for your high-altitude first-aid kit. Overall, education has helped reduce the prevalence of some forms of altitude illness;[123] this is clearly a case of knowledge being a powerful weapon.

There are three major illnesses that are caused directly by altitude: acute mountain sickness (AMS), high-altitude pulmonary edema (HAPE), and high-altitude cerebral edema (HACE). The British spelling of *edema* is *oedema,* so the acronyms would be HAPO and HACO. There are other altitude illnesses that are more common in long-term residents (e.g., chronic mountain sickness) that I will not discuss here. See Leon-Velarde et al.[203] for more information.

Altitude illness can kill, and it can kill quickly. Let's consider the fate of Vladimir Bashkirov, a 45-year-old Russian with over 28 years of high-altitude experience and seven 8,000 m summits (including Everest three times). His friend Anatoli Boukreev spoke with Bashkirov during an ascent of Lhotse (8,516 m):

> *"How are you?" I [Boukreev] asked.*
>
> *"I didn't sleep well. I had a low fever during the night, and now I feel a little tired," he responded.... Encountering Bashkirov about thirty meters below the top, protected from the wind in the couloir, I asked how he was feeling.*
>
> *"Not too well," he replied, "but as leader of the expedition I need to wait for the slower ones, Bagomolov and Pershin, who are coming. Waiting will give me time to do some filming for my sponsors."*

...Bashkirov waited another two hours for his climbers. He did not make it back to camp. When I spoke to the other Russians about his descent, they said he simply became ill, then lost consciousness. His condition deteriorated [to death] even though he was supplied with bottled oxygen. (Boukreev 2001, p. 216)

Trekkers pause on the way to K2 Base Camp, Pakistan.

Here we have a classic tale: symptoms present prior to sudden collapse, the impact of secondary factors (leadership, sponsors), and likely some hubris attained through decades of successful decision making at extreme altitude. Better judgment was shown by Greg Child on the final summit ridge of Broad Peak (8,047 m):

> We are nearly there, thirty minutes away. But my fears about what is happening to me double. A vicious headache rings in my ears and pounds at my temples, and a tingling in my arms grows so intense that my fingers curl into a tight fist, making it hard to grip my ice axe. My last shred of rational consciousness raises a cry of concern over the possibility of a stroke, or cerebral edema. But to articulate this to Pete is difficult, as speech and thought seem to have no link in my mind. (Child 1988, p. 98)

Child's partner, Pete Thexton, managed to get him down, and his symptoms subsided. In a cruel twist of fate, Thexton then developed HAPE and/or HACE and died on the descent.

Stories like these lead some to call altitude a "killer." Death occurs at altitude, but death occurs in the ocean, on the highways, and is the ultimate consequence of living. We now know enough about the variety of altitude illnesses and their treatment to shelve the "killer" concept next to the idea that mountains are inherently dangerous because of the dragons that live there.

ENCOUNTERING ILLNESS AT ALTITUDE

The general rule of thumb is to assume initially that any illness encountered at altitude is altitude illness. For example, there are many possible causes of vision problems, but there are very few of us who can do a proper diagnosis at altitude. So assume that it's altitude illness and proceed accordingly. A common symptom that is not associated with any form of altitude illness is diarrhea.

Physicians at Altitude

Dealing with life-threatening medical problems in the wilderness will be a challenge to even the best physicians.[180] Most physicians are not trained in the specifics of high-altitude medicine, so if you encounter a physician while you are at altitude, will he or she know how to deal with altitude illness? Don't count on it. Physicians from other countries can have the added impediment of a language barrier; they usually know some English but may not understand you well enough to deal with the nuances of diagnosis.

Sometimes the physician's response is startling. While I was at 5,200 m on Aconcagua, a young man suddenly fainted but immediately recovered. His vision then alternated between completely blurred and normal. We asked a nearby (non-English-speaking) doctor, whose diagnosis was, "No problem, no problem." We ignored that recommendation, and the climber was evacuated to Base Camp, where he was monitored for a couple of days in the medical tent. He then relapsed, nearly died, and was flown out. The "no problem" diagnosis was totally inappropriate and would likely have led to the climber's death if he had not descended. To be fair, physicians have equivalent difficulties with patients,[138] so be a good patient if the situation arises.

Physicians pose a more subtle danger—they may be more likely to ignore their own symptoms and succumb to serious altitude illness. In one study, three of the seven bodies autopsied after fatal altitude illness were those of physicians.[98] While I hesitate to speculate about the causes of this, I think that physicians are trained to ignore their own health in pursuit of their duties; a doctor who's afraid to enter a house full of infectious people wouldn't last long in the profession. In this case, the cause of illness—hypoxia—is environmental rather than infectious, so the physician doesn't have any acquired immunity from prior exposure.

Don't get the impression that all doctors are problematic at altitude. Dr. Deb Robertson saved the life of one of my teammates on Broad Peak in 2004, and the literature is chock-full of similar examples of excellent, selfless medical care. Infection, injury, and other illnesses are areas where a physician should normally be able to provide quality care regardless of altitude.

Physicians are seldom experts in rescue and evacuation. Those without wilderness experience may not realize the dangers and difficulty of moving an injured person through rough terrain. An urban injury that would involve a cervical collar and backboard might require the traveler to walk down the mountain. In the end, experienced travelers should consult any available physician but in most cases must make final decisions about rescue and evacuation.

If you are traveling with a physician, you should inquire about his or her training in altitude medicine before you start. Ask about the medications and equipment the physician plans to bring, and compare that list to the list of recommended medications in books on mountain medicine.[332, 378] Ask how many cases of AMS, HAPE, and HACE that the physician has seen. A vague response should set off very loud alarms in your head. Remember, the physician on your team will be in charge in the event of an illness, and it's hard to disagree with him or her when you're sick. Just be a smart consumer of medical care, educate yourself, and be tactful but forceful if you disagree with the diagnosis or treatment. This is especially true if the counsel is to delay descent and wait for the condition to resolve itself. All this being said, I'd much rather travel with a physician than without one.

A General Approach to the Potentially Ill

Even experts can have problems diagnosing and treating altitude illness.[138] There are people who feel sick and who are actually sick, people who don't feel sick but who are actually sick, and people who feel sick but who aren't sick. The last group may be irritating to teammates but isn't in any danger, unlike the middle group. As a member of a team, you have two responsibilities: (1) Be honest with yourself and others about the true state of your health, and (2) observe the state of health of your teammates and act on those observations when necessary.

You have to know the major signs and symptoms of altitude illness. Period. I'll summarize these in a moment. You don't have to know how to diagnose a particular altitude illness; that's why you carry a reference booklet in your pack.

For those on treks or expeditions, porters are particularly difficult subjects. It's a tradition among porters to complain about headaches, stomachaches, and hunger to any member they see. If you give them pills to treat their headaches, they will likely stick the pills in their pockets and trade them to another porter. However, there are porters with true medical problems that could benefit from treatment. Since 90% of the time their complaints don't require treatment, it's easy to become calloused to their complaints. If you have a good translator, you can quickly determine their general condition and make an informed decision.

PRIMARY SYMPTOMS OF ALTITUDE ILLNESS

Here's a list of the primary signs and symptoms* of altitude illness. There are others, but you need to keep these in an easily accessible drawer in your mind.

- Loss of appetite and/or nausea
- Dizziness or light-headedness
- Poor sleep
- Headache
- Mental abnormalities
- Lack of coordination (ataxia)
- Excessive fatigue
- Excessive shortness of breath

The first three are often experienced by those with altitude illness but can also occur for many other reasons. The last five should always be assumed to be caused by altitude illness until proven otherwise.

If you or another person may have altitude sickness, consult (1) a qualified physician, (2) a suitable reference (such as Bezruchka[43]), or (3) the best qualified individuals around. Generally, you'll be doing all three at once.

PREVALENCE OF ALTITUDE ILLNESS

There are different types of high-altitude travel, so it stands to reason that there are different risks of altitude illness associated with each. In a study of trekkers in Nepal, there were only 10 deaths due to altitude illness out of 275,950 trekkers over a four-year period.[320] There were 40 trekker deaths in all during the period. Of the 10 who died of altitude illness,

---

* Symptoms are reported by the patient, while signs are observed by another. I won't differentiate between the two.

80% were members of an organized trekking group. This is even more significant when you note that only 40% of trekkers traveled in an organized group. Among these trekkers, death was six times more likely in organized groups than in trekkers not part of an organized group. This is due to the inflexible nature of group schedules and to the social dynamics in such groups (see Chapters 9 and 11). At extremely high altitudes, the death rate has been about 11% for individuals descending from the summit of K2 without supplemental oxygen;[170] altitude illness was not the direct cause of all of these deaths.

The various types of altitude illness differ in their rate of occurrence. Mild AMS is common; 50% or more of trekkers and expeditionary climbers may experience this. Severe AMS and HACE occur in 1% to 2% of the individuals in the same groups, and HAPE is also found in about 2% of these individuals. It would not be surprising to encounter somebody with HACE or HAPE on a busy trek or mountain. I've seen numerous cases of HACE but only one clear case of HAPE over the years.

RISK FACTORS FOR ALTITUDE ILLNESS

Certain factors will contribute to your chance of developing an altitude illness. Rapid ascent (poor acclimatization) is the most likely cause; the rule of thumb is to increase sleeping elevation no more than an average of 300 m (1,000 ft) per day. Heavy exertion (and the dehydration that goes with it) is also a risk factor. Previous altitude illness increases your risk of contracting it again, while recent time at altitude reduces it.[310] New Zealand mountaineer Gary Hall contracted HACE on K2 and survived, only to die of HACE the next year on Dhaulagiri. Another famous Kiwi, Sir Edmund Hillary, never again climbed high after Everest because he apparently contracted HACE on two subsequent expeditions.[154] There is almost certainly a genetic component to susceptibility, but we don't know the details. People with abnormal lung circulation can be more susceptible to HAPE.[311] Two risk factors that haven't been demonstrated by researchers but have been implicated by climbers: illness, especially a respiratory infection,[296] and high levels of indirect stresses.[90, 91] As always, there is individual variation in susceptibility to altitude illness. At this point, there isn't good evidence to show that these differences are genetic.[298]

Acute Mountain Sickness (AMS)

AMS is a term that describes an illness that varies among individuals. The primary symptoms are headache, loss of appetite, nausea (and possibly vomiting), sleep problems, and lethargy. Appendix B is a worksheet that you can use to evaluate your AMS symptoms. I find it useful to glance at this worksheet daily as I gain chunks of altitude. It serves as a useful check on your state of health. As you look at this worksheet, consider the state of your teammates as well.

Most of us will suffer from mild AMS at some point during our time in the mountains. The presence and severity of AMS are related to the rate of ascent and hydration[26] and by exercise soon after arrival at altitude.[287] While AMS may be caused by brain swelling,[286] there are still many questions about the origins of the illness.

High-Altitude Cerebral Edema (HACE)

HACE is a life-threatening illness that requires immediate treatment. We still don't understand the mechanisms that lead to AMS and HACE, but it is thought that there is a progression from mild AMS to severe AMS to HACE. HACE may result from a disruption of the blood–brain barrier, leading to fluid accumulation and cerebral malfunction.[143] Individuals with HAPE have a higher chance of developing HACE than those without HAPE.[143] HACE usually starts as AMS and progresses to HACE (and/or HAPE) over 24 to 36 hours. This is not to say that AMS *will* progress to HACE/HAPE. Sometimes HACE can arise without previous symptoms, but that's rare.

Brain function is always affected by HACE, but the actual effects are not predictable. Severe lethargy, ataxia (loss of coordination or balance while standing or walking), memory problems, problems speaking, other mental/judgment issues, and vision problems (including blindness) have been recorded by many climbers.[63, 64, 67, 296] While some of these are likely a result of HACE, there are several other neurological causes of temporary blindness or vision disturbance.[28] Since most of us aren't neurologists, the only recourse is to treat any of these disturbances as HACE.

High-Altitude Pulmonary Edema (HAPE)

Peripheral edema, or fluid buildup in the face or limbs, is not unusual at altitude.

Pulmonary edema is excess fluid in the lungs. This fluid leaks from the capillaries, enters the intercellular spaces, and fills the air sacs (alveoli). Recall that a response to hypoxia is pulmonary hypertension; the vessels in the lungs constrict, raising the blood pressure in that circuit of blood flow. This high pulmonary artery pressure likely causes leakage of fluids into the spaces between cells. If these fluids are not carried away by the lymph system, the lungs will lose their ability to serve as the interface between the atmosphere and the blood. While Aleister Crowley[89] diagnosed an "edema of both lungs" in a teammate in 1902, the concept of HAPE wasn't recognized until the 1960s. Individuals susceptible to HAPE show greater pulmonary hypertension at altitude, greater pulmonary hypertension during sea-level exercise, and have smaller lungs than individuals not susceptible to HAPE (summarized by Bärtsch et al.[23]).

Those with HAPE have trouble catching their breath and rapidly fatigue upon exercise. There may be chest pain and symptoms of AMS. The observer may note a rapid heartbeat (over 110 at rest), increased respiration rate (over 30 breaths/min at rest), and higher body temperature. Rales or crackles in the base of the lungs (a stethoscope will be needed) may be the earliest sign of HAPE.[360] Compare the color of the lips and fingernails to a normal

CLOSE ENCOUNTERS WITH HACE

I encountered HACE on Broad Peak in both 2004 and 2005. In 2004, five climbers from my group spent a couple of nights at 6,500 m, then climbed to about 7,200 m. The next morning, the leader noticed that two climbers were kneeling while they urinated. He quickly realized that the two climbers couldn't stand up and likely had HACE. One of them could walk, but they had to descend nearly 500 m to reach the top of the fixed ropes while dragging/lowering one now-comatose climber. Other teams on the mountain helped with the evacuation and supplied a doctor, rescuers, rescue equipment, oxygen, drugs, and satellite phones. After two days they reached the glacier (5,100 m), and the patient with severe HACE was still only slightly responsive. The next morning the helicopter arrived and flew the victims down to Skardu. Once the chopper flew below 4,000 m, the severely ill victim quickly became responsive. The doctors in Skardu diagnosed exhaustion (and no altitude illness).

In 2005, bad weather meant that there was one possible summit day, and several climbers made it up to the false summit at 8,000 m. An Italian climber apparently developed HACE. He became separated from his partner on descent, and instead of returning to the high camp, the mentally confused HACE victim decided to bivouac in a crevasse and then head back up the next day. An American pair saw him the next morning, but due to language difficulties and the altitude (over 7,400 m), they didn't realize that he was ill. His Swiss partner went out that morning, climbed up to 7,600 m to find the Italian, then escorted him back down the mountain. This certainly saved his life.

This climber suffered HACE at 7,500 m; luckily, he had a partner who could rescue him.

person, as HAPE can lead to cyanosis (blueness) in the lips or fingernails in some individuals. Patients with HAPE will show little change as the illness gets worse, then suddenly deteriorate as the lungs fill with fluid.

A pulse oximeter may provide valuable information about HAPE. This device measures blood oxygen saturation (SaO_2), usually by clipping it to the index finger. Always measure a warm finger, and compare the patient's SaO_2 to that of others in the party. The actual value is usually less important than a significant deviation from the other members of the party.

Use the pulse oximeter to help diagnose HAPE.

If the patient is capable of some movement, let him or her rest for 10 to 15 minutes and check the patient's SaO_2. Now have the patient exercise enough to get fatigued (which may be fairly quickly) by walking uphill for 10 to 30 meters, then return. Immediately measure the SaO_2. If it drops more than 3% to 5% after exercise, suspect HAPE. Remember that SaO_2 will vary from measurement to measurement, so don't make too much of small differences.

There is evidence to suggest that it is possible to reascend after an episode of HAPE.[210] It's important to allow time for recovery and then begin a slow reascent with extra opportunities to rest. The ascent must be stopped if you experience any new symptoms of altitude illness. Be careful—this won't be possible for every HAPE victim.

High-Altitude Retinal Hemorrhage (High-Altitude Retinopathy, HAR)

The tiny blood vessels in the retina of the eye can burst, leading to bleeding in the retina. You won't notice this unless a vessel in the more visually sensitive part of the retina is affected. There's no way to prevent this, and it usually resolves by itself upon descent. It's more common at higher elevations; 82% of those climbing high on Everest had retinal hemorrhages, and 10% experienced changes in their vision.[213] Some climbers have lost some vision as a result of severe HAR. Once visual disturbances have occurred due to HAR, reascent in the future is not recommended.[213]

TREATMENTS FOR ALTITUDE ILLNESS

There are a variety of options for treatment of AMS, HAPE, and HACE. If an altitude illness doesn't resolve itself after descent and other treatment, you should suspect some other issue and seek further treatment. In the following discussion, I've noted which of the three illnesses the treatment applies to. Also note that drugs have a limited ability to tolerate environmental extremes,[195] so make sure your medical kit is replenished with fresh supplies as needed.

A CLOSE ENCOUNTER WITH HAPE

As we walked up the well-traveled Baltoro Glacier in 2005, a teammate encountered a porter who complained of headache and difficulty breathing. Luckily, the teammate was a professional rescue medic and not yet hardened to the constant complaints of the porters. As I approached, he yelled, "Find our liaison officer and call a helicopter! This porter has HAPE!" As I approached the porter, I could hear his lungs crackling from 3 ft away. He was cyanotic, breathing rapidly, and obviously in distress. The porter told us that he had been given a pill by another trekker, but he didn't know what the medication was.

We were faced with a real quandary. If the porter had already received the correct medication, a second dose could lead to a fatal crash in blood pressure. Without medication, he could easily die. Luckily, we knew that just a couple of hours behind us was a large *National Geographic* medical team with several doctors and the equipment to match. We sent a note down by porter, alerting the docs that a patient was on the way. Several porters carried our patient down the trail, almost at a run.

The docs got our message and rushed ahead with medical equipment. The patient was put in a Gamow bag (see below) for hours, and after a lot of medical attention, he lived. The physicians said that he had less than 30 minutes to live when they got to him. The porter had never been sick before and had made 16 trips to 5,100 m on the Baltoro Glacier, but he became ill on descent. Why not call the helicopter? Choppers don't fly for natives in most of these countries unless the members pay for the flight ($6,000 in this case).

Descent (all). Descent is the one treatment option that is almost always possible. In many ways it's the best option, as you are removing the original cause of the illness. The rule is to descend until symptoms are gone or to the last sleeping altitude where no symptoms were present. If a person has a severe illness, descend as low as possible, preferably to a hospital.

Hydration (AMS). Altitude headaches may be dehydration headaches, and the first signs of a headache should signal the need to down a liter or two of fluids. Nausea may prevent this, but constant sips of a palatable fluid should be taken if possible. If vomiting or other severe dehydration has occurred, try to get some sugar and electrolytes into the fluid as well.

Acetazolamide (Diamox) (all). A 125 mg dose twice a day prevents AMS symptoms,[25] though some advocate higher rates. There are side effects: tingling in the extremities, increased urination, and a temporary inability to taste the "fizz" in carbonated beverages. Personally, I find taking about 90 mg (three-quarters of a 125 mg tablet) is a low enough dose to minimize side effects. Acetazolamide may decrease exercise capacity and increase leg fatigue,[127] so using it when it's not necessary may reduce performance.

Acetazolamide will improve sleep in most cases,[366] which may be its most useful effect outside of reducing AMS symptoms.

Severe AMS (which will involve extreme fatigue and/or ataxia) should definitely be treated with acetazolamide and descent. There is no clear dividing line between AMS and HACE, so any mental involvement in AMS should be treated as HACE. If HAPE or HACE is suspected, give acetazolamide if the patient can swallow and retain the pills. Acetazolamide is a sulfa drug, so consult your doctor if you have had an adverse reaction to such drugs.

Aspirin (AMS). Headache may be relieved by aspirin.[70] Ibuprofen is also used to treat altitude headache. I find that neither works very well for me.

Dexamethasone (HACE). This is a powerful steroid that is useful in the treatment of HACE. Because severe HACE can prevent patients from taking oral medications, an injectable form should be available, along with the knowledge to use it. It appears to reduce pulmonary artery pressure and may help with HAPE,[214] and it reduces mental problems that may be associated with HACE.[198] Dexamethasone is also useful for rescue teams or others who must rapidly ascend to very high altitudes without acclimatization. It's also used by some as a performance aid at altitude, although in my opinion, and in the opinion of others, this is not ethical.[312] There are many possible side effects, such as immune suppression and psychosis. If you stop taking dexamethasone while at altitude, symptoms can return and be as bad as or worse than they were prior to taking "dex."

Nifedipine (HAPE). Nifedipine dilates blood vessels, including those in the lungs. This reduces pulmonary hypertension and reduces fluid entry into the lungs. The drawback is that blood pressure drops throughout the body, sometimes to the point of fainting. This can obviously be a problem. Self-administration of nifedipine is tricky as a result. See Bezruchka[43] for dosages and methods for safe administration.

Sildenafil (Viagra) and tadalafil (Cialis) (HAPE). Promising potential replacements for nifedipine are sildenafil and tadalafil. These relax blood vessels in the lungs as well as in the penis. A clinical trial showed that tadalafil is effective against HAPE,[214] and it's highly likely (but not proven) that sildenafil is effective as well. Both drugs reduce pulmonary hypertension without lowering overall systemic blood pressure.[284, 394] Self-administration is therefore much safer than with nifedipine.

Ginkgo biloba. Numerous studies have tested the effectiveness of the herbal medication ginkgo in preventing AMS. There really isn't any good evidence to support this idea.[21] Some work suggests that ginkgo supplements will reduce the severity of AMS symptoms.[129] That being said, I do take ginkgo at low altitude and have taken it at high altitude. It's unlikely to hurt you, but acetazolamide is far better for AMS.

Oxygen (severe AMS, HAPE, HACE). If rapid descent is not possible, then administration of supplemental oxygen is indicated. This is an expensive option, and many teams don't carry any oxygen due to the cost and weight. Emergency oxygen is carried by most responsible high-altitude expeditions, so even if you don't have any, somebody else might (but expect to pay a premium for it).

Hyperbaric bag (HACE, HAPE). Also called a Gamow (pronounced GAM-off) bag after its inventor, this is an airtight plastic bag with a zipper and a pump to inflate it. After the patient is put into the bag, it's sealed and inflated, effectively lowering the elevation and increasing SaO_2. You can't transport the patient in the bag unless you have a vehicle. The bag may not work as well for HAPE as it does for HACE,[43] and patients will be more comfortable if you raise the head end of the bag about 30 degrees.[103] Claustrophobia is a serious issue, and constant vigilance is necessary while the patient is in the bag. Bags can be rented; check the Web.

Pulse oximeter (all). Don't overestimate the value of a pulse oximeter. Sitting around the mess tent comparing SaO_2 values is a common pastime during expeditions. Pulse oximeters may overestimate (by a few percentage points) saturations at the low values experienced on high peaks[200, 341] and in individuals with dark skin pigments.[44] If you use a pulse oximeter, take your measurements at the same time every day and in the same position. If you take measurements in the morning before you get up, you can get a resting pulse and SaO_2 at the same time while you're nice and warm. The SaO_2 measurements can be used to assess your level of acclimatization, but only after you've accumulated some experience with the pulse oximeter. If an individual is receiving supplemental oxygen, it's necessary to wait for at least 20 minutes after the end of treatment before taking SaO_2 measurements, because breathing is temporarily stimulated by oxygen therapy.[243]

OTHER MEDICAL ISSUES AT ALTITUDE

Any medical problem that can arise at sea level can arise at altitude. Because the body is struggling to maintain homeostasis, a hidden preexisting condition might appear due to the unusual stress experienced by the body. While the rule is to treat anything that could be altitude illness as altitude illness, misidentifying a problem as altitude illness means that the proper treatment may not be given.[28] Such is the challenge of high altitude.

Basnyat et al.[28] examined a dozen non-HACE neurological problems that have arisen at high altitude, and I recommend that anyone traveling at extreme altitude read this paper. Neurological problems related to altitude illness will be preceded by the typical headache/nausea/fatigue of AMS, while those problems not related to altitude illness will generally occur rather suddenly and without the buildup of other symptoms. Bezruchka[43] contains a short discussion of several of these potential issues; case reports concerning global amnesia are provided by Litch and Bishop,[209] and cases of double vision are discussed by Shlim et al.[321]

Nonneurological medical issues can also provide a challenge for diagnosis at altitude. Does the person have HAPE or pneumonia? HACE or carbon monoxide poisoning? A sore muscle or deep venous thrombosis? The only good defense is self-education. See Basnyat et al.[24] for a summary of nonneurological issues.

KEY CONCEPTS

1. There are three major types of altitude illness encountered by hikers, trekkers, and climbers: acute mountain sickness (AMS), high-altitude cerebral edema (HACE), and high-altitude pulmonary edema (HAPE).

2. There are several symptoms that always should be considered to be caused by altitude illness.

3. There are a variety of treatments depending on the situation.

4. Unless you are a medical expert on altitude illness, a reference book should be carried during longer and more remote trips to altitude.

5. Not all physicians are skilled at treating altitude illness or other wilderness medical problems.

6. Individuals with preexisting medical conditions need to consult with a physician skilled in altitude medicine prior to a trip to high altitude.

The *viento blanco* (white wind) gets ready to hit Aconcagua.

Experiences at Altitude: Circulation, Respiration, Nervous System, and Immunity

The next three chapters provide a summary of the common effects of altitude on the different systems of your body. The topics are not presented in any particular order, so consult the index to quickly locate any particular topic. Again, I'm assuming you're a healthy person with no medical problems.

CIRCULATORY SYSTEM

Your resting heart rate goes up with altitude. The amount of blood pumped per beat (stroke volume) doesn't change, but more beats per minute means more blood is reaching the tissues. At the same time, your maximum heart rate decreases as you gain altitude. Lundby and van Hall[212] measured maximum heart rates before and during an Everest expedition. At sea level, average maximum heart rate was 186 beats per minute (bpm). After one week at 5,400 m, the average decreased to 155 bpm and remained constant thereafter. Peak heart rates of 143 bpm were recorded at 8,750 m. Each of us has a different resting and maximum heart rate (see Chapter 12 to learn how to measure these), so it's difficult to estimate just how much yours will change.

A rapid climb in elevation (by plane or auto), coupled with a bit of exercise, can lead to a racing pulse. Any near-maximal exercise can lead to a pounding chest or hearing your heartbeat in your ears. At altitude you are more likely to experience this because of increased blood flow to the brain and increased activation of the sympathetic nervous system. Your blood pressure doesn't increase unless you are engaging in heavy exercise.[360]

After you are acclimatized, stroke volume decreases, and overall blood flow decreases. This may be the result of the increase in the number of red blood cells that occurs after one to three weeks of acclimatization. More red cells equals more hemoglobin, which means more oxygen-carrying capacity per pint of blood (refer back to Fig. 14). But more cells and less plasma means thicker blood that's harder to push through the system.* Resting heart rate is likely still elevated, but it does drop down closer to sea-level values as you acclimatize.

There is no pain associated with the heart at altitude, merely anxiety on occasion due to the faster heart rate. The obvious solution is to rest and allow your heart rate to decline, then resume your movement at a slower pace. Any significant chest pains should be dealt with as if you're at low altitude.

Carbon Monoxide Poisoning

We have become increasingly aware of the dangers of carbon monoxide (CO) in our homes, and several tragic deaths have apparently been caused by carbon monoxide in tents or caves at altitude. Carbon monoxide is only generated when fuel is burned, so no burning means no carbon monoxide. The atmosphere normally contains no measurable carbon monoxide. As carbon monoxide concentrations rise, the effects on your body are severe, ranging from headache to coma to death. One study showed that 12% of the climbers studied (on Denali) tested positive for carbon monoxide exposure.[293]

Leigh-Smith[201] reviewed the studies done on carbon monoxide in tents and snow caves. He found that (1) carbon monoxide production is higher with a pot on the stove, (2) carbon monoxide production is higher with a low flame, (3) carbon monoxide levels will increase if either air supply or exhaust is restricted, and (4) some fuels (e.g., kerosene) produce more carbon monoxide than others, such as white gas and butane (see also Schwartz et al.[315]).

In general, a yellow flame means carbon monoxide is being produced. Any cooking done in an enclosed space requires adequate cross-ventilation. This means both an inlet and an outlet. If you're cooking inside, it's likely the weather is bad, but that still means two air holes. In a snow cave/igloo you still need a vent other than the door. Since carbon monoxide will tend to accumulate near the top of the tent/cave, always put the exhaust near the top of your shelter and your air intake as low as possible.

SYMPTOMS OF CARBON MONOXIDE POISONING

Symptoms of mild CO poisoning may mimic those of the flu: headache, nausea, shortness of breath, dizziness, and fatigue. However, there is no fever. As your blood binds with more CO, you may become confused, lose judgment, experience hallucinations, have chest pains, and lose consciousness. It's possible that the lips and nail beds will turn a bright cherry red, but don't count on it.

---

* Excessive red blood cell production (polycythemia) can lead to chronic mountain sickness,[203] which is seen in individuals spending longer periods of time at altitude than I deal with in this book—generally more than six months.

It took several hours of digging to clear the snow from these tents so they could be used safely.

Carbon monoxide binds tightly to the hemoglobin and doesn't let go. Continued low-level exposure will lead to gradually increasing blood carbon monoxide levels. So long days simmering the stove in your shelter could lead to eventual carbon monoxide poisoning. A headache and increased heart rate are signals to turn the stove off and get out of the tent. The worst situation is a storm, which can freeze up a tent and restrict the normal air exchange through fabric and zippers. Storms also fill in vent holes in snow caves. Keep your vents open and tents clear of snow and ice.

RESPIRATORY SYSTEM

You'll breathe more deeply and more often at altitude. The benefits should be obvious: More air into the lungs means more oxygen into the blood. Recall that this is called the hypoxic ventilatory response (HVR). While the heart doesn't work much harder at altitude than at sea level, the lungs clearly work much harder.

Did you catch the mistake in that last sentence? The lungs don't do the work; they just expand and contract as the result of pressure changes caused by muscular movement of the diaphragm and rib cage muscles. What happens when you strenuously exercise muscles that generally aren't trained very well? They get tired! Since you have to keep breathing to stay alive, one could imagine the need to preserve sufficient "breathing muscle power" in any situation. At 5,000 m, your respiratory muscles may be consuming 25% of the oxygen you're taking in, five times as much as at sea level.[82] Your brain is most likely monitoring the fatigue in these muscles and will force you to cease exercise if fatigue becomes critical. For high-intensity exercise at high altitude, I recommend training these muscles (see the training regimen in Chapter 12). Some unpublished data show that training the ventilatory muscles leads to better exercise performance at altitude.

There's a lot of variability from person to person in HVR. You may be breathing like crazy, while your partner may barely be breathing hard at all. So who's responding better to altitude? Schoene et al.[314] found a clear relationship between the maximum altitude reached and HVR (higher HVR, higher altitude reached on Everest). But a more recent study[41] found the opposite: A lower HVR meant better summit success on K2 and Everest. A low HVR was predicted to lead to an increased risk of acute mountain sickness (AMS), but there is too much variation among individuals to identify such a relationship.[22]

High-Altitude Pulmonary Edema (HAPE)

Let's suppose that you're hiking and you feel like you can't get enough breath. You stop and rest and feel fine. You start walking again, and the excessive breathing starts again. The key observation is that you're breathing much harder than you should be for that level of exercise and altitude. This could be a sign of HAPE. Another sign is frothy and/or bloody sputum. This requires immediate treatment (Chapter 5).

Periodic Breathing

Another issue is periodic breathing (also called Cheyne-Stokes breathing), which is a change in the frequency of breathing over time while at rest. Think of this as alternating periods of faster breathing (hyperventilation) and slower breathing (hypoventilation) or a total cessation of breathing (apnea). I'll talk about this more in the Sleep section of this chapter because we all suffer from it when sleeping at altitude. If you encounter this when awake, you'll suddenly find yourself gulping for air, breathing rapidly a few times; then your breathing will return to normal. It's nothing to worry about, though it is irritating. The only time I've experienced this during the day was after three weeks at 5,000 to 6,500 m, so acclimatization must not eliminate this altogether.

Cough

High-altitude cough is very easy to contract, often difficult to cure, and a very important cause of bad experiences up high. This is a dry, nonproductive cough that is very common—in one study, 42% of trekkers in Nepal complained of cough.[242] Cough frequency increases with altitude (or possibly just with a longer exposure time to altitude).[20] Mason and Barry[218] suggest that there are two different types of altitude cough. The first is an exercise-related cough, occurring at any altitude, that doesn't go away when you descend. The second is caused by high altitude (above 5,000 m), and not directly by exercise. This cough will go away upon descent. In either case, the coughing can be quite debilitating. Strained rib cage muscles and even cracked ribs are possible. The incessant coughing can leave you exhausted and your teammates contemplating euthanasia.

A wet cough (you're hacking up gunk of some kind) can occur for a number of reasons and should be monitored closely. Sometimes a dry altitude cough can cause the throat tissues to slough off and to be coughed up. The color and consistency of anything you cough up should be noted. Any red (bloody) and/or foamy sputum is a likely sign of HAPE and should be treated immediately.

The exercise form of high-altitude cough rarely responds well to treatment. Throat lozenges and hard candies help prevent coughing but don't cure anything. On any extended trip you should have 40 to 50 lozenges, just for your personal use. They will disappear in days once you need them. Codeine is a great cough suppressant at low doses (~10 mg) but shouldn't be used at higher altitudes. It's probably fine for occasional use at any base camp or while trekking. Tessalon Perles (benzonatate) are also recommended by many physicians; this drug numbs the stretch receptors in the lungs. Regular cough syrups are not effective. Maintain the airways at high humidities, rest, and hope for the best.

Try to avoid irritating the airways. Dry, dusty air is a common irritant that can be minimized by wearing a bandanna over the nose and mouth or by using a commercially available dust mask. This is especially important if you're driving along dusty roads on the way to the trailhead.

Pleurisy

In the absence of an injury, any sharp, localized pain when breathing is likely pleurisy, an inflammation of the lining of the chest cavity. There are a number of causes (which may themselves require treatment) but no real treatment for the pain. The chest can be splinted with tape, but only on one side at a time. Extreme coughing can crack ribs (causing a more diffuse pain). Nonsteroidal anti-inflammatory drugs (NSAIDs) such as aspirin and ibuprofen may help.

Smoking

A surprisingly large number of people smoke at altitude. Even the godfather of high-altitude medicine, Dr. Charles Houston, enjoyed "a restful cigarette" at 7,300 m on K2. In at least one study,[390] smokers suffered fewer symptoms during acute hypoxia in a pressure chamber, possibly due to the acclimatization effects of a lower blood oxygen content. This is caused by carbon monoxide binding to hemoglobin. I'm not suggesting that you acclimatize by smoking! Smoking increases the risk of frostbite[151] and definitely isn't good for you, but in small doses it probably won't hurt you at altitude. Giving an adult porter a cigarette is preferable to giving him candy and rotting his teeth.

THE NERVOUS SYSTEM

In the words of Ward et al. (p. 191),[360] "The central nervous system is exquisitely sensitive to hypoxia." The brain and spinal cord make up the central nervous system, and even

Mario Panzeri enjoys a cigarette at 7,000 m after reaching the summit of Gasherbrum II (8,035 m).

minor changes in oxygen and carbon dioxide (CO_2) levels in those tissues can disrupt the brain's functions. These functions include all thought processes and thus your moods, emotions, decision making, and communication.

There is very little solid science to explain how the brain malfunctions at altitude,[272] but there are some interesting observations that have generated a number of theories.[161] If you hold carbon dioxide at normal levels and reduce oxygen availability, blood vessels in the brain dilate, and blood flow through the brain increases. If you hold oxygen at normal levels and reduce the carbon dioxide content of the air, blood vessels in the brain constrict, and brain blood flow decreases.

Recall the description of HVR: As oxygen levels in the blood decrease, the rate and depth of breathing increase. Some folks have a stronger HVR than others. One consequence of increased ventilation is that carbon dioxide is lost from the blood. So a strong HVR means more oxygen is transported to the muscles, but the vasoconstriction that occurs in the brain due to low carbon dioxide will reduce overall blood flow to the brain. At moderate altitudes (3,800 m/12,500 ft), blood flow (and oxygen delivery) is not reduced,[385] but at higher altitudes, oxygenation likely decreases. It's been speculated that a strong HVR allows those individuals to attain greater heights than other travelers, but this leads to a lower blood supply to the brain and greater long-term brain dysfunction.[272] Sounds good, but nobody really knows if it's true. At more moderate altitudes, it does appear that hypoxia alone isn't sufficient to explain brain dysfunction.

Proper brain function requires energy (adenosine triphosphate, ATP) harvested from glucose. As neurons in the brain become active, blood flow and glucose use increases more than oxygen use. The glucose comes from glycogen that's stored in astrocytes, which are cells that pass materials from capillaries to the nerve cells. The glucose can be broken down without oxygen by using glycolysis (see upcoming Fig. 27 in Chapter 7 for the details).

Now let's add sleep into the equation. One of the purposes of sleep might be to recharge the astrocytes with glucose,[39] allowing proper brain function. We all know that lack of sleep leads to behavioral changes, and sleep disruption is essentially universal at altitude. Raichle and Hornbein[272] suggest that hypoxia will have direct effects on the brain (reduced blood flow) and indirect effects on the brain due to lack of sleep (lack of glucose).

After summarizing some of the intricate ways in which the brain works, Raichle and Hornbein (p. 394)[272] state that an important consequence of hypoxia may be that your brain will rely on reflexive behaviors when stressed. They conclude:

> [I]ndividuals without well-honed mountaineering skills (i.e. reflexes or habits) could be at a distinct disadvantage in the presence of a life-threatening emergency.

In fact, different areas of the brain are involved in storing new memories and storing ingrained skills.[306] This provides a biological basis for the saying "Practice makes perfect." A newly learned skill (such as ice-axe arrest or even tying a knot) may be very difficult to accomplish at altitude. This is one of the greatest dangers of the current trend of inexperienced climbers buying their way up 8,000 m peaks.

Behavioral Effects

Like all other aspects of high-altitude travel, people differ in their behavioral responses to altitude. In general, impairment is greatest just after arrival at a new high point. Tasks require more time, but generally they can be done as accurately as at sea level. Lassitude/lethargy and a general disinclination to do anything are common. People are grouchier, more anxious, and less tolerant of others. At extreme altitudes, the effects on perception can be severe:

> Taken prisoner by hypoxia...our "reality" began to more closely resemble a surreal fantasy. (Webster 2000, p. 436)

Indeed, Arzy et al.[12] suggest that hypoxia may predispose some individuals to mystical revelations.

There are many examples of visual and auditory "hallucinations" at high altitude (Table 4). These are almost always experienced by climbers who are alone, tired, and at very high altitudes. There is a clear pattern of "wishful thinking" in most of these, as you can see. Frank Smythe[326] was at 27,600 ft on Everest and saw two "kite balloons," which he then

Table 4

Examples of Phantom Companions at Altitude*

Climber	Perception	Reference
Rob Taylor	A "companion watcher"	Taylor (1981)
Jerzy Kukuczka	Feeling he was cooking for other people	Kukuczka (1992)
Doug Scott	Feeling of more people on the mountain than were actually there	Tasker (1982)
Joe Tasker	An American family accompanied him on descent, complaining that he was slow	Tasker (1982)
Ed Webster	Buddhist monks holding a blessing ceremony	Webster (2000)
Jean Troillet	A marching band playing music and skiers gracefully skiing by	Webster (2000)
Herman Buhl	An imaginary partner who cared for and belayed him	Buhl (1956)
Stephan Venables	An old man who both gave and sought support	Venables (2000)
Reinhold Messner	An invisible companion who asked him to get the cooking done	Messner (1989)
Frank Smythe	Divided his mint cake in half to give to his imaginary companion	Smythe (2000)
Frank Smythe	Pulsating objects	Smythe (2000)

* One might assume that all of these individuals were suffering from dehydration and lack of sleep as well as hypoxia. Most examples are from extreme altitude (over 7,700 m). Taylor was also seriously injured.

described as black objects, one with underdeveloped wings and one with a beaklike protuberance. They pulsed with "some horrible quality of life" at a rate slower than his heart rate.

This last example corresponds with other sensory distortions that are likely due to sleep deprivation. Ed Drummond, after an incredible ascent of the low-altitude Troll Wall, heard imaginary people talking just below the summit.[101] After long-distance trail runs without sleep (27 and 43 hours), I've experienced vivid hallucinations; people turn out to be mailboxes, basketballs in the middle of the forest are rocks, hockey sticks are trees. Technically, none of these are true hallucinations as defined by psychologists.

At the highest elevations, one's perception of time is often affected. On one hand, you're moving slowly,[42, 193] and time drags along. On the other hand, the sun seems to move across the sky very quickly, and you can be surprised by darkness.[191] Further examples of mental issues are presented in the section on decision making in Chapter 11.

Critical Altitudes

How high is high enough to worry about mental/behavioral/emotional changes? Minor changes have been seen at 5,000 to 8,000 ft, the altitude to which aircraft are pressurized, and the altitude of many cities (e.g., Denver). These changes are unlikely to be noted except through carefully controlled tests, however. By the time you reach 4,500 m (~14,800 ft), it is clear that changes can be noticed in a significant minority of people (most 8,000 m peak base camps are higher than this). It's likely that each person will have a critical altitude above which symptoms become noticeable. No Western climber has ever claimed to feel "normal" while summiting Everest without oxygen. As you go from 5,000 to 8,850 m, mental dysfunction increases ever more rapidly. This is likely a major cause of the high death rates in those climbing without oxygen on the more technical higher peaks, such as K2.[170]

Peripheral Nervous System

Parts of the body can go numb or exhibit burning or shooting pains when carrying a pack, regardless of altitude. Over one-third of backpackers experienced such symptoms on the Appalachian Trail.[59] These sensations disappear after removing the pack in most cases. The best defense is a pack that fits well and is not overloaded.

SLEEP

Sleep disruption is a common problem at altitude. There are three reasons for this: (1) a disruption of the normal sleeping schedule due to travel, (2) changes in sleeping comfort, and (3) physiological disturbances. By far the most important are the physiological disturbances.[366]

Sleep at altitude is constantly interrupted as the result of **periodic breathing**. Also known as Cheyne-Stokes breathing, this is a pattern of hyperventilation followed by a lack of breathing (apnea). Recall that breathing is controlled by both the amount of oxygen and the amount of carbon dioxide in the blood. If oxygen is too low, breathing is stimulated. If carbon dioxide is too high, breathing is stimulated; if carbon dioxide is too low, breathing is repressed. Increasing oxygen through hyperventilation will decrease carbon dioxide.

A possible explanation for this process is summarized in Fig. 26. Low oxygen levels stimulate breathing, followed by suppression due to low carbon dioxide. The cycle time between the start of one apnea period and the next may be shorter at high altitudes. All lowlanders suffer from periodic breathing at altitude, and while the amount of periodic breathing is thought to decrease through time, it may not go away completely.

Sleep can be disrupted for other reasons. I don't sleep well the first couple of nights when camping; the sleeping bag, extra noises, and other distractions can take some getting used to. Cold air can make it difficult to sleep soundly, especially if you keep getting

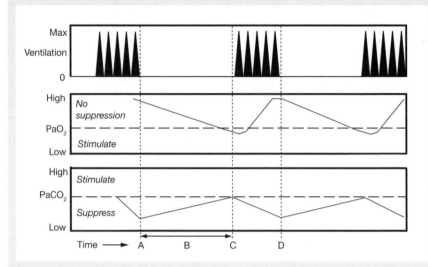

Fig. 26. One explanation for periodic breathing. The upper panel represents ventilation rate, the middle panel represents arterial partial pressure of O_2 (PaO_2), and the bottom panel represents arterial partial pressure of CO_2 (PaCO_2). The horizontal axis represents time in all three graphs. The horizontal dashed lines represent the homeostatic set points for PaO_2 and PaCO_2. High PaO_2 does not inhibit breathing, while breathing is stimulated if PaO_2 falls low enough (dashed line). High PaCO_2 will stimulate breathing, while low PaCO_2 will inhibit breathing. At time (A), immediately after a period of hyperventilation, O_2 is adequate, but hyperventilation has reduced CO_2, and breathing is suppressed. (B) A period of apnea follows, due to adequate O_2 and low CO_2. (C) Blood O_2 levels finally drop enough to trigger another bout of hyperventilation. (D) The cycle begins again. The set point for PaCO_2 moves downward during acclimatization, leading to less suppression of breathing.

frost in your face. On most treks the staff seems to get up at 4:00 A.M. and cough and spit and yell "Good morning" to each other, then bang pans in the kitchen. And at least one of your partners will snore, cough, or speak in tongues most of the night.

Jet lag is a well-known sleep disrupter. This, of course, doesn't directly relate to altitude, but it does contribute to prealtitude stress, and you should minimize the effects of jet lag as much as possible.

Practical Advice

The best cure for periodic breathing is acetazolamide (Diamox). I keep some acetazolamide handy at all times during an ascent to higher altitudes. This drug isn't a sleeping pill, but it affects blood carbon dioxide by inhibiting the action of the blood cell enzyme carbonic anhydrase (refer back to Fig. 8). Periodic breathing is clearly reduced, and sleep is improved as a result. Other sleeping pills should be avoided. There are many cases of consequences of sleeping pill use at high altitude; see the section on performance aids in Chapter 4.

Sleeping pills can be a useful adjunct to help with adjustments to jet lag. They all have their positives and negatives, but try to use a sleep aid that has a short half-life so that you are able to function well after six hours. Melatonin, a natural sleep-inducing compound, may be useful if you don't like medications (it may be useful at altitude as well).

A good pad, a roomy sleeping bag, a proper pillow, and earplugs are all hallmarks of the seasoned traveler. Try out your earplugs in advance, as there are many different types, and everyone seems to have a preference. Some folks can sleep in the middle of mayhem; they should count themselves lucky.

Daytime Somnolence (Excessive Sleepiness)

Most accounts of life at high altitude stress the difficulty of sleeping, especially at the highest camps (~8,000 m). The flip side of the coin—excessive sleepiness (or somnolence)—is rarely discussed except in anecdotal reports. While descending from 7,900 m after a failed attempt on Broad Peak, I found myself nodding off in the warm sun, dreaming vividly for a few minutes, then waking up and descending some more. While awake, I was thinking normally, evaluating the route, weather, and my own condition.

The mountaineering literature reveals a number of cases of daytime somnolence:

> I was consumed by total torpor; my mind and body melted in the warm sun. John lay next to me, apparently asleep. (Ridgeway 1980, p. 277)

> Up! 8,400 metres....
>
> Soon after that we discover Mrufka [Dobroslawa Wolf].
>
> She is leaning, immobile, into the steep slope above the small rocky shoulder. "She's asleep!" says Julie, amazed. I don't trust my eyes. Can she really be sleeping here?
>
> Before, earlier in the day, at the end of the traverse where the last fixed rope was, Mrufka had dozed off with her head on her arms. It is obviously not "her day." (Diemberger 1991, p. 515)

> I slumped forward on my ice axe and dozed for awhile. When I opened my eyes Ed was only slightly closer. I dozed again, sinking into blissful semi-consciousness, perhaps even falling asleep. This time when I opened my eyes Ed too was sitting down; but after awhile he stood up and moved a few steps closer.
>
> I had been dozing intermittently for an hour when Ed finally arrived at a spot just below me. I had been alone for nearly twelve hours and it was good to have company again. I asked Ed if he would do a spell in front. He replied sleepily, muttering something about not being able to stay awake. (Venables 2000, p. 168)

When I finally caught up with him, I either fainted or simply drifted off to sleep briefly (I remember dreaming). John muttered something about "your fainting spells" and complained I was making him nervous. (Wickwire and Bullitt 1988, p. 273)

I felt sluggish and lethargic, ready to doze off midstep—whether from hypoxia, boredom with my snail's pace, or simple lack of sleep over the previous several days, I couldn't say. (Viesturs 2006)

What could cause this somnolence? The cases listed here were not due to hypothermia, and all climbers descended safely to their camps after their experiences. The easiest explanation is that lack of sleep the previous night(s), coupled with the relative warmth of the midday sun, may lead some individuals to involuntarily fall asleep. Supplemental oxygen wasn't in use by any of these climbers, so hypoxia may be a direct contributor.[366] Fatigue is certainly a contributor, but none of these climbers appear to have suffered from exceptional fatigue. Since scientists still don't understand clearly why we need to sleep, a good explanation for high-altitude sleepiness isn't going to appear soon.

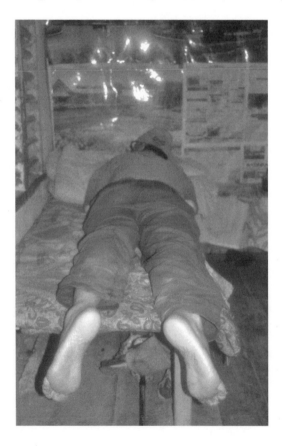

The more important question: Is this dangerous? Somnolence is listed as a symptom of high-altitude cerebral edema (HACE) by some authors, but by itself it isn't a definitive indication of HACE. It should probably be considered along with general fatigue level and mental status when you make your up/down evaluation. In the example of Mrufka Wolf, her sleepiness was combined with irrationality and a slow climb rate. Her partner, Al Rouse, convinced her to turn around just below the summit of K2 (both died days later as the result of a terrible storm and high-altitude deterioration).

Sleepiness while moving is one thing; severe sleepiness or excessive lassitude to the point of not wanting to leave the tent is likely a more serious issue (possibly HACE) and needs

After 10 weeks, a weary climber realizes his dream: a bed.

to be monitored by teammates. This feeling is normal after a summit attempt due to severe fatigue, but willpower should win out over somnolence if mountaineering judgment dictates movement. Finally, sleepiness might be a symptom of other problems:

> [John Evans] was feeling very lethargic and had been sleeping constantly for the past twenty-four hours. Jim [States, M.D.] thought this was due to exhaustion and hypothermia from the previous day. He couldn't know Evans was coming down with hepatitis. (Roskelley 1987, p. 201)

THE IMMUNE SYSTEM

Your body is a wonderful habitat for bacteria, viruses, and parasites. The immune system is responsible for resisting this onslaught of homesteaders and repelling any successful invasion. In addition, any injury needs to be repaired.

There are three different facets to the immune system. **Nonspecific defenses** such as your skin may also serve other purposes. **Circulating components** (immune cells and proteins) travel throughout the bloodstream and lymphatic fluid, ready to attack any invaders. Finally, the **fixed components** (spleen, lymph nodes, bone marrow) either produce circulating components or help destroy invaders that are carried to them.

It appears that the immune system is not strongly affected by hypoxia.[223] However, we don't know much about how exercise and altitude together affect the immune system. If we consider only infections, an important question is: Are infections more likely at altitude? Infections could increase in two ways: You could have a normal immune system but be exposed to more (or different) infectious agents, or your immune system could be compromised and be less adept at resisting infection.

Exposure to certain infectious agents is more likely at altitude. Even on a day trip in the United States, one sip from a polluted stream could give you any number of bacterial diseases or parasites. On a trek you'll be exposed to lots of human and animal feces, and your cooks and food servers are unlikely to strictly follow sanitary procedures. The porter who just coughed behind you may have sprayed you with some exotic respiratory disease. Living and eating in close proximity to others always contributes to higher exposure to infectious agents (ask any college dorm resident). Moist tropical areas harbor diseases that haven't even been identified yet. The bacterial community in the gut changes at high altitude,[187] and exposure to a new set of bacterial symbionts is likely a cause of many infections.[27]

A cold environment and high levels of ultraviolet (UV) radiation will likely result in fewer infectious agents. Cold-climate military and research facilities have little infectious illness until new recruits arrive. UV radiation kills bacteria, viruses, and some parasites.

Several factors may depress the immune system at altitude.[223] Stress, both physical and psychological, clearly affects immune response. While short-term stress will stimulate the immune system, long-term stress can seriously depress the immune system.[306] Stress causes the release of cortisol from the adrenal gland, and this hormone reduces both inflammation and infection-fighting immune responses. Cortisol levels may or may not increase at altitude.[6, 36, 357] Dry air may make the airways more prone to physical damage, allowing easier infection. Finally, hypoxia and hypobaria (low air pressure) could directly contribute to depression of immune function. However, one study[187] showed that the immune system produces more infection-fighting proteins while at high altitude. The net result is that infection is more common at altitude, but two of the major contributors—stress and hygiene—can be managed with effort.

Injuries heal more slowly at altitude. Major injuries will dictate quick descent, and minor cuts will need to be watched more carefully than we would at home. Slow healing means a longer period of potential infection. If you do get infected, the immune system might be compromised enough to allow the infection to take hold and spread. You may be tempted to keep the injured area covered and warm. This isn't a bad idea, but you have to continually change dressings and check for infection. The warm, moist darkness under a bandage is a great place for bacteria to start a family!

Practical Advice

Minimizing stress and maximizing hygiene are the keys to avoiding infection. Strenuous physical activity hinders your immune system, so adequate rest is crucial. Mental stress needs to be minimized by whatever means you find useful. Dealing with your hygiene is simple; getting others to embrace proper hygiene can be tricky. Of course, being a germophobe means that you are going to pile on more mental stress, so don't develop hygiene hysteria.

While most of us are aware of bacteria, viruses, Giardia, and other internal threats, be careful of external threats while traveling abroad. Fleas, lice, and bedbugs sound unpleasant, but they can drive you to distraction due to the itching and scratching (think of poison ivy or poison oak). These can be found in any blanket, mattress, sleeping bag, or tent used by locals. In 1939 the great American alpinist Jack Durrance visited a local habitation on his way to K2 and picked up some fleas that pestered him for weeks.[182] On Broad Peak in 2005, my teammate moved into a sleeping tent used by our cook and was overrun by fleas for the rest of the trip. There's not much you can do about this, except stay out of obviously filthy buildings. Bedding in trekking lodges is usually suspect. Any infestation should be dealt with ruthlessly so that you don't transfer them to all of your gear. Cold temperatures and bright sunlight can help.

KEY CONCEPTS

1. The heart beats faster and your maximum heart rate decreases with increasing altitude.

2. Ventilation rate (breathing) increases with altitude, though this varies dramatically among individuals. The depth of breathing increases as well.

3. Periodic breathing occurs in many individuals, especially at night. This can disrupt sleep.

4. A number of issues can affect the lungs and muscles controlling ventilation.

5. The brain and nervous system are very sensitive to hypoxia. This can affect many physical and psychological characteristics.

6. Sleep is disturbed in practically all travelers to altitude.

7. Many altitude trips will expose you to new infectious agents. This reinforces the need for proper hygiene and for the reduction in stress during longer trips to altitude.

Paiju, Pakistan, may have the most scenic sinks in the world.

Experiences at Altitude: Food, Digestion, Hydration, and Hygiene

APPETITE, DIGESTION, AND WEIGHT LOSS

"An army travels on its stomach" and "The way to a man's heart is through his stomach" may be clichés, but eating is part of the essential triad of activities (along with sleep and sex*). Altitude can cause significant changes in your appetite and digestive processes, possibly leading to lowered physical and mental performance and weight loss.

Let's use a 19-day trek to Makalu Base Camp as an example of the general patterns of food intake seen at altitude.[215] They measured energy intake for the low-altitude (480 to 2,500 m) and high-altitude (3,500 to 5,200 m) portions of the trek, as well as total weight loss. In the five-day period at low altitude, trekkers consumed an average of 3,200 calories** per day. During the nine days at high altitude, 2,600 cal/day were consumed, and on the descent phase (four days) they consumed 3,700 cal/day. Protein consumption dropped at high altitude, while fat consumption stayed constant. Trekkers lost an average of 4.2 kg (9.2 lb), some of which was due to water loss.

This weight loss could be due to inadequate energy intake or due to the inability of the body to digest and absorb the energy in the food. Let's first examine appetite, digestion, and energy balance/weight loss more thoroughly, then I'll offer some practical advice.

---

* I mean for living organisms in general, not necessarily for your trip to altitude.

** The term calorie is in standard usage in the United States, so I'll use it. Technically, these are kilocalories (kcal). The proper units would be kilojoule (kJ), which is 0.239 of a kcal.

Appetite

Appetite is the desire to ingest food (hunger is the need for food). Appetite is stimulated by a lower body temperature, lower blood sugar, and higher palatability of the food. Appetite is suppressed by the reverse of these factors, by stretch receptors in the stomach (a feeling of fullness), and by increases in certain hormones. One of these hormones is leptin, which is released from fat cells when fat is formed (suggesting that it's time to stop eating). Stress can either increase or decrease appetite, and psychological conditioning can also do both.

The higher you go, the less your appetite.[375] Loss of appetite is known as anorexia. Anorexia may be due to increased leptin concentrations at altitude,[348] but others have found a decrease in leptin at altitude.[393] Regardless of the physiological cause, it appears that most people become much more picky about what they eat and have a decreased ability to force down unpalatable food at altitude. Cold temperatures by themselves don't seem to influence appetite,[199] while hot temperatures can depress it. Your only recourse, especially at the highest altitudes, is sheer determination to eat, eat, eat:

> Willi [Unsoeld] and I attacked the problem of eating with a stubborn determination born of our Masherbrum experience. There I lost twenty pounds, which didn't leave much. [On Everest,] as long as there was food, we ate. We would neatly clean the leftovers of those whose appetites were jading, and we competed even in this....[W]e lost only four pounds each during the weeks preceding our final push. (Hornbein 1966, p. 106)

> Everything smelled and tasted disgusting and the other two refused to eat the chocolate-coated granola bars that I had found. However I managed to sit up and eat two bars, concentrating stubbornly on the unpleasant task and swilling them down with sips of dirty melted snow. (Venables 2000, p. 197)

> Without wishing to boast I think the feat of eating a large mugful of pemmican soup at 27,200 ft. performed by Lloyd and myself is unparalleled in the annals of Himalayan climbing and an example of what can be done by dogged greed. For greed consists in eating when you have no desire to eat. (Tilman 1948/2003, p. 443)

Food cravings are common. Reynolds[277] recorded the food cravings of climbers on an Everest expedition. The most common craving on the climb was for cheese or yogurt, followed by fresh fruit and "better food." Here's an incredible (and clearly British) meal eaten at 8,200 m in preparation for the first ascent of Kangchenjunga:

> They made orangeade from crystals, and followed it up with sweet tea. Supper consisted of asparagus soup from a packet, lambs' tongues from a tin, and mashed potato. Then they drank again, this time chocolate, drinking it slowly

in order to keep it down. It was a meal which they really enjoyed.... (Evans 1956, p. 120)

My only response is, "Urp."

Digestion

Once you get food into your body, it needs to be broken down and absorbed into the bloodstream for transport to the tissues. Below 5,500 m, it seems that there is no problem with digestion and absorption.[360] While earlier research suggested that fats were not digested well at high altitude, diets consisting of 47% fat were digested properly in exercising individuals at 4,700 m.[271] Above that level (which falls into the altitudes generally experienced only by climbers), the jury is still out, but there are likely problems with absorption. This means that even if you eat enough, much of it might just pass on through:

> *[T]he shrimp creole I had eaten the day before now exited in a form similar to that which it had earlier entered.* (Bettembourg and Brame 1981)

> *There were zippers and [V]elcro and more zippers and flaps. I was starting to panic. Finally everything was aligned and out came the Sherpa mash. I thought the stuff hadn't changed that much.* (Burgess and Burgess 1994)

Danielle pets somebody's dinner.

Cellular Respiration and Fuel Supplies for the Cells

The food we eat is just a bunch of molecules. There's energy stored in those molecules, and this energy can be transferred to other molecules using a series of biochemical pathways called **cellular respiration.**[*] Don't confuse breathing (also called respiration) with cellular respiration. In its simplest form, the biochemical pathway of cellular respiration that occurs in cells looks like this:

Glucose (sugar) + $O_2 \rightarrow CO_2 + H_2O$ + 38 ATP (energy),

where O_2 is oxygen, CO_2 is carbon dioxide, H_2O is water, and ATP is adenosine triphosphate. The energy in a single sugar[**] molecule (glucose, $C_6H_{12}O_6$) is transferred to ATP. ATP is a small molecule that stores energy and moves around the cell quickly and easily. It's often called an energy currency, because, like money, it's easily transported, and its value (energy) can be used to do many different things. About 38 ATP are formed from each glucose molecule under ideal conditions; each ATP molecule contains only a fraction of the energy found in a glucose molecule. That's good, because most reactions that use ATP need only one or two of them at a time. There's simply too much energy in a glucose molecule to be used effectively at one time, similar to paying for a candy bar with a $100 bill; it's very inefficient.

Cells can use three different biochemical pathways to create ATP, depending on the circumstances (Table 5, Fig. 27): the **creatine pathway, glycolysis,** and **aerobic respiration.**[***] Muscle cells use all three pathways, so we will use those cells as an example. The creatine pathway is just a single reaction. Creatine phosphate is a secondary energy storage molecule that is found in the muscles. When a muscle begins to contract after a rest, energy stored by creatine phosphate can very quickly be transferred to ATP. It is thought that this pathway is important for only a few seconds of muscular contraction, until the other pathways in the muscles get cranked up. This is one reason why creatine supplements are good for some sports but probably not important for trekkers or climbers.

All cells conduct glycolysis and aerobic respiration. Glycolysis means "splitting sugar," and that's exactly what it does. Glucose molecules from the bloodstream or from glycogen (starch) in the cell are broken down, and a small amount of ATP is formed. If there is oxygen available in the cell, the product of glycolysis is pyruvate, which then enters the aerobic respiration pathway, and many more ATPs are formed. If no oxygen is available in the

---

[*] This energy transfer is never 100% efficient, so some energy is always lost as heat. This heat is what keeps our bodies warm.

[**] A sugar is a molecule with a particular chemical formula. Table sugar, or sucrose, is composed of a glucose and fructose molecule. Starches (like glycogen) are usually formed of glucose molecules, as is cellulose (plant cell wall material).

[***] My term *aerobic respiration* is shorthand for the Krebs cycle (or citric acid cycle) followed by oxidative phosphorylation (or electron transport).

cell, lactate is produced instead. Lactate is likely an important source of portable fuel for cells to use when under stress (see discussion in Chapter 3).

Fats and proteins can also be used as fuel to make ATP. These require oxygen to be broken down and so must enter the aerobic respiration pathway.

The body needs to store, release, and transport fuel molecules to ensure adequate ATP production in every cell. The three major types of fuel are carbohydrates (sugars and starches), proteins (composed of amino acids), and fats (composed of glycerol and fatty acids). Sugars are stored as glycogen (a starch) in the muscles and the liver. While some fat is stored in all cells, a vast majority of the fat is stored in fat cells found beneath the skin and between the organs. Protein is not stored per se, but is found in large concentrations in muscle cells. All enzymes are proteins, and the body has a circulating pool of amino acids, the building blocks of proteins, in the bloodstream.

While all cells need access to fuel, let's focus our attention on two types of organs: the brain and the muscles. The brain appears to use glucose as its primary fuel. It doesn't use fats or protein as other cells can to produce ATP. This means that the brain gets priority for any glucose circulating in the bloodstream. The muscles have the largest range of energy demand of any type of cell. Upon heavy exercise, ATP production needs to skyrocket to keep pace.

Table 5

Comparison of the Four Metabolic Pathways That Produce ATP in Cells

	Creatine Pathway	Glycolysis	Aerobic Respiration*	Anaerobic Respiration
Where it happens	Muscle cells only	All cells, outside mitochondria	All cells, inside mitochondria	All cells, outside mitochondria
Speed of reaction	Very fast	Slower	Slower	Slower
Fueled by	Creatine phosphate	Glucose	Pyruvate, O_2	Pyruvate
Products	Creatine	Pyruvate (if O_2 present) or lactate (if O_2 absent)	Water, CO_2	Lactate, CO_2
ATP production	Varies, but not sustainable	Low, sustainable	Many, sustainable	Very few

* I am combining the Krebs cycle and oxidative phosphorylation.
ATP, adenosine triphosphate.

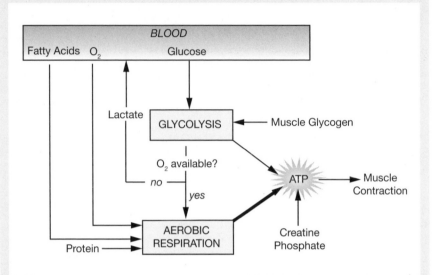

Fig. 27. A summary of the paths of fuel use in cellular respiration. The primary fuel is glucose, which can come from muscle starch (glycogen) or from the bloodstream. Fatty acids and proteins can also be used as fuel if oxygen is available. See text for a complete explanation. ATP is adenosine triphosphate.

The key organ in fuel management is the liver (Fig. 28), which can turn a number of different substances into glucose. This glucose enters the bloodstream for use by the brain. Any extra glucose can be used by muscles or other cells as needed. The liver can store glucose in the form of glycogen. Upon demand, such as during exercise, this glycogen is broken down into glucose and sent into the bloodstream. A liver containing maximal glycogen can hold enough fuel to sustain 90 minutes to 2 hours of exercise.

Glycogen is also stored in muscle cells. These cells will break down the glycogen into glucose as needed. Under anaerobic conditions, the lactate that is formed (Fig. 27) can be transported to the liver and turned into glucose. Even pyruvate can be transported for the same purpose when oxygen is present. When carbohydrate stores are exhausted in the body, the proteins in the muscle tissue will break down into amino acids, which are then transported to the liver for conversion to glucose. While this results in muscle loss, remember that muscles aren't useful without a brain to control them, and that brain has to be constantly fed.

The fat cells contain the primary energy reserves in the body. When needed, fats are broken down into two components: glyercol and fatty acids. The glycerol goes to the liver for conversion to glucose. The fatty acids are transported in the bloodstream to muscle and other body cells. There, the fatty acids enter the aerobic respiration pathway, and

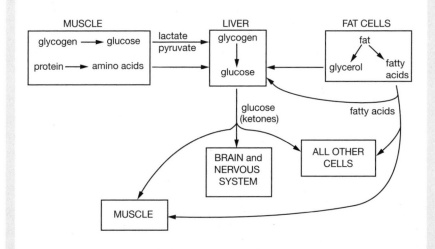

Fig. 28. Management of fuel stores in the body after digestion is complete. The brain is always supplied with fuel (glucose and some ketones). The role of fat and protein breakdown depends on the length and severity of exercise. When you digest food, the liver, muscles, and fat cells all store energy (just reverse the arrows within those boxes).

ATPs are formed. Note, however, that fat can only be used when sufficient oxygen is present in the cells. Finally, some of the fatty acids can be transported to the liver for conversion to other molecules.

What happens if you've just eaten a meal and the digestive system is flooding the blood with sugar from your piece of cake? In general, you can reverse most of the arrows in Fig. 28. Glycogen is stored in the liver and muscles, fat is produced from fatty acids and glycerol and stored in fat cells, and there is enough glucose for brain, muscles, and all other cells.

Insulin and Other Hormones

These processes are controlled by a number of hormones. You're most familiar with **insulin,** which is produced in the pancreas. Higher insulin levels lead to storage of starch and fats, while lower insulin levels lead to their breakdown (Table 6). What controls insulin production? Blood glucose levels are an obvious factor. Low blood sugar leads to low insulin, which leads to mobilization of stored fuel reserves. High blood sugar (say, after a meal) leads to high insulin and net fuel storage. There are other signals as well. There's a hormone that signals the body that you're eating and that you should begin to secrete insulin. High amino acid concentrations also lead to insulin secretion.

Table 6

The Effects of Insulin on Fuel Management in the Body

Area Affected	Increasing Insulin	Decreasing Insulin*
Muscle cells	More glucose uptake into the cell; glycogen synthesis and storage; more amino acid uptake; protein synthesis	Breakdown of glycogen and protein; export of amino acids; fatty acid uptake into the cell and use in aerobic respiration
Fat cells	More glucose uptake into the cell; more fat synthesis	Less glucose uptake; breakdown of fats and export of fatty acids and glycerol
Liver cells	More glucose uptake; glycogen synthesis and storage	Breakdown of glycogen; synthesis of glucose from other molecules; increased glucose release; ketone synthesis and release

* A decrease in insulin is accompanied by an increase in glucagon, cortisol, and/or epinephrine concentrations to achieve the changes listed.

There are several hormones that act in opposition to insulin. Glucagon is a hormone that's released when blood glucose levels are low. Glucagon increases glycogen breakdown and glucose synthesis in the liver. Yet another hormone, cortisol, is released as a response to stress. This hormone stimulates the breakdown of glycogen and fats, prevents muscle and fat cells from taking up glucose, and promotes the formation of glucose in the liver. Finally, epinephrine also leads to fat breakdown, glycogen breakdown, and formation of glucose in the liver. All of these hormones lead to an increase in blood glucose levels, leading to more insulin, and the circle goes round and round.

Energy Expenditure by the Body

The energy used to do the business of life (**metabolism**) comes from the food we eat. The amount of energy we use will be determined by a number of internal and external factors. Internal factors include sex, age, body weight, and genetic makeup. External factors include temperature, altitude, load, and type of exercise. Given the importance of load carrying and moving uphill and downhill at altitude, some consideration of the energy costs is appropriate.

Basal metabolic rate (BMR) is the minimum amount of energy needed to keep a person alive. It tends to increase by 10% to 15% as a response to altitude, at least up to 6,000 m.

Exposure to cold also will increase BMR. Women have a lower BMR than men, and older people have a lower BMR than younger folks. Of course, most days we do more than just lie around and watch TV, so our caloric needs are higher than the BMR. The typical male needs about 1,500 to 2,000 calories per day at sea level, while a woman needs less. Running 30 miles a week will burn about 3,000 calories. Climbers consumed about 5,000 calories per day on an Everest expedition,[278] and polar explorers who pull their own sleds require about 6,000 calories per day.

Walking without a load requires the least amount of energy on a 10% downhill grade (that's a drop of 1 m vertically for every 10 m walked). Walking (or should I say climbing) up a 45% slope requires about 15 times as much energy as walking on the flat. Downhill walking on a 45% slope requires only about three times as much energy as walking on the flat.[233] The optimal uphill gradient for hiking trails has been theorized to be 25%.[231] These data were all collected from treadmill tests; the roughness of a typical mountain path will certainly have an impact on the energetics of walking.

It's been theorized that human body proportions may have evolved in response to the effects of carrying a load,[358] and load carrying is certainly central to much high-altitude travel. There is remarkably little useful information beyond what you already know: It takes more energy to carry a bigger load. Nag et al.[244] suggests that porters should carry a maximum of 25 to 30 kg at 3 kph (2 mph), which is a typical load and pace.

Other activities at altitude can require considerable energy. Snow shoveling takes almost two and a half times as much energy as walking on level ground,[1] and heart rates can exceed 90% of your maximum while shoveling.[121] So digging tent sites, making walls to protect tents, and digging snow caves all require considerable energy. In 2004 we had to clear two buried tents after arriving at 7,300 m. It took six of us a couple of hours, and some of us felt afterwards as if this energy expenditure prevented us from moving fast enough to summit the next day. As stated earlier, the amount of energy required to do a given amount of work doesn't change with altitude; the work seems harder because our peak work capacity is lower and because of enhanced fatigue at altitude (refer back to Fig. 21).

Fuel

There is disagreement over the relative importance of carbohydrates, proteins, and fats as fuels at altitude. For example, the percentage of carbohydrates, fats, and proteins consumed by Everest climbers did not vary with altitude.[279] Other studies suggest that carbohydrates are a preferred fuel at altitude.[65] It appears that climbers spare muscle mass and burn fat at altitude,[278, 336] but long trips to altitude will lead to muscle loss. After a 16-day climbing/trekking trip to high altitude, 66% of the weight lost was fat, while 33% was lean muscle mass.[9] Women may burn fewer carbohydrates and more fatty acids (Fig. 28) than men at altitude.[62]

There is a lot of variation among individuals in the relative amounts of fat and carbohydrate used at rest and at exercise, even at low elevations (Fig. 2).[132] In that study of 61 trained cyclists, 9 were using fats for more than 80% of their energy needs, 6 used fats for less than 40% of their energy needs, and the rest used fat for between 40% and 80% of their energy needs while at rest. The same level of variation was seen at different exercise intensities. If you are one of the significant number of people who depart from the norm, any diet advice you get will likely be suspect. You are unique, remember? Don't let the sports industry and nutritionists convince you otherwise.

Practical Advice

The different types of altitude travel have different challenges, food-wise.

Short trips (one day to a few days). For those day or weekend trips to altitude, eat what you want. You don't need any special diet, vitamins, or supplements. Do eat during your activity, however, and carbohydrates are important if you are working hard for a number of hours. Unless you're acclimatized, you might find high-fat foods (e.g., salami) to be less appealing at altitude. While taking 30 gel packets may sound like a good idea until you try and choke down the eighth packet, bagels and some cheese might actually get eaten.

Self-supported longer trips (up to two weeks). A high-altitude backpacking trip requires more planning as food weight becomes a major factor. Unfortunately, the lighter the food, the worse the taste. Freeze-dried food is light and nutritious, but it has a peculiar taste and often causes digestive malfunctions. Bulk food (pasta/tuna/cheese, etc.) tastes better but is heavy. As long as you keep eating, it's unlikely that there will be any nutritional consequences. One expedition consumed dehydrated foods during a 31-day trip to altitude without ill effect.[386] A good cookbook for this type of trip is by Richard et al.[283]

Treks (including expeditions, up to Base Camp). Now you're not in charge of choosing or cooking your food, and you're going to have to eat this food for two to three weeks or more. Trekking food is extremely variable and depends on the country in which you're trekking, the cost of the trek, and the quality of the cooks. You have control over the first two, but the cook is the wild card. He can have your best interests at heart, or he can be totally indifferent to your desires. In general, the higher the price, the better chance you have of a good cook. Experience doesn't ensure quality, as this observation from a French expedition shows:

> [The cook] was conservative and in spite of his efforts—and ours—he would produce the most horrible recipes—recipes that would have appalled the lowest of scullions in the scruffiest of soup kitchens. Glutinous rice, boiled potatoes, chicken roast in water, and boiled water flavored with smoke were some of his more remarkable specialities. But we were ready to condone these faults when we learnt that he had started his career under the auspices of our British friends. (Franco 1957, p. 60)

Hungry climbers enjoy pizza, baked beans, and french fries at Kangchenjunga Base Camp, Nepal.

The first step is to evaluate your likes and dislikes and compare that list to the food you're supposed to get on the trek. If you can't stand the food to be served, you're in trouble. A team member on my trip to Kangchenjunga couldn't stand daal bhat (lentils and rice); since this is the national dish of Nepal, he might have expected to eat it regularly! Unless you're willing to pay top dollar for pure Western-style meals, assume that you'll eat the local starch and vegetable dishes, along with local meats and some tinned fish.

Westerners get meat wrapped in plastic from the grocery store. Your meat on the trek will be very fresh and often walking beside you on the trail. Once killed, the meat is generally cut into 1-or 2-inch cubes with no regard to the actual structure of the animal, so don't count on a nice chicken breast or leg for dinner. After our goats were slaughtered at Paiju in Pakistan, our cook told us to expect the best parts. Unfortunately, the British influence dies hard, so we got a platter of heart, kidney, liver, and other organs at dinner that night while the staff ate the "inferior" meat.

Unless it's a very small group, don't expect the kitchen to cook your food to order. It is appropriate to ask the kitchen to prepare enough food to keep you full. It's also OK to suggest that the eggs be cooked in just a little grease and not coated in salt. If you approach the cook correctly, he will often appreciate learning tricks to help improve his cooking (and his tips). In the long run, a cast-iron stomach is your best friend on a trek. This is not because the food is necessarily bad, but because the combined stresses of travel can make your digestive system more tender than normal.

Expedition members with a Base Camp cook can expect more and less than those on a simple trek. Since the kitchen isn't moving, the cooks can pursue more time-consuming dishes. In isolated situations, deliveries of fresh vegetables or meat may be rare, so by the end of the trip you might be eating a lot of cabbage and tuna.

Leaders should be proactive about food issues. There needs to be a clear understanding among you, the cook, and the trekking agency as to the type, quality, and quantity of food to be served. Meat (fresh or canned) is the most expensive part of any food budget, so have an agreement as to the amount of meat, eggs, and cheese to be provided. If possible, inspect the food before it is packed so you'll know what's actually leaving the trailhead. On Kilimanjaro, we were surprised to get fresh watermelon on the third night of the hike (which explains why we needed so many porters).

On the trek, the leader needs to make sure that the cook is meeting expectations of quality, quantity, and cleanliness for both food and water safety. Any issues must be dealt with quickly and firmly. Most Americans (myself included) tend to be too laid back and let the cooks get away with too much. Sometimes the "chain of command" will go through your local guide or sirdar, so learn and follow local protocols. It's far better to establish your authority early on than to be stressed the entire trip (more on this in Chapter 9).

Diet and Supplements

These comments really only apply to extended trips to altitude (say, a week or longer). Butterfield[71] suggests that you need to eat 500 calories more than you want to every day you're at altitude, and the data of Worme et al.[386] support this claim. This really isn't that much if you consider foods like chocolate and nuts. Five hundred calories of rice is a lot of rice! Take a variety of different snacks that you know you like. Assuming you're trekking or climbing, you should eat as much as you want, plus the extra 500 calories. Even given the evidence discussed above, most researchers feel that a high-carbohydrate diet is best.

Boukreev[57] stated that a limited intake of easily digestible food is best. He was extremely fast, and his quick forays to high altitude probably didn't lead to the same weight loss as more extended forays would for a normal climber, so I can't agree with his recommendation. In my experience, most climbers crave meat as the trip proceeds. Here are two comments from the same expedition:

> We realised that variety was important to ensure that we continued to want to eat. We knew how one starts to crave for strong flavours, hence all the mustard and mayonnaise. We knew that at altitude a vegetarian diet induces better health. (Venables 2000, p. 107)

> Our mostly vegetarian diet had left several of us craving meat.…(Webster 2000, p. 367)

It's clear that heavy exercise increases protein requirements,[202, 337] but it's not clear that more protein helps at altitude.[238, 374] The U.S. recommended daily allowance (RDA) for protein is 0.8 to 1.0 g/kg body weight/day. A 155 lb (70 kg) person would require between 56 and 70 g of protein per day. There is general agreement that this is too low and a variety of sources suggest that the protein intake for an exercising person should be more like 1.5 g/kg/day. For a 120 lb (54 kg) person, this would be 80 g/day, and for a 170 lb (77 kg) person, the protein intake would be 115 g/day. You can get this much protein at home, but it's difficult to obtain that amount of protein while at altitude.

These intakes clearly aren't possible at altitude, so my recommendation is to plan some snacks and foods with decent amounts of protein, and certainly don't worry about overconsumption; I know from experience that it's easy to eat 30 slices of precooked bacon for breakfast after a trip to 8,000 m. Four members of the 1935 Everest Reconnaissance Expedition ate 140 eggs at one meal. Protein supplements or meal replacement powders are an excellent adjunct on long expeditions; try them in advance, as the flavor must appeal to you even under stressful conditions.

Vitamins and other supplements may not be necessary. After 30 days on tinned rations, acclimatized subjects living at 3,600 m required no additional vitamin supplements.[330] Others suggest that some supplements are necessary.[322] Frankly, if you think they help, go ahead and take reasonable amounts of supplementary vitamins (I do). A useful guide to

Salty, crunchy foods are hard to come by on long trips, so bring a secret stash of molded potato snacks.

vitamins and minerals is by Stampfer.[331] While it may seem that iron supplements should be required, it appears a healthy male has sufficient iron stores to manufacture new hemoglobin. Menstruating women may want to have an iron supplement available, but don't overdo it. Your physician can help here.

Do watch for "hypervitaminization." Most energy bars, gels, and drinks contain lots of vitamins. If your favorite energy bar has 100% of the RDA for vitamins, what happens if you eat five of them a day, take a multivitamin, then eat a balanced diet? This is just plain silly and is strictly a marketing gimmick to sell more stuff. I strongly recommend that you keep your vitamins, electrolytes, and sports nutrition in separate packages. Do you put oil in your car every time you gas up? So why combine fuel with large amount of vitamins? There are energy gels (e.g., Hammer Gel) and energy bars (read the labels) that don't have added vitamins; use these. Take electrolyte capsules instead of relying on a sports drink for sodium and potassium. While it's not possible to avoid some overlap, don't triple-dose yourself every day.

Performance-Enhancing Aids

These are covered, briefly, in Chapter 4 and more thoroughly by Twight and Martin.[351]

Oral and Gastrointestinal Experiences
Mouth and Throat

Canker sores, cold sores, sunburn, and cold sensitivity of teeth are covered in Chapter 8. This leaves other dental problems. While accidents happen, you're a real dunce if you don't have your teeth checked thoroughly before any long trip. The last thing you need is some frontier dentistry in a third-world country. Tell your dentist that you're traveling and make sure everything is in top shape.

Tooth pain can occur as you ascend if a tiny amount of air is trapped in a filling or decaying tooth. If that happens, there's really nothing you can do about it except kill the pain—if you can. If you experience any toothache on a plane flight, get to your dentist to deal with the issue before a long stay at altitude.

If you do experience a toothache or gum infection, there is little that can be done at altitude unless you have a dentist along. Filling repair kits available in pharmacies will have oil of cloves (for the pain) and some temporary material to replace a lost filling. An infection will require serious antibiotics and painkillers and may require descent for treatment. This can be prevented in almost all cases with proper preventive care. Joe Tasker's description will serve as a precautionary tale of what may befall the dentally deficient:

> On the second day of the walk to Base Camp I developed a toothache....I con-
> sumed antibiotics and extra-strong painkillers. By morning I was delirious....I
> writhed all night....I visited the Army compound....I saw the pedal-operated
> drill and rusty instruments....[The doctor] prescribed penicillin injections. An

orderly performed the injection, fishing the syringe out of a glass of murky
water and squeezing it hard into my arm before realizing there was a blockage
in the needle.... (Tasker 1982)

He got better, luckily.

Gastrointestinal Issues

Your digestive tract is full of bacteria that aid in the digestion of food and the packaging of feces.[395] These are beneficial, and we certainly don't want to kill them. But sometimes this community gets invaded by new bacteria, or the current community gets decimated (say, by certain drugs). This is often the cause of gastrointestinal (GI) distress. Viruses and parasites can also cause GI distress, as can certain chemical compounds (e.g., syrup of ipecac is used to induce vomiting). GI distress due to infection can be prevented with proper hygiene.

The diagnosis and treatment of GI distress is a medical matter that is beyond this book. Travelers on long trips need to have appropriate medications available and the knowledge to use them. Some forms of GI distress strike quickly, some may take a couple of weeks to hit you. For any trip, it's prudent to carry some antidiarrheal medicine in case you get hit during a plane or bus trip. Your first step is to consult with a physician prior to foreign trips to learn about common ailments and the proper medications to have on hand.

There is no evidence that altitude directly causes GI distress; most problems are associated with poor hygiene or altitude illness. One study showed that the chance of diarrhea

Dysentery can bring the strongest climber to a complete standstill.

on an expedition was influenced by the length of the trip (= exposure to pathogens) and the presence of sick teammates.[222] My personal experience has been that a rapid ascent to new heights seems to bring on an occasional bout of diarrhea and that I often have less warning before an urgent bowel movement. And pity the technical climber who's hanging from his anchors. Proper clothing systems with strategically placed zippers are a must for high-altitude or technical climbers. Trekkers and the like don't need any special clothing.

The opposite of diarrhea is constipation, which can easily occur at altitude if you're not drinking enough. Severe constipation may require medical intervention. Minor constipation is not unusual and will usually clear on its own (albeit with a bit of effort) after you rehydrate.

Hemorrhoids (piles) are enlarged veins in the rectum. They can be external or internal, and sometimes burst and leave spots of bright red blood on your toilet paper. **Anal fissures**—small cracks in the anal tissue—are also common and leave blood spots. High-altitude climbers seem prone to hemorrhoids and fissures, possibly due to cold, too much sitting, straining to defecate—who knows. As usual, prevention and pretreatment can block any serious problems at altitude. If you need to treat them, don't do what one poor soul did; he grabbed the Ben-Gay instead of the hemorrhoid cream!

DEHYDRATION AND THIRST

It is difficult to determine the direct effects of altitude on fluid balance because dehydration is a common response to stress; travel to altitude, exercise, and exposure to heat or cold all cause dehydration. Because it affects so many different organ systems, the homeostatic responses to dehydration are complex. Another complicating factor is that sodium, potassium, and other ions **(electrolytes)** are also involved. The only way to excrete excess sodium is to excrete water, so maintaining sodium balance may lead to further dehydration. Controlling hydration is a key requirement of a successful experience at altitude. Noakes[249] has a thorough discussion of dehydration during low-altitude exercise.

You are mostly water (about 70% by weight). This total body water is found in three major compartments: within cells **(intracellular volume)**, between cells **(extracellular volume)**, or in the blood **(plasma volume)**. The amount of water in these compartments and the distribution of water among these compartments are crucial to proper bodily function. There is another source of water that's not accounted for in this compartment model—let's call it metabolic water. This is water that is formed or released as a consequence of chemical reactions. We also have water consumed by reactions, so the actual change in the amount of **metabolic water** is a balance between formation and degradation of water.

Total body water first decreases, then increases at altitude. In one study,[175] three days after being flown from sea level to 3,500 m, resting individuals showed a decrease in body weight of 3% and total body water of 3.5%. Plasma volume decreased by 8%, and extracellular volume decreased only slightly. After 10 days, plasma volume dropped even more, while the other compartments showed little change.[175] After 10 weeks at 6,000 m, Anand et al.[6] found that total body water was 20% above normal, and plasma volume was 30% above normal. In addition, total blood volume was 84% above normal, and total body sodium was about 15% above normal.

Few people spend much time at altitude without engaging in significant exercise. Exercise has almost the opposite effect on fluid balance, as described in Table 7. Exercise at altitude results in a pattern similar to exercise at sea level.

Pathways of Water Loss

There are three major routes of water and electrolyte loss: respiration, perspiration, and urination. If you have diarrhea, then defecation is route 4. When you exhale, water is lost from the lungs. In the cold, you can "see your breath" because water vapor is condensing as it hits the cold air. At low altitude, a typical trekking day in subfreezing temperatures would lead to the loss of about 1.0 L of water in a day.[122] While some authors feel that respiratory water loss is an important contributor to dehydration,[360] others do not.[334] There's no way to reduce respiratory water loss in any event.

Perspiration can be a major avenue of water loss; over 1.5 L/hr can be lost at high levels of exertion in warm weather.[235] There is tremendous individual variation in perspiration rates, so don't watch others to judge your own water loss. It's possible to sweat in even the coldest temperatures by overdressing or dressing incorrectly. Dry skin doesn't mean no sweat. A dry atmosphere or the wicking power of your clothes can lead you to believe that you're not losing as much water as you actually are.

Keeping ahead of dehydration requires a lot of work above snowline.

Urine is produced by the kidneys, which have several functions. The kidneys regulate body water content, sodium concentrations, and blood acidity. The kidneys also produce erythropoietin (EPO), the hormone that stimulates red blood cell production in bone marrow. The amount of urine produced is determined by the amount of fluids ingested unless the body is trying to correct a problem with sodium, acidity, or some other molecule that must be excreted. In that case, urination will occur even if it causes dehydration.

I've included simplified mechanism of plasma volume control (Fig. 29) because it nicely shows how many factors can influence fluid balance. Higher pressures in the right atrium

Table 7

A Comparison of the Effects of Altitude and Exercise on Fluid Balance

Characteristic	Low Altitude Exercise	High Altitude, No Exercise	High Altitude, Exercise
Urine volume	Decrease	Increase	Decrease
Plasma volume	Increase	Decrease	Increase
Extracellular volume	Increase	Decrease	Increase (?)
Sodium excretion	Decrease	Increase	Decrease

Source: Summarized from Withey et al.,[383] Anand and Chandrashekhar,[5] Ward et al.[360]

cause stretching of the atrial wall, which releases a hormone called atrial natriuretic peptide (ANP). This leads to sodium and water excretion, lower plasma volume, and less stretching. It's important to remember that the pressure in the right atrium will be determined by both the current plasma volume and the amount of vasoconstriction/vasodilation. For example, cold causes vasoconstriction, forcing the plasma into a smaller volume and thus increasing the pressure in the atrium. This leads to ANP release and increased urination. There are several other hormones that control body water content (such as antidiuretic hormone [ADH] and aldosterone), so this diagram leaves out much of the complexity that exists.

Effects of Dehydration on Performance

Dehydration is often studied along with heat stress, which tends to confound the direct effects of dehydration on performance. I'll try to keep heat stress out of this discussion when possible. Dehydration (a 4% decrease in body weight) decreases muscular endurance but not muscular strength.[237] In a treadmill running test at 70% of maximal oxygen uptake ($\dot{V}O_2$max), not drinking during the run decreased exercise endurance by 24%.[113] A similar study using stationary bikes found that not drinking during moderate exercise decreased endurance during near-maximal exercise by nearly 50%.

Dehydration has a number of other effects that may (or may not) contribute to this decrease in exercise endurance. Dehydration reduces plasma volume,[137] which reduces stroke volume[134, 236] and increases heart rate and body temperature.[236] Blood flow is reduced to the skin and muscles,[135, 136] and a number of hormones (e.g., ANP) increase in concentration in the blood.

Dehydration clearly affects the brain. Researchers have noted ataxia, apathy, moroseness, aggressiveness, listlessness, and a general lack of will and purpose in dehydrated individuals,[34, 107, 333] and rehydration reversed all of those mental issues rather quickly.

Normal function can continue until dehydration reduces body weight by about 6%. Organ damage will occur with a loss of 15% to 20% body water. Care must be taken in doing these calculations, however. Weight loss during exercise does not equal water loss. Some of the weight loss is due to consumption of fuel and release of the metabolic water mentioned above. One calculation suggests that over 2 kg (almost 5 lb) of weight loss during a marathon (in which 1.5 L of fluid were ingested) was due to these two factors.[262] Or it may be less, but in any case this weight loss doesn't come from just the three water compartments. So don't sweat the loss of a couple of pounds during a long endurance performance.

Thirst

Thirst is a subjective sensation that compels us to drink. Several factors contribute to the feeling of thirst, the simplest being dryness of the mouth and throat. This is a strong sensation, but you only have to wet your mouth and throat to relieve it. The digestive system monitors water intake and can "turn off" the feeling of thirst. The two main physiological triggers of thirst are decreased plasma volume and an increased concentration of sodium (or other osmotically active solute) in the blood.

Altitude depresses the sensation of thirst,[48] complicating the mental calculus used to prioritize your activities at altitude (sleep versus melt drinking water). By the time you're thirsty at altitude, you are usually pretty dehydrated. Don't rely on the sensation of thirst to guide your drinking.

Electrolytes

Sodium, potassium, magnesium, chloride, and other elements are known as electrolytes. These elements are essential for normal cell function, and their amounts are carefully reg-

---

A SIMPLE DRINK OF WATER

The North Face of Kangchenjunga was my first attempt at an 8,000 m peak, and dinners were to be provided by the organizer. Well, the "dinners" were ramen noodles and the occasional tins of tuna. These ramen noodles included a spicy oil packet that, while tasty, had a long-term aftertaste. Of course, nobody (including me) was interested in washing dishes on the hill. As we moved up to 7,000 m and then 8,000 m on our summit push, we would melt snow for drinks in the camp pots that were tainted with this ramen oil slime, so our tea tasted like ramen. Coffee tasted like ramen. Orange drink tasted like ramen. Everything tasted like ramen.

After a couple of days I started to gag at the smell of any ramenish liquids, so I didn't drink. By the time we got to 8,000 m, I was dehydrated and certainly couldn't have reached the summit (the monsoon and a fatality canceled our attempt). Since then I carefully keep a "water only" pot with me so I can melt water that doesn't taste like anything. And I still have trouble eating ramen noodles.

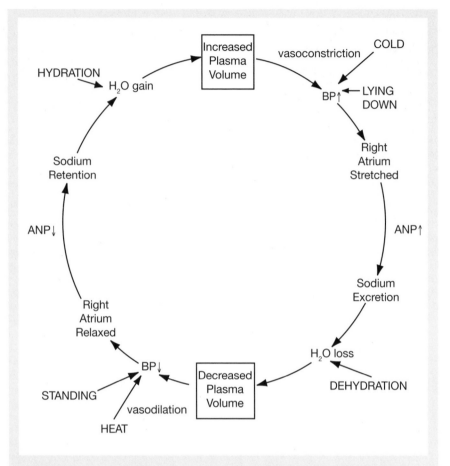

Fig. 29. Some factors involved in controlling plasma volume. This is a homeostatic system that maintains adequate blood pressure in the face of the various stresses listed. Several other control systems also influence plasma volume. ANP is atrial natriuretic peptide; BP is blood pressure. Modified from Ward et al.[360]

ulated by several hormones and the kidneys. You also lose electrolytes through sweat, and individuals differ in the composition of their perspiration. Heat acclimatization leads to a lower sodium content in the perspiration.

It appears that the body tends to preserve sodium at high altitudes, and at least one expedition has taken no salt with them as a result.[279] The sodium content of sweat varies on different parts of the body,[319] among individuals, with the seasons,[184] with fitness, and with acclimatization to heat (summarized by Noakes[249]), so you should be prepared to supplement your diet and drink as needed.

Paul brews up at 7,700 m on the north face of Kangchenjunga, Nepal.

Overhydration is a growing problem in low-altitude endurance events. In an event like a marathon or longer triathlon, participants are urged to hydrate before and during the event. Drinking plain water (or the partial-strength sports drinks commonly served) can lead to a dilution of sodium and the development of **hyponatremia** (low blood sodium [Na^+]).[250, 329] Overhydration is not necessary to maintain performance,[249] and those with high-sodium sweat need to replace sodium even at moderate hydration levels.[235] This overhydration is seldom an issue while at high altitude unless you are participating in an organized endurance event lasting three hours or longer.

Practical Advice

At low altitude it is possible to overhydrate; the recommendations here apply only to travel at altitude. It is difficult to overhydrate even at moderate altitude, given the relative difficulty of procuring clean drinking water and the decreased thirst sensation. At the highest altitudes, several hours may be required to melt the water needed to maintain hydration. While your needs will vary, most will need to drink 2 to 4 L/day. This can be in any form (tea, soup, drink mix, etc.), but keep in mind that the caffeine in coffee, tea, and chocolate increases urination and therefore cuts down net water gain. Alcohol does the same.

Urine color is the best indicator of hydration.[11] A lightly colored urine is optimal; clear may indicate overhydration, and yellow or orange-brown indicates increasingly severe dehydration. Some vitamins cause the urine to be bright yellow regardless of your hydra-

Urine this dark means the traveler isn't drinking enough. The square pee bottle can't be confused with your water bottle at night.

tion state. While we're on the subject, a pee bottle is a necessary accessory for the hydrated traveler (more in the Food and Water Safety section).

Drinks that taste great at home can make you nauseous at altitude. Bring along a variety of drinks on longer trips so that you will have something that tastes good. Boiled water is flat (no gases, remember?), and warm boiled water is unappetizing to most people. I try to boil a liter of water in the evening for use the next day. In the perverse world of high-altitude travel, you're often craving a nice cold drink even at the highest elevations. I've also found that what tastes good on one trip doesn't necessarily taste good on the next trip.

MAKE YOUR OWN SPORTS DRINK

There's no need to buy drink mix that's laden with the wrong stuff. Go to the local brewer's supply store and buy some maltodextrin, which is just starch made up of long chains of glucose. Use this as the base for your drink, then add enough sugar (but not too much) for good taste, some flavoring (Kool-Aid), and maybe some whey protein for good measure. Get out the measuring cups and experiment until you find the recipe that tastes good to you.

The other option is to take a commercial high-sugar mix and cut it with maltodextrin. Take your electrolytes as separate capsules and make sure you get some protein either in the drink or in your food.

Ad-lib drinking seems to be sufficient at sea level;[94, 249] there's no need to attempt to maintain your body weight throughout exercise at low elevations. At altitude you need to monitor your fluid intake and make a conscious effort to drink even when you're not thirsty. At the highest elevations you must set a goal (e.g., 4 L/day) and focus on achieving it.

As discussed earlier, it is common these days to buy carbs, water, and electrolyte as a single drink. These "sports drinks" are formulated primarily to taste good (= sweet) and not necessarily to provide what your body actually needs. During exercise at altitude, these drinks form a useful flavor base to make treated water more palatable, but don't depend on them to adequately replace electrolytes. Cold fluids with some electrolytes (either in the fluid or a pill) and some carbs will be absorbed by the bloodstream more quickly than plain water alone.

If you take electrolytes, make sure that they don't include a lot of other ingredients— just sodium, potassium, and maybe magnesium compounds. Succeed and Saltstick are two brands that I recommend. You will have to adjust your electrolyte intake to take into account your unique physiology, your degree of heat acclimatization (if relevant), your effort level, and the environmental conditions (temperature and humidity). I didn't take any salt on my last expedition and ended up borrowing some (but not a lot). Oversalting your food isn't a good idea, though many fast-food fanatics find foreign food less palatable just because it isn't coated with salt.

FOOD AND WATER SAFETY

More high-altitude trips get ruined by poor hygiene than by the direct effects of altitude. Poor hygiene usually manifests itself through GI illness, which can range from a mild case of indigestion to a severe illness that requires immediate evacuation. It doesn't take much of a GI illness to keep you from reaching your goals, and prevention is by far a better tactic than counting on drugs to cure you. One study[93] reported that over 20% of individuals traveling in developing countries experienced GI problems.

What is poor hygiene? Any act that leads to the ingestion of unclean food, water, or other substances is poor hygiene. I'll also consider an infectious agent that enters the body from a cut or through the eye to be the result of poor hygiene. Somehow, the pathogen or toxin has to get into your digestive system or bloodstream. My goal here is not to catalog the various illnesses and their treatment (that's the doctor's job), but to outline a strategy that you can use to avoid problems in the first place.

In water, the largest organisms of common interest are cysts of parasites such as *Giardia* and *Cryptosporidium*. Bacteria (*Escherichia coli* [*E. coli*] and *Salmonella*) are smaller than parasites, and viruses are the smallest infectious agents that we need to deal with in most cases. Prions, which cause mad cow disease, can be avoided by not eating brains or spinal tissue. Table 8 lists some current purification technologies and their effectiveness against the major critters.

Even if all these biological agents are killed, the presence of small particles such as silt can cause digestive distress. These are best removed by filtration. If you're chemically treating your water, take a reusable cloth coffee filter with you to strain the worst of the particles from the water. Pakistani porters extol the medicinal virtues of drinking the waters of the Baltoro River, which is more mud than water. At the same time, they report to sick call in the afternoons complaining of stomach pains!

GO AHEAD AND IGNORE IT

You'll never get sick, right? After a deadly summer on K2 in 1986, Jim Curran trekked out:

> At Paiju I succumbed to a violent attack of dysentery and the miles to Askole seemed endless. When I got there I collapsed and spent a nightmarish day and night camped in pouring rain on my own in a field of mud. Racked by vomiting and stomach cramps, I could barely reach the tent door to throw up into a puddle. Then a stray dog would lap up the mess. (Curran 1987, p. 169)

In 2004 I returned from Broad Peak to Skardu after spending the night at our cook's house in the Hushe Valley. The next evening we were in the hotel at dinner and I proudly noted my record of never getting sick on an expedition. At 9 p.m. I felt a little funny, then thought, "OK, I'm going to throw up now." I spent the next twelve hours experiencing projectile vomiting and diarrhea. By noon the next day I was completely exhausted and lay in sheets streaked with my own filth. While the worst was over, I lived on antidiarrheal meds to survive the two-day bus trip to Islamabad.

Bruce filters water on Mount Moran, with Grand Teton in the background.

Table 8

Various Water Treatment Methods and
Their Effectiveness at Removing or Killing Biological Agents*

Method	Example Product	Crypto-sporidium	Giardia	Bacteria	Viruses
Filtration	Various	Yes	Yes	Yes	No to partial
Lifesaver filtration	Lifesaver	Yes	Yes	Yes	Yes
Boiling	–	Yes	Yes	Yes	Yes
Iodine[1]	Various	No	Yes	Yes	Yes
Chlorine bleach	–	No	Yes	Yes	Yes
Chlorine dioxide	Aquamira, Pristine	15 min to 2.5 hr[2]	Yes	Yes	Yes
Silver	Micropur (Katadyn)	Up to 4 hr	Yes	Yes	Yes
Various oxidators	MIOX (MSR)	4 hr	Yes	Yes	Yes
Ultraviolet light	SteriPen (Hydro-Photon)	Yes	Yes	Yes	Yes

* These will be effective only if you follow the directions for that method and use
water of proper temperature and clarity. Other products use these technologies.
Effectiveness is based on manufacturers' claims in some cases.

Yes = effective.

[1] There are several chemical forms of iodine that can be used for disinfection;
when used properly, all share these qualities.

[2] According to Pristine.

Finally, the organisms can produce toxins that can make you sick. These are the direct
causes of food poisoning. Many of these toxins can be disabled by heat. While most cases
of food poisoning come from prepared food that is not refrigerated, occasionally canned
food is contaminated. A bad tin of sardines gave Peter Habeler[142] food poisoning on his
and Messner's first attempt to climb Everest without supplemental oxygen.

Keep in mind that some people are very sensitive to some of these organisms/toxins,
while others are not. In other words, the "cast-iron stomach" is a real phenomenon. However, nobody is completely immune to these agents, so don't get too cocky.

Practical Advice
Alpine Climbs, Hikes, and Backpacking Trips

All surface water in the United States (and likely Europe as well) is contaminated with viruses that come from the human digestive system,[15] and there is a general feeling that parasites such as *Giardia* are nearly ubiquitous as well. Untreated water of any kind can lead to illness. The standard recommendation is to treat all water. Tap water is safe, and food is generally assumed to be safe as well. Since you are cooking your own meals in the mountains, it's easy to maintain proper hygiene. Overall there is very little danger of GI illness during one of these trips unless you get lazy.

Less-Developed Countries

Travel to the mountains in less-developed countries is perhaps the most difficult in terms of risk management. Certain precautions are easy to remember: Don't brush your teeth with local tap water, for instance. Eating in restaurants is a real game of chance. Most hotels that cater to Western travelers have learned to prepare safe food, but be willing to pass on anything that doesn't meet your own standards. While the standard rule is "Don't eat anything fresh that you can't peel," I've had no problems with salads and other foods in decent hotels in any country, but you should follow the rule (or so the lawyers tell me). I do avoid ice in all cases.

Street food (charcoal-grilled beast and vegetables) is a no-no. The meat isn't kept refrigerated prior to cooking, so you can imagine what's growing in it. Exceptions are freshly roasted vegetables and freshly peeled fruits. As you cut a fruit or vegetable, the knife will draw bacteria from the skin into the cut, so wash the skin and knife prior to cutting.

Bottled water is safe, but watch for used bottles that are refilled from the local spigot. There is generally a tear-off plastic seal around the cap; if that's missing, just say no. Carbonated drinks are safe. Uncarbonated fruit drinks and other nonfizzy drinks are available, but you have to decide if they are safe. Again, avoid ice.

Treks and Expeditions

Here we have a cook who is responsible for preparing clean food and water during the trek or your time in Base Camp. The cook will often have assistants, depending on the size of your group. It is the cook who sets the tone in the kitchen and ultimately determines how likely you are to get sick. The leader of the group is responsible for dealing with the cook, so expedition members should work through the leader when dealing with the staff.

Unless you've had prior experience with a particular cook, you'll not know what you are getting until the kitchen staff actually gets to work. I've gone from being a rather laid-back, "the cook knows best" kind of a guy to a pretty strict disciplinarian. I've had some of the nicest guys in the world as cooks but also some quite rascally fellows who frankly could care less if you survived their food. Don't be afraid to stick your nose into everything the cook does at the very beginning of the trip and establish your authority as a leader.

You may want to see who's washing the dishes (Nepal).

Here are some specific issues:

- Hot water and soap must be available outside the kitchen area for all to use throughout the entire day. Kitchen staff must wash every time they reenter the food preparation process—after using the latrine, after visiting another camp, after going to their tents. There should be several hand towels in the group for drying hands, with a clean one being used each day. These rules apply to members as well.
- Alcohol-based gel disinfectants are great and belong in the kitchen and mess tent and in each member's toilet kit.
- Confirm that all drinking water is brought to a rolling boil for two minutes. Most cooks will skimp on this step to save fuel and time. If you're in a hurry for tea, then the water won't be boiled. Also, be sure you ask for "boiled water" and not "hot water" in the native language (e.g., *umaaleko paani,* not *taato paani,* in Nepali).
- The cooks should use different cutting boards for raw meat and vegetables. Both plastic and wooden cutting boards can harbor disease organisms, even when cleaned properly.[84] A clean board is useless if knives aren't cleaned and hands aren't washed properly.
- You can watch the kitchen practices without being overbearing. I sit with the cooks, talk to them about family, show them photos, and generally do some bonding while at the same time seeing how they do things. Try to avoid correcting the cook in front of his underlings (at least initially) so he doesn't lose face.

- The first step upon reaching a new campsite is to establish the location of the water supply, which dictates the location of the latrine. The heavy use of many areas makes the cleanliness of the water suspect. Most of the time an assistant cook will be responsible for carrying water to the kitchen, and he'll consider the closest source to be the best source. Revise his thinking as needed.
- If water is provided at a tap (not unusual in Nepal or Pakistan), the tap is contaminated. All samples (save one) taken from taps and sinks along the Baltoro Glacier (Pakistan) in 2005 were contaminated with human fecal bacteria.
- For an expedition with a base camp, climbers should bring one or two food-grade plastic barrels that can be used for water storage. The barrels available once you arrive in-country may be clean or may have been used to store some nasty chemicals. Your sanitary barrels can be used to transport gear during the approach.
- All the sanitary food and water in the world won't help if your eating utensils are dirty. Plates, silverware, and cups must be properly cleaned. Washing is seldom a problem, but rinsing and drying are. One recommended system uses three containers: one for a prewash (water and detergent), the second for a final wash (10 mL of 4% household bleach per 5 L of water), and the final rinse (drinkable water).[147] This means you need bleach and a couple of pairs of dishwashing gloves. Don't use too much bleach! Others have used iodine or potassium permanganate as a rinsing agent. The final rinse removes the smell of the disinfectant. Your dishwasher will feel compelled to dry each item with a greasy, dirty towel prior to use. Being gentle but firm, stop this practice immediately.

The water in this barrel should be considered contaminated. Plaza de Mulas, Aconcagua.

- Bring your own mug or plastic glass, or assign mugs to individual trekkers/climbers. This prevents unintentional sharing of germs.
- The toilet is usually nothing more than a hole in the ground. The staff is responsible for maintaining it, so don't be afraid to complain if it gets too icky.

A climber collects ice to melt at Camp II, Kangchenjunga.

Away from Base Camp or the Kitchen

The same rules apply here. If you have high-altitude porters, they may do some cooking for you. Enforce the rules of sanitation here as well, but be a little reasonable. Locate a latrine area and an area for water collection (liquid or frozen). Avoid dumping garbage or pee right outside the tent; in a storm you may want that snow for drinking water.

Your situation will determine the best method for portable water purification. If the water is silty, a filter would be preferred over boiling or chemicals. If you're above the snowline, then you need to melt snow or ice in most cases. I always carry chemical disinfectants in my pack while hiking or climbing below the snowline. These work fine if they are fresh (opened bottles should be discarded if they won't be used in a few weeks) and if you give them enough time to work. In the future I'll likely consider taking an ultraviolet (UV) sterilizer instead.

Garbage

Burgess and Burgess (p. 420)[67] provide a hilarious but accurate account of how garbage is handled on expeditions. They conclude that it's the leader's job to deal with garbage, and I agree. Your staff just won't understand why you're concerned about proper waste disposal. On some mountains (e.g., Aconcagua) you have to demonstrate that your garbage has been removed, so it's easier to get help from the staff. Here are some suggestions:

- Discuss garbage with your trekking agent prior to departure and confirm that rubbish removal is part of the cost of the kitchen that you've paid for. If possible, talk with both the cook and the trekking agent at the same time so everyone is clear on the rules of the garbage game.
- Staff members believe that just about anything can be burned, and once they attempt to burn something, they have no further responsibility. Don't allow them to get away with this.
- Separate all metal cans and other nonburnables like plastic from the items that are clearly burnable. If you're trekking and must carry this stuff with you, make sure the cook has a place for it in one of the kitchen loads. If he says there's no room, ask how the food you ate was carried.

Sadly, this is a typical mess left on the glacier after many expeditions.

- The metal cans should be rinsed out (bring a bottle brush along, or you'll be treating cuts from the metal edges), then flattened.
- While at Base Camp, establish containers for burnable and nonburnable garbage and inspect them regularly to be sure that they're being used.
- Before departure, personally supervise any burning and make sure everything is undeniably and reliably burned. All other garbage must be carried out. Do not pay the porter who carried the load until you personally inspect it at the trailhead; otherwise the load will end up getting dumped at the first possible opportunity.

KEY CONCEPTS

1. A decrease in appetite and a craving for unavailable foods are common at altitude.
2. Willpower to eat the food that's available is a key to minimizing weight loss on longer trips.
3. Dental issues can ruin a trip; deal with them in advance.
4. Thirst is a poor indicator of the need to drink, and dehydration reduces performance and causes changes in mood.
5. Urine color is the best indicator of hydration.
6. Electrolyte replacement is a controversial topic in high-altitude travel.
7. Poor water quality and poor hygiene practices lead to gastrointestinal problems, which are a major issue on trips of any length.
8. Proper garbage disposal is the responsibility of trekkers and climbers visiting less-developed countries.

A climber hides from the sun at 4,200 m on Aconcagua.

Heat and Cold

Your body is constantly losing and gaining heat energy. Heat transfer happens in three ways: **Conduction** is heat transfer directly between two objects (bare feet on a cold floor), **convection** is heat transfer via a gas or liquid (a hot wind blowing on your face), and **radiation** is electromagnetic transfer (from the sun to you). These are discussed in more detail below. Fig. 30 summarizes the ways in which you gain and lose heat. Clothing will significantly slow down the rate of heat exchange. If heat loss is greater than heat production plus heat gain, body temperature will fall. The reverse will lead to a higher body temperature.

We consider "normal" body temperature to be 37°C (or 98.6°F), but this can vary by 1°C among individuals. There's variation in the temperature of different parts of the body, and skin temperature can vary dramatically depending on the environment. Body temperature fluctuates during the day, with the highest body temperatures recorded during midafternoon. However, alititude reduces these daily fluctuations.[53] By now, I hope you'll assume that normal, healthy individuals can have different body temperatures.

At altitude you will find yourself dealing with severe heat and severe cold, occasionally at the same time. The thin atmosphere means that air temperatures are determined by the sun, which doesn't as much rise and set as snap on and off like a light switch:

> One moment, in the morning sun, it was stupefyingly hot...then in a matter of minutes, when the afternoon cold rolled up the mountain, you were freezing cold, toes nipped by frostbite.... There was no in-between—just blazing heat or icy cold.... (Bonington 2001, p. 137)

Most people can acclimatize to chronic heat, but the degree of possible acclimatization to chronic cold is under debate.[248] Heat acclimatization takes about two weeks. Cold acclimatization is less successful, though any cold-climate resident knows that the sensation of cold is less intense at a given temperature after living in the cold for some weeks. There's a lot of variation in individual response to heat and cold, and most people have a clear preference for a particular range of temperatures.

Fig. 30. Pathways of heat transfer between you and the environment. Short-wave radiation from the sun is the source of all other heat energy. Long-wave infrared (IR) is both absorbed and radiated by the body. Wind or water can transfer heat to or from the body via convection. Conduction via direct energy transfer between solids, such as your feet and the snow, isn't labeled.

COLD

The obvious consequence of cold is that parts of your body get cold. The most vulnerable parts are those that are long and skinny and far from the internal organs.* But you already know that from personal experience. The consequences of reduced tissue temperature depend on the duration and severity of cooling. Let's call the cooling of fingers, toes, feet, arms, noses, and so on, **peripheral cooling** (possibly leading to frostbite), to distinguish it from a more general lowering of core body temperature **(hypothermia)**.

As long as you're not actually immersed in water, heat loss from the body (or any single part) is determined by the air temperature and wind speed. These two factors interact; cooling is faster in windier conditions. The "windchill" describes the effect of wind by giving us a temperature that would lead to the equivalent amount of cooling in still air. The National Weather Service (NWS) revised the Windchill Temperature Index in 2001. You can find it, along with a windchill calculator, at www.weather.gov/os/windchill. The old NWS windchill scale overestimated the effects of moderate winds on cooling of the body. Interestingly, lower air density means that the cooling effect of wind is less at altitude than at sea level.[169]

General Effects of Cold

Cold affects almost all bodily functions. Nerve function (both sensory and motor nerves) decreases at air temperatures below 8°C to 12°C. This leads to a loss of sensation (numbness) and a decline in motor skills. Muscle function also decreases. For example, hand grip strength is significantly reduced for 40 minutes after immersion in a 10°C water bath.[87] The combination of decreased nerve and muscle function leads to a loss of dexterity; finger dexterity decreases about 15% when air temperature decreased from 18°C to 10°C.[217] Colder temperatures lead to greater loss of function.

Cardiac output (volume of blood pumped per minute) increases in cold conditions. Heart rate doesn't increase, but the amount of blood pumped per beat (stroke volume) does increase. Blood pressure increases as a result of a decrease in peripheral blood flow to skin and limbs. Cold has been found to increase pulmonary artery pressure in animals, and probably does the same in humans.

Cold exposure leads to increased fluid loss. While it is difficult to separate out the interacting forces of cold, altitude, and exercise, there appears to be a direct link between cold and fluid loss through increased urination (refer back to Fig. 29).

Mental function decreases as body temperature decreases. Work rates and performance decrease with cold,[108] apathy increases, and decision making becomes increasingly poor. Hypoxia and fatigue will have similar effects on mental state. Since your defense against cold injuries depends on constant vigilance, impaired mental functions lie at the root of almost all cold injuries.

---

* This is a result of relatively high surface-to-volume ratios for small cylinders (like fingers).

How does your perception of cold relate to your body's actual status? If you think, I'm freezing! are you? This is a critical point, as proper decision making depends on accurately gauging the state of your body (refer back to Fig. 22). If you put a group of people in a cold environment, their perceptions will vary quite a bit. These are likely not just differences in perception, but differences in the physiological responses of each individual to cold.

The physiological effects of cold may depend on sex, age, fitness, and general state of health. Response to cold may be determined more by body composition than by age[112] or sex.[343] So if you feel extremely cold and your companions do not, listen to your body—it's telling you something (you're different than they are).

Maintaining Temperature Homeostasis

Young et al.[391] group the body's homeostatic responses to cold into three categories: behavioral avoidance of cold, vasoconstrictive reduction in heat loss, and metabolic increase in heat production. Behavioral responses include the use of clothing and minimizing exposure to cold conditions. The rest of this discussion will deal with reduction of heat loss and increase in heat production.

When the skin is exposed to the cold, the blood vessels in the skin constrict and limit blood flow to that area. After a short time, the blood vessels relax, and blood flow increases. The peripheral vessels continue oscillating in a pattern of vasoconstriction and vasodilation. Vasodilation is reduced at altitude, which could lead to a greater chance of cold injuries. It appears that vasodilation (leading to warmer skin temperatures) is greater in individuals who are acclimatized.[92]

Split fingers are a common problem at altitude as a result of the cold, dry conditions.

Increased heat production means increased metabolic activity. This can occur by (1) increasing basal metabolic rate (BMR), (2) increasing muscular activity through exercise, or (3) increasing muscular activity through shivering. BMR is increased by cold.[178] Eating also increases BMR. Exercise produces heat by muscular contraction. It turns out that a given work rate requires more energy in the cold simply because it takes 10% to 15% more energy to exercise in heavy clothing that restricts movement. Shivering is rapid muscular contractions that do not result in limb movement; the result is increased heat production.

Cold, altitude, exercise, and malnutrition all interact to affect homeostatic responses to cold. Heavy exercise can reduce the response to cold by reducing the body's ability to reduce heat loss through vasoconstriction while not affecting rates of heat production.[76, 77] After a nine-week Army Ranger training course that included chronic fatigue, underfeeding, and sleep deprivation, cold tolerance was reduced considerably.[392] This was likely the result of reduced insulation (due to loss of body fat) and lower metabolic rate (due to malnutrition and high exercise levels).

As with altitude, prior experience in cold environments usually results in better tolerance to cold. The great Austrian climber Hermann Buhl described how he was able to tolerate winter rock climbing without gloves:

> What a good thing my hands were so tough; I had been out and around without gloves the whole winter, and now it was paying off. I had also improved on that by carrying a ball of snow in my hand on most occasions, even after my fingers had gone green and blue with cold—evidently a rewarding experience.
> (Buhl 1956, p. 99)

Nonfreezing Peripheral Cooling

Virtually all peripheral cooling is resolved without injury, but not always without pain. Ice climbers sometimes experience "hot aches" or the "screaming barfies" in their hands. After a strenuous, cold pitch, the hands may be numb. As blood begins to flow back into the hands, it feels as if you've stuck them in boiling oil, and the sensation is often accompanied by severe nausea. While this passes in a minute or two, the discomfort is exquisite. I've found that it usually occurs only at the beginning of the climbing season and only happens during harder climbs. There is no permanent damage.

Some folks suffer from Raynaud's disease, or "dead man's hands." Vasoconstriction is extreme upon exposure to cold, and the skin turns a deathly white. Skin color can progress to blue, then red. Calcium channel blockers may help prevent the attacks.[340] Be careful! If you normally don't suffer from this problem, the "deathly white" color may indicate frostbite.

Cold exposure can result in neuropathy (pain) and burnlike injury on the feet.[276] A significant number (8%) of climbers treated by one expedition doctor over several years complained of continuous pain and/or numbness in the feet. There was no clear direct injury.[280] The pain responded to treatment with carbamazepine, and the numbness usually receded after several weeks. I've personally experienced this numbness several times. My totally nonscientific theory is that it is caused by a combination of cold and the extreme pounding that the feet take on a long expedition or trek. I've also experienced similar foot numbness after 100-mile trail runs in which cold exposure wasn't an issue.

Some people's teeth are sensitive to cold and/or heat. This also results in a unique pain sensation that will respond to nonprescription pain relievers. Those who have experienced this know that it can be almost debilitating, so don't belittle the problem. Acidic drinks, such as soda, and tooth whiteners can increase sensitivity. Sufferers should brush with special toothpaste (containing potassium nitrate and strontium chloride) for cold-sensitive teeth before and during your trip. If this is a severe problem for you, your dentist can use stronger products than you can get over the counter.

Another common problem in cold, dry conditions is fissures in fingertips. These can be quite painful and can reduce dexterity. Water-based lotions seem to exacerbate the problem; petroleum jelly seems to help, or even cooking oil in a pinch. Human tissue adhesive can be used to glue the fissures closed,[14] which may be the best approach if they become too painful. There's been a suggestion that individuals with certain diseases (like diabetes) may be more susceptible to this type of injury.[380]

Frostbite

For years the most widely known frostbite case in the climbing world was that of Maurice Herzog, who made the first ascent of Annapurna in 1950. He graphically describes the amputations that occurred on the march out, with various toes and fingers being swept out of the train as startled Nepalis looked on.[153] Herzog has now been supplanted by Beck Weathers, the 1996 Everest climber who lost his nose and most of his hands after being left for dead at 8,000 m.[364]

While the actual frostbite injury can often be precipitated by a single event—removing a mitten to take a photo,[365] for example—the path toward frostbite starts much earlier. Dehydration, exhaustion, illness, smoking, alcohol, and drugs can all predispose you toward frostbite. Frostbite will occur when (1) your body simply can't provide enough heat to the affected part to overcome the effects of extreme cold or (2) your body refuses to provide heat to the affected part in order to preserve the temperature of the central core.

Inappropriate clothing was listed as the main cause of frostbite in a group of Iranian mountaineers, followed by lack of equipment, incorrect use of equipment, and lack of knowledge about living in cold temperatures.[148] Probably the most important issue is to know the sensory differences between simple cold numbness and actual freezing of tissue.

The NWS windchill chart lists frostbite on an exposed face occurring in 30 minutes at windchills of about –28°C (–20°F), in 10 minutes in windchills of –36°C (windy) to –50°C (calm) (–33°F [windy] to –59°F [calm]). Frankly, nobody is going to carry a thermometer and wind gauge to determine the windchill temperature, but this gives you an idea of the temperatures that are generally tolerated. Interestingly, my personal, unscientific limit for running outside has been a windchill of –25°F, which corresponds with the frostbite threshold in calm air.

Frostbite is much more likely as elevation increases. A large study of Pakistani frostbite victims showed that 71% were affected in a one- to three-hour period,[151] though at very high altitude frostbite occurs in a matter of seconds. Over a 10-year period, 11% of Pakistanis who were treated for frostbite died.[151] This number is much lower for Europeans because of far better access to high-quality, long-term care.

Practical Advice

Frostbite can be avoided in almost all nonemergency situations. Proper clothing and footwear are key, of course. Gloves and mittens must fit properly for two reasons: Constrictions can lead to decreased blood flow, and poor fit can lead to the removal of gloves/mittens to perform tasks. There is a lot of variation in hand size and shape, and most manufacturers use a single shape in their designs. Make sure fingertips are not jammed into the fabric of the mitten or glove and the thumb is sized properly. Be very, very picky.

Boots are critical as well. Your feet will often swell at altitude, making sizing difficult at sea level. Swollen feet combined with clean, fluffy socks can cause constrictions and lead to frostbite.[42] As you shop for boots, try on many different brands. Look for boots with enough room in the toe box to allow you to wiggle and bend your toes a bit and don't allow your toes to bang the front of the boot while going downhill. Carry both regular-weight socks and a slightly thinner pair that you can put on if your feet swell up.

Don't forget your head; ears, nose, and cheeks are often frostbitten. A balaclava and possibly a Neoprene face mask should be in your kit. Avoid metal frames on eyeglasses. Elbows and kneecaps are also susceptible due to a lack of fatty insulation and little blood flow. Guys, don't forget the genitals; windbriefs are important, especially if you are engaged in highly aerobic activities (running, skiing) in cold temperatures.[363]

The road to frostbite often starts as you transition from a warm sleeping bag to the cold reality outside the tent. Jamming on cold gloves and boots isn't smart; warm up your gloves, socks, and even boots in your sleeping bag first. Boots take a long time to warm up, so this isn't always practical. Climbers using double boots can warm the inner boots prior to use.

Another route to take is to use chemical heat packs in your boots and/or gloves. These release heat when exposed to oxygen. When they work, they're great, but I've found that the quality of the packets is very inconsistent. The packages must be kept intact until use (throw them out if they feel caked), and the packet must remain dry to work. This a big problem if you have sweaty feet or hands. If you're climbing at extreme altitudes, the limited oxygen in the air means lower heat output. I've had some work just fine at 7,500 m and others not work at all. Use them as an adjunct to proper equipment and technique. They are great early in the morning before you and the atmosphere warm up.

While you're out and about, you must continually monitor your extremities. If they go numb, it is critical to keep the affected parts moving. Toes should be flexed every step. Hands can be clenched and unclenched. Loosen mitten gauntlet straps, ice axe straps, and other constrictions as much as possible.

When skin temperature falls to 10°C, the tissues go numb. Actual freezing doesn't begin until skin temperatures fall below 0°C. The key is to know when you are crossing the line between numbness and actual frostbite. Unfortunately, there is no simple signal that will tell you when it happens. If you can flex and extend your fingers and toes, they are likely not frozen. Serious frostbite on the limbs will generally be progressive (tips of fingers or toes back toward the body) unless you have an equipment malfunction. Your face, elbows, and other parts can be covered with additional insulation—improvise if need be.

You can develop frostbite in your sleeping bag. A crowded tent or sloped tent site can lead to your feet pressing against the side of the tent. Blowing snow can pack around the tent, compressing your sleeping bag material and cooling your toes enough to cause frostbite.

TREATMENT FOR FROSTBITE

The Medical Committee of the International Commission for Alpine Rescue recommends the following treatment protocols for use by nonphysicians in a wilderness setting:[335]

Emergency Treatment in the Open

Get out of the weather; retreat to camp if possible; drink warm fluids.

Remove boots if swelling will allow you to put them back on.

Replace wet clothing with dry if possible.

Warm the cold bits in armpits or groin of a partner for a maximum of 10 minutes.

Take one aspirin or ibuprofen if tolerated.

DO NOT RUB the cold parts, especially with snow!

DO NOT APPLY direct heat (stove, car exhaust).

Give oxygen if available.

If sensation returns, it's probably OK to continue toward your goal. If not, get back to a warm place.

Emergency Treatment in Base Camp

Replace wet clothing with dry; remove rings from fingers.

Drink warm fluids.

Take aspirin (500 to 1,000 mg) or ibuprofen (400 to 800 mg) for pain and circulation.

Rapid Rewarming

NEVER rub or use dry heat; always use water.

Immerse the affected part in a 37°C (99°F) water bath. If a thermometer is not available, use a warm elbow to test the water, which should feel comfortably warm but not hot. Use disinfectant in the water if available.

Continue warming until color returns and/or the part is the same temperature as the rest of the body.

Dry, then apply loose (preferably sterile) bandage; elevate the part.

Don't walk on thawed feet, so don't thaw until transport is possible. This may mean walking to a lower camp with frozen feet.

General Concerns

Don't rub frozen parts, especially with snow.

If the victim has hypothermia, deal with that issue first.

Don't rewarm a part if there is a chance it will refreeze.

Seek qualified medical help as soon as possible.

Circulation must be restored within 48 hours, or the frozen part may be lost.

At some point you may feel that actual damage is taking place. At that point follow these treatment recommendations.

Hypothermia

The minute the setting sun left us, we became conscious of the intense cold of high altitude, a cold that seemed almost liquid and entered our very bones. (Bates et al. 1939, p. 270)

I woke up at 3 a.m. to a numbing cold that didn't so much come from the outside as from right inside of me and which then seeped slowly outwards, through my limbs. (Bonington 1973, p. 239)

The cold was a kind of inner-cold from lack of food and fluids....I had the kind of feeling you have when you hear of four bodies being found months later and you wonder what happened. Didn't anybody move? Did they just continue lying there until it got colder and colder? (Burgess and Burgess 1994, p. 198)

We suffered little from the cold in the acute way, but rather from a chronic effect. (Crowley 1969, p. 319)

Hypothermia is best defined as having an abnormally low body temperature. Normal oral temperature is 37°C, with rectal temperature slightly higher. Ward et al.[360] define core temperatures between 32°C and 35°C as mild hypothermia and core temperatures below 32°C as severe hypothermia. Durrer et al.[105] break the severe category down into several more categories to allow for better treatment in the field (Table 9).

The effects of hypothermia are most strongly felt at the cellular level. Colder temperatures slow down both diffusion and chemical reactions. As temperatures fall below a critical level, cell membranes are damaged, and the movement of materials between cellular compartments is disrupted, precipitating organ failure.[60]

Body temperature will fall when heat loss to the environment is greater than heat production by the body. The amount of heat you can produce will be limited by your fuel stores (starches, proteins, and fats) and the amount of oxygen available. So as elevation increases, your maximal possible heat production will decrease, and hypothermia will be more likely to occur. Fatigue also reduces your ability to produce heat.[76, 77, 392]

Whole-body heat loss will be affected by windchill (as described above) and also by moisture. Immersion in cold water results in massive heat loss and rapid, severe hypothermia. Falling into a glacial pool or stream can lead to death in a few minutes. Cold rain and fog can also result in rapid heat loss. Even if the weather is mild, hypothermia is possible if you are extremely fatigued. Noakes[249] summarizes a number of cases of hypothermia in marathon runners, including a case that occurred in dry but windy 12°C conditions.

In dry air, it's possible to survive for a surprisingly long time, even in cold temperatures (Table 10). I include this table primarily to convince your brain that it can survive longer than it thinks during a cold bivouac. As core temperature decreases, the body's homeo-static mechanisms begin to fail, accelerating the cooling process.

Table 9

Stages of Hypothermia*

Signs and Symptoms	Core Temperature (°C)	Core Temperature (°F)	Stage of Hypothermia
Normal consciousness with shivering	32–35	89.5–95.0	HT1
Impaired consciousness without shivering	28–32	82.5–89.5	HT2
Unconsciousness	24–28	75.2–82.5	HT3
Apparent death	13.7–24.0	56.5–75.2	HT4
Actual death	< 13.7? (< 9?)	< 56.5? (< 48?)	HT5

* The temperatures that indicate actual death are conjectural.
Source: Adapted from Durrer et al.[105]

Practical Advice

Hypothermia can occur at temperatures far above freezing, so the main goal is to prevent hypothermia by keeping the skin dry and warm. It's amazing how rapidly deterioration can begin. We were retreating down a gully during a vicious storm, and I was rappelling last. All at once I realized that I was standing under a waterfall and was shivering uncon-trollably. Luckily, I heard the "Off rappel" call at that moment and was able to clip in and descend before I lost complete control. After a few minutes I recovered completely (I did leave my camera at the base of the cliff and had to walk 7 miles back the next day, but that's another story).

Along with the self-examination, as described in the frostbite section, it's important for team members to monitor each other. Hypothermia, altitude sickness, hypoglycemia, and a host of other problems are often unnoticed by the affected person. Changes in mental state, ataxia (loss of coordination or balance while walking), and inability to maintain a steady pace all may be indicators of hypothermia. All of the advice in the frostbite section applies here as well.

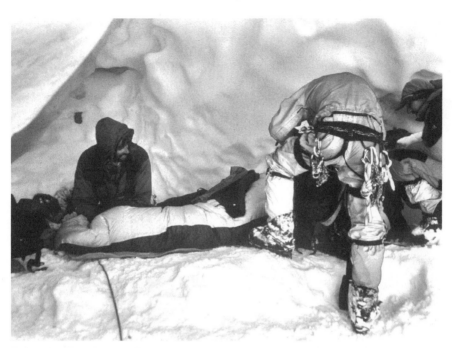

Rewarming Galu Tamang after he nearly succumbed to hypothermia at 6,800 m on Kangchenjunga.

Table 10

Theoretical Survival Times in Cold Air for an Average Healthy Male

Temperature (°C)	Temperature (°F)	Nude, 1 km/hr Wind	Two Layers of Loose Clothes, 5 km/h Wind
−50	−58	−	4.0 hr
−40	−40	−	5.6
−30	−22	1.8 hr	8.6
−20	−4	2.5	15.4
−10	14	4.1	> 24
0	32	9.0	−
10	50	> 24	−

Source: Adapted from Tikuisis.[342]

TREATMENT FOR HYPOTHERMIA

The Medical Committee of the International Commission for Alpine Rescue has made recommendations for the treatment of hypothermia in mountains where quick evacuation to a modern hospital is available (e.g., European and North American mountains[105]). Refer back to Table 9 for the classification of the stages of hypothermia.

Always treat hypothermia before frostbite!

All Stages

Shelter from wind.

Improve insulation as much as possible.

Apply hot packs on trunk but not on skin.

Warm air or oxygen if possible.

Change to dry clothing when possible.

Specific Stages

HT1 (shivering, normal consciousness): Provide food, hot sweet drinks. Active movements allowed.

HT2 (not shivering, conscious): Hot drinks if the victim can swallow; carefully watch for further deterioration; minimize movements; evacuate as soon as feasible.

HT3 (unconscious but alive): Constant vigilance; prepare for cardiopulmonary resuscitation (CPR).

HT4 (apparently dead): CPR until arrival of doctor.

Further information for physicians is available in Durrer et al.[105]

True Wilderness Situations

Reviving individuals who are unconscious is problematic in the true wilderness situation. Here are suggestions based on Ward et al.:[360]

Rewarm slowly and treat the victim as gently as possible to avoid triggering heart problems.

If the patient is not breathing: Use standard airway management (CPR) techniques.

If the patient has no carotid pulse for 60 seconds or cardiac arrest within the last 2 hours, start standard chest compressions (CPR). Don't start compressions unless you can continue throughout the evacuation or until good faith efforts can be made to warm the victim by delivering tent/sleeping bag/stove.

Avoid other techniques to restart the heart, as you might induce arrhythmias.

Do not declare a victim dead until the victim has been warmed to normal body temperatures. In a true wilderness survival situation, this simply may not be possible.

A CLOSE ENCOUNTER WITH HYPOTHERMIA

We were in Camp II on the North Face of Kangchenjunga (8,586 m), heading up on our summit push. That morning the winds were howling, and it was clear that we would be taking a rest day. After breakfast, Chris walked 100 m from camp to shoot some video of the Rock Band. As he panned his camera, he saw a speck of color on the ropes; somebody was coming down in atrocious conditions, and he didn't appear to be moving. After watching for 30 minutes and seeing no motion, we knew somebody was in deep trouble.

Two climbers took off immediately, and two of us followed with gear and food. Stu shot up the ropes and found a nearly unconscious Galu Tamang stuck on a long horizontal traverse on steep, ice-coated rock. Stu had to chop the ropes clear of water ice that had formed over previous days. He manhandled Galu onto the start of each rappel, and Galu then slid down the ropes like a sack of potatoes. Meanwhile, the rest of us had set up a camp inside a nearby ice cave, melting water and fixing ropes over to the cave.

Once Galu arrived, he could tell us his name, but he didn't know the mountain he was on. We removed his many layers of clothing; spindrift was packed between each layer and next to his skin. He was unable to drink much, so we put him in my sleeping bag, and Stu (the smallest among us) crawled in with him.

After two to three hours, he began to revive. Another Sherpa had arrived and was able to engage Galu in simple conversation. At this point Galu was able to start drinking and revived fairly quickly. We then descended 200 m to Camp II, where Galu continued to rehydrate. The next morning he descended to Base Camp, where he nursed some mild frostbite. I think that Galu was as lucky as he was inexperienced, and only his incredibly strong constitution kept him alive.

HEAT AND SOLAR ISSUES

The atmosphere not only provides us with oxygen, it also protects us from solar radiation. Without the ozone layer, life wouldn't be possible on land—the ultraviolet radiation would fry your DNA. Understanding the effects of the sun requires a tiny bit of knowledge about the nature of light.

Light is a form of **electromagnetic** (EM) **radiation.** EM radiation is described by its wavelength. The waves are equivalent to the waves seen on a body of water or the waves you can generate by rhythmically moving the end of a long piece of rope. The distance between the top of one wave and the next is known as the **wavelength.** If we count the number of waves per second, we know the **frequency;** longer waves mean a lower frequency. Finally, radiation of a shorter wavelength has more energy.

The light we see is only part of the EM radiation spectrum. The wavelengths we see are between about 400 and 700 nanometers (1 nm = 0.000000001 m) and are known as visible light. Wavelengths from 290 to 400 nm are in the ultraviolet portion of the spectrum. Shorter wavelengths include x-rays and gamma rays. Wavelengths from 700 to 10,000 nm form the infrared portion of the spectrum. Longer wavelengths include microwaves, radar, and radio waves. Different colors represent different wavelengths of visible light. Blue light is around 400 nm, red is around 700 nm, and green and yellow fall between these extremes. Your red shirt looks red because the material reflects red light and absorbs all other wavelengths.

One last issue: EM radiation is absorbed by all objects, living or not. Even on a cold day, a sunny rock may be warm to the touch as a result. All objects also emit EM radiation. The wavelengths emitted are determined by the temperature of an object. Almost all objects on Earth are relatively cool and emit low-energy, long-wave radiation. If you stand close to that warm rock without touching it, you can still feel the warmth due to this radiation. The sun (or any nuclear blast) has a very high temperature and emits short, high-energy waves.

Peripheral Heat Injury

Just as with cold stress, we can experience peripheral heat problems and central core heat problems. Unlike cold, the peripheral heat problems can occur on any surface of the body. Also unlike cold, you can experience heat injuries without actually feeling hot. Let's discuss some common heat/solar issues.

Sunburn

Sunburn is primarily caused by wavelengths from 290 to 320 nm (known as ultraviolet B [UVB]) and to a lesser extent by ultraviolet A (UVA) radiation (320 to 400 nm). The ozone layer absorbs a lot of UV and even more is absorbed as light passes through the atmosphere. At higher altitudes, there is more UV radiation striking you than at sea level.

A safari-style hat provides excellent protection against the sun.

Several factors influence your likelihood of sunburn. Skin pigmentation is a major player. Melanin is the pigment that darkens the skin. Some racial groups have higher levels of melanin, and certain people produce more melanin (get a tan) in response to exposure to the sun. Those with low melanin levels will be more likely to burn. People with certain diseases and people who are taking certain drugs are also more sensitive to the sun. Always check any new medications before you take a trip up high.

You can get burned in some strange places while at altitude. Ever sunburned the roof of your mouth? The inside of your nose? Your tongue? It's not uncommon at altitude, especially when walking on snow or ice. The light reflects off the snow and travels upward, finding your nostrils (which are normally well protected) and your mouth (which is hanging open as you breathe). On Aconcagua, I used trekking poles without gloves (it was hot) and promptly burned the back of my thumbs and palms. Even a mesh hat can allow enough light through to burn exposed scalp. The lips are especially sensitive. "My lips," Carlo Mauri wrote afterwards,

> were terribly split: ears covered with cracks, and scaly. A few hours' sleep at night with the mouth closed was sufficient to blister the lips together. It was a painful business—in the morning you had to open them very, very carefully. My throat was full of sores. Coughing could mean loss of blood. (Maraini 1961, p. 264)

When traveling at altitude, the same advice applies as at sea level, only more so. If you are fair-skinned, use clothes and a hat as your first line of defense. Manufacturers are making money by promoting certain fabrics as having a higher level of sun protection than others. While this may technically be true, as long as you're wearing a normal-weight fabric, you're likely getting enough protection. I find an umbrella to be an essential piece of gear on a trek or expedition. Buy one that's not black and that can be inverted by the wind without damage. They are usually less than $5 in non-Western countries. This provides a cool and colorful shelter against sun and rain. Your comrades will start by laughing at you and end by borrowing it from you.

Sunscreen is essential. Don't just buy any ultra-high SPF sunscreen and assume that you're covered. SPF stands for sun protection factor; higher numbers mean longer protection. There are different chemicals used as active ingredients by various manufacturers;[207] recent consumer reviews have shown that many advertising claims surrounding the safety and performance of sunscreens are just plain false (see the Recommended Reading for this chapter).

Most people carry too much sunscreen in an overly large bottle. This means you have to lug it around in your pack the whole trip and dig it out each time you want to use it. I use a small (2 to 3 oz) bottle that I can clip to my pack. This way I can apply sunscreen when I need it without taking off the pack. I prefer alcohol-based sunscreens in very hot environments because they don't clog my pores as much as a cream. Many creams also freeze, which is an issue for glacier travelers. As the sun rises, the risk of sunburn goes from 0% to 100% in a couple of minutes. Your frozen cream won't thaw on its own for hours, so keep it in your sleeping bag if possible (and imagine the mess if it opens).

Carefully protect the hands, feet (if you're wearing sandals), ankles, backs of ears, insides of ears, nostrils, and underside of the chin. The mouth and tongue are problematic. A bandanna over the mouth, bandit-style, can help, or a disposable dust mask (though this can restrict breathing). Some hats come with an extension that covers the back of the head and the ears. I often wear very thin liner gloves even when it's warm to protect my hands. Burned hands lead to loss of dexterity, which means you're an accident waiting to happen.

Sunburn should be treated as any other burn. Get out of the sun, cool the area, and apply aloe vera or cortisone cream. Nonsteroidal anti-inflammatory drugs (NSAIDs) such as acetaminophen and ibuprofen can help. Severe sunburn can lead to infection, which may require more advanced treatment.

Canker Sores, Cold Sores, and Fever Blisters

Canker sores are ulcers, often whitish, that occur inside the mouth, on the gums, or on the tongue. It's unclear what causes them (though it's apparently not a *Herpes* virus), and they're not contagious. Cold sores (fever blisters) are red sores around the lips, or on the chin, cheeks, nose, and rarely on the roof of the mouth. They are contagious, so no smooching while you have an outbreak. Sun exposure will often trigger outbreaks of any these lesions. Stress also seems to be a trigger, as well as certain foods.

These lesions can make your life miserable. After I lost my hat on the second day of an attempt on Denali, I burned my mouth and sprouted something like nine canker sores inside my lower lip. The pain was so intense that there was no way I could climb; luckily, I was stuck at 4,300 m in a 10-day storm. It was hard to eat, hard to drink, hard to talk, and hard to sleep. Cold sores dry out, cause cracking around the lips, and are just as painful.

There is no truly effective treatment; you'll just have to wait the 7 to 10 days it takes these lesions to heal. There are prescription medications that will shorten the length of a cold sore outbreak; ask your physician. A warm saltwater solution helps kill the pain, while a Vaseline-type lubricant can help prevent cold sores from drying out too much. Aspirin, acetaminophen, or ibuprofen can help the pain. I was taking codeine on Denali just to make it through the day.

Snowblindness

Sunburning the eyes is another very unpleasant high-altitude problem that can be avoided 99% of the time by proper use of the proper equipment. Snowblindness often occurs like this: It's foggy or snowing, your glasses are fogging up, and you're trying to pick a complex route through a glacier or along a snowy ridge. You take off your glasses; it doesn't seem very bright. That night or the next morning, your eyes start to feel as if there is sand in them. That's snowblindness. You forgot that UV radiation penetrates the clouds or fog, even though visible light is reduced. You've burned the outer layers of your cornea, which have fallen off and exposed the nerves underneath.

Like regular sunburn, the only thing that will heal you is time. You should use an anesthetic only if you must descend to a safer location; don't use it continuously. Cover the eyes, and take aspirin or ibuprofen. Some people recommend moist teabags on the eyes.

Prevention is the best cure. Your sunglasses must be fitted properly so that light doesn't sneak in around the edges. Don't be afraid to use some duct tape to add some extra shading. Always carry goggles (with UV protection) for those nasty days. Improvise glasses with tape or cloth if you lose yours. And carry a spare pair of sunglasses on long trips.

Overheating the Core

Once heat production (by the body) and heat gain (from the environment) become greater than heat loss, body temperature will increase. The body attempts to maintain homeostasis by behavioral means (taking off clothes or finding some shade) and/or by physiological means (increasing heat loss).

The primary physiological method for increasing heat loss is perspiration (sweating). Perspiration works because it requires heat energy to evaporate water. A lot of energy. Everyone has watched a pot of water on the stove and asked, "Why is this taking so long to boil?" It's because of the large amount of energy required to evaporate the water. Your body takes advantage of this by secreting water (and salts) through the sweat glands onto the surface of the skin. As this water evaporates, it carries a lot of heat away with it, cooling your skin.

If water is to evaporate from your skin, the atmosphere must accept it. Here are the basics of atmospheric water vapor:

- The atmosphere can only hold a certain amount of water at any given temperature.
- The amount of water that can be held increases as the temperature of the air increases.
- If the air is holding the maximum amount of water that it can at that temperature, it is 100% saturated; this is described as 100% relative humidity.
- Relative humidity describes how saturated the atmosphere is with water, from 0% (completely dry air) to 100% (completely saturated air at that temperature).

Long ago I forgot my hat and my sunglasses on a climb of the Middle Teton Glacier. I don't know how I avoided snowblindness.

If the relative humidity is 100%, then there will be rain, snow, or fog. Because the water-holding capacity of air decreases at lower temperatures, we can raise the relative humidity to 100% by cooling the air. When you open your freezer on a hot summer day, the warm, moist air in your kitchen is cooled, relative humidity increases to 100%, and fog forms. Note that the actual amount of water in the air hasn't changed, just the capacity of the air to hold water.

Why is this important? Well, the sweat from your body needs to enter the atmosphere to carry away heat. If the relative humidity is 100%, that can't happen.* Relative humidity isn't normally 100%, but the higher the humidity, the slower the evaporation and heat loss.

Exercise increases heat production and therefore the need for increased heat loss. Some people lose heat more easily due to body size (short and skinny), body fat (skinny), and age (younger). Diseases and drugs can affect heat loss as well.

General overheating leads to a continuum of problems that can be broken down into three categories:[360] glacier lassitude, heat exhaustion, and heat stroke.

Glacier Lassitude

> I was fully acclimatized to the height. Yet I found it terribly difficult to make any progress, and I was breathing five times to each step I took. The sun was beginning to be unbearably hot, too. ... [T]he snow is dry, the air cold, yet the sun's heat is merciless, parching my body, drying out the mucous membrane, beating heavily on my whole being like a ton load! (Buhl 1956, p. 274)

> The heat and stillness were oppressive. Sometimes I would want to take my temperature to make sure I wasn't sick, but it was only glacier lassitude—we called it the "Cwm gloom," which was not gloom but a delightful lethargy that must be the Himalayan substitute for sex. (Hornbein 1966, p. 104)

Walking on a glacier or snowslope and carrying a load on a sunny glacier can be one of the most trying experiences you'll ever have, and nobody besides Hornbein[159] has described it as "delightful" or "a substitute for sex." Under these circumstances you are sweating a lot, but you can't always tell it. You're also losing water from the lungs, and as a result dehydration is a part of all heat injuries. But glacier lassitude is more than that. The combination of dazzling light, heat, and snow seems to suck the will to move from your veins and makes walking or climbing a horrible chore.

Glacier lassitude can be minimized by getting up early and completing your trip in the dark. However, you still will likely be camping on the glacier, and your tent temperature can easily exceed 40°C (105°F). At 6,500 m on Gasherbrum II, I had to put my sleeping bag on

---

* A practical note: A reading of 100% relative humidity means precipitation, which usually increases heat loss because in above-freezing temperatures, the rain leads to conductive heat loss (unless it's very hot).

TREATMENT FOR HEAT EXHAUSTION AND HEAT STROKE BY NONPHYSICIANS

This information was modified from Ward et al.[360] and Noakes.[249]

Patient Is Conscious (even after a < 1 minute fainting spell)

Remove from sun.

Elevate legs and pelvis.

Provide water with carbohydrates and electrolytes as victim desires.

If improvement is not rapid, proceed as below.

Patient Is Unconscious

Check rectal temperature.

If rectal temperature is > 40°C (> 104°F), begin cooling procedure below.

If rectal temperature is < 40°C, check blood pressure and pulse rate. If these are reasonable, then the patient may have some other problem (low sodium, low blood sugar, etc.). Remove patient from sun, recheck rectal temperature, and examine for other problems as you are able (altitude illness).

Evacuate as soon as possible; other organs may fail over time, even if the patient appears to recover.

No liquids by mouth until instructed by physician.

Cooling Procedure

Place cold liquids, ice, snow, or any liquids < 30°C (< 86°F) on the trunk and around the neck to promote rapid cooling.

Massage limbs gently to promote blood flow.

Monitor body temperature; as it approaches normal, reduce the cooling.

---

the roof of the tent to provide some shade and cooler temperatures. In the evening I could smell hints of burning nylon from the sun's intense rays.

The trusty umbrella can help, though it can't cut down on the glare from the snow. Wear light-colored clothes; a white cotton zip-neck turtleneck works well. The only other hope is to have cold drinks available during your hike. Recovery is usually rapid once shade and fluids are available.

Heat Exhaustion

As the limits of homeostasis are reached, body temperature remains near normal, but sweating starts to clearly decrease. The brain still functions normally (except for lassitude), but cramps, vomiting, nausea, and fainting may occur. Noakes[249] suggests that individuals who cease heavy exercise may faint due to the sudden drop in blood pressure that can naturally occur when you stop and not due to dehydration.

Heat Stroke

The body has now lost temperature homeostasis. Sweating ceases, and core temperature rises to a rectal temperature of over 40°C.[249] Mental function deteriorates, with coma or convulsions possible. If the person suddenly becomes aggressive, irritable, or nonresponsive and has stopped sweating, immediate treatment is imperative.

KEY CONCEPTS

1. Exposure to heat or cold will change a number of bodily functions as the body attempts to maintain a constant temperature.
2. Cold can lead to nonfreezing injury, frostbite, or a lower body temperature.
3. A person who is apparently dead due to hypothermia must be warmed before being pronounced dead.
4. Some standard treatments for cold injuries, such as rubbing snow on frostbitten areas, lead to further damage and should not be done.
5. It's easy to get sunburn in short periods of time and in unusual places when traveling at altitude.
6. The eyes can be sunburned, leading to snowblindness.
7. Overheating the body can lead to a loss of willpower, nausea, or coma, depending on the amount of overheating.

Interpersonal Relations

Your experiences at altitude are going to be heavily influenced by other people. These may be your traveling companions, other groups, staff (porters, cooks, and guides), officials (liaison officers), and local residents. Long after the thrill of the physical experience subsides, you'll remember the people. Often these will be fond memories, sometimes they won't be. Interpersonal relations can be a significant source of stress (refer back to Fig. 21), which can affect your performance at altitude. My main purpose here is to acquaint you with some of the possible issues that you might face so you can minimize stress and maximize your performance.

What are your travel plans? A day trip with a close friend? A weeklong trip with some friends and others? A three-week guided trek to a foreign country with a group of strangers? A two-month expedition with a group of foreign climbers, and you're the only one who speaks English? The joys and challenges will differ considerably among the different types of high-altitude travel. I'll focus on the most extreme situation—an expedition to an 8,000 m peak—to illustrate the range of issues involved. If your trip is simpler, just focus on those issues that apply to you.

THE TEAM

These are your traveling companions or partners. We usually talk of climbing teams and trekking/hiking groups, but I'll use the word *team* to cover all types of groups. I'll use *member* or *teammate* to describe individuals on the team other than the leader, guide, or staff; *member* is the label that locals will apply to trekkers or climbers in the Himalayas.

Your level of dependence on other team members will differ considerably on different types of trips. Trekkers don't rely on other teammates all that much, while climbers have

In this one mess tent are five people, five countries, five languages, and five cultures.

to trust their lives to other teammates. Throwing a group of people (or even animals) together activates the stress response in the body.[306] The composition of the team will impact how members interact and how group decisions are made.

Friends versus Strangers

Teams of friends are not unusual, even on the highest peaks. Highly technical climbs are often tackled by friends, if only because of the requisite trust involved. Few larger expeditions or treks are composed solely of people who know one another. Strangers may be from your country, from another English-speaking country, or from a non-English-speaking country. This last group may or may not speak English. It will be easier to get to know (and predict the behavior of) people who are more like you. I'll talk about language a bit more below.

Keep in mind that you must have something in common with these strangers because you're interested in doing the same thing. On trips where mutual trust must be developed, such as technical climbing, seek to develop that trust from the very first day. If English is the language of choice, pay special attention to those who can't speak it well to make sure they are included and understand what's going on. I've been on the other end of this (the only English speaker), and believe me, it gets real lonely real fast.

It's common for teammates to compare notes on your climbing, trekking, or other travel experiences. This isn't just an easy conversation topic, but it allows members to figure out the experience levels of group members. The quietest people are usually either the least or most experienced members. While a certain amount of one-upsmanship is common (especially among male climbers), it's quite tedious to have to listen to a member constantly brag about his accomplishments. These folks are often insecure, and you might want to keep an eye on them in critical situations. Keep in mind that your goal is to have a functional relationship with each member so that necessary tasks can be accomplished, just like at work.

How were members chosen? Trips can be classified as commercial or self-organized. Self-organized groups are noncommercial trips, while a commercial trip is organized and advertised by another individual or business. On commercial trips the organizer may have criteria that members have to meet, such as previous experience, but many only require that your check doesn't bounce. Self-organized trips almost always have requirements for joining the team. For example, the old-style national climbing expeditions either invited particular climbers or solicited applications that were then screened by the leader or a selection committee. The same process goes on, far more informally, on almost any self-organized trip. ("Should we invite Joe to come?" "No, he snores too much. Let's ask Christy instead.")

Which type of trip works better? There's no way to tell in advance. Friendships can shatter or form and success can be won or lost on both commercial and noncommercial trips. On the whole, self-organized trips offer the best chance of assembling a compatible team. Keep in mind that a self-organized trip may use commercial outfitters (e.g., trekking agents) to arrange logistics.

Guided Trips

Commercial trips may be led by one or more guides, but they can also be unguided in many cases. Unguided commercial trips are usually found only on the highest peaks as a result of government permit requirements. The cost of these permits is high (several thousand dollars), and commercial outfitters will buy a permit and sell the slots to individuals or groups. These expeditions can be teams in name only, with the different subgroups operating independently on the mountain. These unguided, commercial groups offer special challenges for decision making, as described below.

Why use a guide? Maybe you want to try out mountaineering or backpacking (or some other altitude activity). A guided trip up Rainier or the Grand Teton is an excellent introduction to alpine climbing. If you already have the skills, you might still use a guide if you want to visit a foreign country where you have no experience; much trekking falls under this category. Organizing a climb of Everest or another high peak can be overwhelming even for experienced climbers, and a guided trip relieves the climbers of leadership responsibilities. Even experts may be unable to find a partner for a particular climb, so a guide can serve as a partner-for-hire. I'll again use a high-altitude climbing expedition as an example.

Guided trips actually vary quite a lot in terms of the guide–client relationship. Krakauer[191] describes the clear differences in guiding philosophy between Rob Hall and Scott Fischer on Everest in 1996. Hall emulated the old-school guides, who set strict rules, made all decisions, and the clients followed the guide's orders. Fischer let clients make many of their own decisions within a general strategy set up by the guides. These have been called the "legalist" and "situationalist" philosophies.[58] The legalist approach tends to squash self-responsibility and judgment in clients; you're not there to think, just to follow orders.[63] The situationalist approach may lead to misplaced self-confidence in clients. If you're going on a guided trip of any kind, it's important to determine the structure of the guide–client relationship and how much freedom you'll have to make decisions on the trip. If you need lots of freedom, then a guide may not be a good idea.

How experienced are the guides and company in the country you're visiting? For example, a guide with lots of experience in Nepal will find things to be very different in Pakistan. Ask for references and use the Web to locate more feedback from previous clients. Don't be scared off by a couple of negative comments (you know the way people complain on the Web). How many guides are there on your trip? A single guide is a dicey proposition on any sort of remote trip. What if somebody, such as the guide, becomes ill or gets injured?

As a general rule, guided climbers have less experience than their nonguided brethren. This will have an impact on you (as a fellow team member) and on other teams on the hill. At 7,000 m on Everest, IMAX filmmaker Dave Breashears encountered some guided climbers and noted:

On some faces I saw an odd expression—a mix of desperation, innocence, and hope. One look, and you knew a lot of them had no idea what they were in for.
(Breashears 1999, p. 253)

Some clients seem to think the word guide means "servant." This can be especially true on the high-end and expensive guided trips. This is partially the fault of the companies themselves, who splash their brochures and Web sites with over-the-top marketing claims. Luxury is a relative thing at 5,000 m, however. When I see clients who complain when they have to help around camp or otherwise participate in normal expedition activities, I wonder what motivates them to climb. An experienced climber on such a trip remarked:

Sherpas put in the route, set up the camps, did the cooking, hauled all the loads. This conserved our energy and vastly increased our chances of getting up Everest, but I found it hugely unsatisfying. (Krakauer 1997, p. 168)

Anatoli Boukreev was criticized for not pampering Scott Fischer's Everest clients.[191] Boukreev[57, 58] clearly indicates the dangers of overindulging clients.

As a client you have the right to expect a good-faith effort by the guides to deliver promised food, equipment, services, and support. But keep in mind that the guide can't control everything. You'll only increase group stress by continually whining, "I paid $$$$ and I expect blahblahblah." Help out where appropriate, but don't be too zealous. In some situations (e.g., a Kilimanjaro climb), you'll find it difficult to do anything other than walk, eat, or sleep, as the staff is usually rather large (we had nine staff for two members).

A good guide will not just get you from point A to point B but should also serve as a teacher. Don't be afraid to ask questions—both you and the guide will find the trip more interesting. Even the most laid-back guide will have occasion to become authoritarian and may start barking out commands, like when somebody falls into a crevasse. At these times you need to be a good soldier and follow instructions, no questions asked, unless you spot a new danger.

These comments refer mostly to guided high-altitude mountaineering. Guided treks, backpacking trips, and alpine climbs will face a subset of these issues. Try to remember that you are spending money to purchase the *opportunity* to do these trips and experience these places. There is never any assurance that your actual experiences will meet your prior expectations. This is, of course, true for any aspect of life, but the high cost of some trips can lead to unrealistic expectations.

Experience

Nobody is born with experience. If we again use the example of high-altitude expeditions, it wasn't that long ago that climbing a high peak required both an extensive climbing résumé and friendships in the right places. Now, anyone with money can buy their way onto an Everest expedition. But is this really a recent phenomenon? In 1939 a U.S. expedition nearly climbed K2 and then succumbed to tragedy. Dudley Wolfe, the American who died, was a very inexperienced but wealthy climber who was only on the expedition because of his money. Team member (and highly experienced climber) Jack Durrance concluded:

> The Himalaya is a poor place for a man to learn mountaineering. (Kauffman and Putnam 1992, p. 155)

During the 10-year period leading to the 1996 Everest tragedy, guided high-altitude climbing really took off, and the proportion of inexperienced climbers in the high mountains skyrocketed. Describing an older group of Americans climbing in India, Joe Tasker observed:

> They struck us as people who like the mountains and buy the equipment recommended without a proper appreciation of when to use it....Age equated with experience and numbers with safety. (Tasker 1982, p. 112)

And just prior to the 1996 Everest debacle,

> What worried me was that many of these people lacked any real apprenticeship in the mountains. They hadn't mastered fundamental skills. (Breashears 1999, p. 253)

After the first couple of days of climbing on the North Face of Kangchenjunga, a difficult route up the third-highest mountain in the world, I realized that one member could barely put on his harness or tie into a climbing rope. Luckily, he bailed out before the difficult climbing started. During my three summers on 8,000 m peaks in Pakistan, it was clear to me that a large number of climbers lacked the basic mountaineering training to safely climb these peaks. Data from Mount Everest reveal that climbers with previous experience climbing in Nepal have almost a 50% greater summit success rate than climbers without experience in Nepal.[171]

Why is experience so important at altitude? Lack of oxygen may make it more difficult to think, forcing you to rely on instinctive actions.[272] Practice indeed makes perfect, and skills that require no thought at sea level will also require little thought at altitude. It may take more concentration and time to accomplish those tasks, though your accuracy will not decline very much if you have enough time.[360]

Even more important is decision making (Chapter 11). The inexperienced climber relies completely on others to make nearly all decisions; that climber moves, eats, pees, and poops and only must decide on the latter two. The inexperienced climber can't evaluate any novel situation: bad anchors on fixed ropes, a crevasse bridge that has deteriorated, avalanche conditions, weather—the list is endless. The inexperienced climber also can't evaluate the quality of the decisions made by others, so must blindly accept their word.

Gain experience on easy trips before trying harder trips.

Experience also leads to an economy of movement and lower energy expenditure over the course of a day. I think that this is a cumulative process, so by the end of an expedition, the experienced climber can have more reserves for that big summit push. There are dozens of little tricks to save energy (many of which are in this book), but you must come up with your own suite of energy-saving tricks that fit your style and body. That can only happen through experience.

Inexperience may also lead to you to overestimate your achievement. Hiring a guide to shepherd you up Mount Rainier, then Denali, then Cho Oyo, then Everest is sorta like riding shotgun in a stock car race, then claiming the win along with the driver.

If we move out of the realm of high-altitude mountaineering and into trekking, backpacking, or alpine climbing, experience is still important but is perhaps less critical. The greenhorn trekker or backpacker may find major challenges in daily activities: using a squat toilet, sleeping on the ground, and eating unusual food, for instance. However, there are few technical challenges during treks or backpacking trips, so it's a matter of endurance in most cases. Guided treks/backpacking trips are usually graded by difficulty or strenuousness, so it's possible to pick an easy trek if you're new to the activity. Similarly, alpine climbing guides won't take you on a technical climb that's beyond your experience level.

In summary, you can't get experience without trying things. If you're a relatively fit person, you can physically accomplish most treks or easy climbs. Rob Hall stated that he could get any fit person to the top of Everest,[191] but is that really a good idea? Regardless of your altitude activity, start easy. You may be physically capable of completing a trek/climb, but you will find a lot of "psychic energy" goes into dealing with all of the other aspects of the activity. If you're just trying out alpine climbing, the most common mistake is to attempt climbs that are technically too difficult. You may be able to lead 5.11 in the climbing gym or M6 at the ice crag, but that's generally irrelevant on a real mountain. Fifteen pitches of 5.6 and some AI2 after a 2,000 ft approach is a whole different ball game, so get humble and pick routes that challenge your route-finding skills and ability to move fast (roped or unroped).

You can hire a guide and learn a lot about your activity very quickly. It is more satisfying and you will make more progress if you can hook up with other experienced individuals. The right partner is a key feature of success at higher difficulty levels.[351] Twight and Backes, Shipton and Tilman, Messner and Habeler, and Troillet and Loretan are examples of famous climbing partnerships that accomplished far more as a team than these individuals could have accomplished on their own.

RELATIONSHIPS AMONG TEAM MEMBERS

> *Age and differing motives were against us from the start. Not only did we have older members of unknown physical strength, we had untested, inexperienced youth.* (Roskelley 1987, p. 38)

Regardless of how your trip was organized, your activities will be dominated by interactions with others. You will interact most often with other team members, and these interactions can make or break your trip. The importance of team interactions is clear from the amount of time spent discussing them in written accounts. I'll focus again on the more extreme situation of a climbing expedition, though the concepts are universally applicable to almost any endeavor.

Choosing the Team

Self-organized trips have the luxury of choosing their members, unlike the commercial expeditions. Probably the best bit of advice comes from longtime expedition organizer/leader Sir Christian Bonington:

> *An expedition is comprised of a pattern of tensions in human relationships.* (Bonington 1973, p. 137)

There is considerable discussion in the literature about the best "type" of climber to include on an expedition. There are the "prima donnas" (technically gifted, highly motivated top climbers who often lack the social skills needed to work with others) and the "plodders" (the decent climbers who are moderately motivated and who are easier to work with):

A partner you can trust is the key to success on technical routes.

Top-class climbers have a touch of the primadonna in their make-up, are often self-centered and are essentially individualists; in some ways the best expedition man is the steady plodder. (Bonington 2001, p. 8)

What about the individual dreams? How do you reconcile the personal ambitions of nineteen climbers with the notion of a group goal which if achieved by some is thereby achieved by all? Nineteen prima donnas could yield a highly explosive mixture. (Hornbein 1966, p. 52)

Bonington assembled teams from a mixture of prima donnas and plodders with much success, primarily because he personally knew most of the climbers. The more difficult the objective, the more important team makeup becomes. John Roskelley spearheaded the first ascent of the high-altitude granite spire Uli Biaho, Pakistan:

Uli Biaho demanded a team. T-E-A-M: A group of people organized for a particular purpose. Not a P-A-R-T-Y: A group of people out for fun and games. Too many American expeditions organized a party and expect to put one together that works, functions, and performs. What drives me to pursue a peak or route may not drive another, equally motivated climber. Not only did I have to find three more compatible individuals to make a team of four, but each had to possess skills that, when added to those of the others, would lead to success. (Roskelley 1993)

This highlights the key issues in team choice: Both complementary skills and social compatibility are required to form a successful team. Simply assembling a team of varying abilities without considering how these individuals will work together is likely to lead to difficulties.

> If one puts two different ability levels in the same climbing group, then someone is constantly being reminded of their weakness. And that is demoralizing. (Burgess and Burgess 1994, p. 335)

> Beyond a shared love of the mountains and a common fascination with the hardships, pressures, rewards, and challenges of climbing, our styles of climbing, our motivations to climb, and our approaches to climbing problems varied greatly, sometimes bringing us into conflict. (Harvard and Thompson 1974, p. 30)

However, teams composed of too many prima donnas have their own difficulties:

> Were we a team? I wondered. A collection of fiery, strong-willed individuals, yes, but not a cohesive group striving for a common goal. We probably couldn't climb "as one," or "for the good of the group," if we tried. Alpine-style climbing is a sport of individualists rather than team players. (Child 1988, p. 74)

> [T]he team, some of America's climbing immortals and legendary prima donnas, would succumb to personal ambition, inexperienced judgments, emotional interference, and, in general, amateurish mistakes. (Roskelley 1993)

> Before we left England I had joked that what the team needed was a psychiatrist, not a film-maker.... (Curran 1987, p. 35)

The highest peaks seldom require the top technical climbing skills of the prima donna. Instead they require the intense passion and will to succeed that differentiate these folks from your average individual. However, without some "top guns" on the team, it will not likely succeed on a really tough climb. Similarly, these top guns are more likely to dislike doing the important but unglamorous tasks such as carrying loads.

Interactions within the Team

It's interesting that American K2 expeditions provide the best examples of teams that were well-adjusted (1953)[165] and maladjusted (1975).[297] The 1978 American K2 expedition, though successful at reaching the summit, was another fairly dysfunctional team.[284] To be fair, the 1970s saw the emergence of the "true confessional" expedition book, and prior expeditions certainly had their share of problems that were swept under the rug in the official accounts (e.g. Roberts[290]).

Everyday life has taught us that some people are easy to get along with, while others are not. When we put people into close proximity 24/7 and add hypoxia, cold, dehydration, hunger, exhaustion, and danger, it's not surprising that interactions become more difficult. We're fighting lots of other stresses, and most of us lose the ability to look past simple issues that would be meaningless in other circumstances:

> Your friend in civilisation may become your enemy on a mountain; his very snore assumes a new and repellent note; his tricks at the mess table, the sound of his mastication, the scarcely concealed triumph with which he appropriates the choicest [tidbits], the absurd manner in which he walks, even the cut of his clothes and the colour of the patch on the seat of his trousers, may induce an irritation and loathing almost beyond endurance. (Smythe 1937, p. 368)

During the first ascent of Everest, Wilfred Noyce gave voice to a common thought at altitude:

> The 25th was for me, I confess it, a day of internal grumps. Every climber must have such days; thank Heaven they are rare. On them it would give the greatest pleasure if all his colleagues fell into the largest crevasse available. (Noyce 1954, p. 155)

It's important to clear the air occasionally and openly discuss the minor and major complaints:

> I am sure that a certain amount of grumbling and character-stripping helps to relieve tension. It is just a matter of keeping it all in proportion. (Bonington 2001, p. 104)

The problem arises when these arguments fester and cliques develop within the team. Another key element is the balance between personal desires (say, to reach the summit) and team goals (to get somebody to the summit). Referring to the 1978 K2 expedition, Jim Curran concluded:

> How could it possibly help to climb the mountain when half the team were locked in combat with the other half? And why, after nearly two months on the mountain, were so many people still deluding themselves they could reach the top? (Curran 1995, p. 145)

The subjugation of personal goals is a topic team members need to reconcile within themselves. Balancing personal and team goals is a major issue in team leadership (discussed below).

Every family has arguments, and a trek or expedition quickly becomes a family. Tolerance is a personality trait that we must all cultivate at altitude:

> You get extremes of selfishness and extremes of selflessness. The funny thing is, you tend to forgive the selfishness—as long as it's not too exaggerated—because everyone suffers a lot. (Mo Anthoine, quoted in Alvarez 2001, p. 73)

Chip in and help. Help unload the bus. Help sort out loads. Help set up tents. Go get water. Do the cooking. Wash dishes. Even if you don't have to, even if you've paid big bucks to be guided, pitch in.

> It was the unspoken sharing of tasks between us that made us such a tight-knit team. (Burgess and Burgess 1994, p. 296)

> [Wanda Rutkiewicz's] lack of involvement and work on the mountain angered her teammates and prevented her from really bonding with them. (Jordan 2005, p. 159)

> In this godforsaken place, I felt disconnected from the climbers around me—emotionally, spiritually, physically—to a degree I hadn't experienced on any previous expedition. We were a team in name only, I'd sadly come to realize. (Krakauer 1997, p. 163)

Every positive interaction you have with fellow travelers is another connection you have to them. Every negative interaction breaks connections. You're more likely to accomplish your goals if others are willing to help you, and if you get into trouble, you can't have too many friends. You don't need to be overbearingly sweet; honest and appropriate interactions are all that are necessary. Sometimes you'll have to stand up for your own interests, so don't be a doormat.

A group of competitive people will be competitive. Some peer pressure is good and serves as a positive motivation. However, it can be carried too far. The 1975 K2 expedition[297] is a wonderful case study of overbearing macho posturing, with continual competitions to see who could carry the most the fastest on both the approach and the climb and a constant barrage of macho verbal taunting. It reminds one of a bunch of 15-year-old boys. Ed Webster was on an American expedition to the West Ridge of Everest in 1985 and recounts similar tales. One day he realized that he needed to acclimatize by sleeping at a lower camp:

> I decided to drop my load and return to Camp Two for the night to "sleep low." Jay, Kevin, and Dan thought my decision was ridiculous. "This is Everest!" Jay exclaimed. "You've got to tough it out, man!" (Webster 2000, p. 70)

This "tough it out" philosophy is generally not productive for either the teammates or the team. It also prevents team members from carrying out an essential duty—monitoring each other for signs of illness or deterioration. It's not unusual for a person to have an altitude illness and have no indication that something is wrong. Minor behavioral changes can be an important clue, so if you don't get to know people when they're well, you might not know that they are sick. Constant bickering, put-downs, or other antisocial behavior can prevent people from truly understanding each other.

Women and Men

We've come a long way from 1961, when Sir Edmund Hillary wouldn't allow women to go above 5,800 m and tried to keep women out of his Makalu Base Camp altogether. In 1978 a team of American women climbed Annapurna (8,091 m), unfortunately with two fatalities.[47] Today, women are commonly members on both commercial and self-organized climbs. Scott Fischer's former company, Mountain Madness, was run by Christine Boskoff until her untimely death in 2006. I've noticed refreshingly little gender bias in backpacking, hiking, or trekking over the last 15 years.

From the standpoint of member interactions, Arlene Blum (leader of the 1978 Annapurna expedition) notes that the main issues for women are the psychological ones:

> What are considered admirable traits in men—assertiveness, independence, ambition, competitiveness—are still often seen as undesirable in women. Yet most successful climbers, male or female, possess these characteristics. (Blum 1998, p. 176)

Women, while generally smaller than men, are just as strong and may have more endurance. Cherie Bremer-Kemp carried loads very high on Dhaulagiri while several months pregnant. The biographies of female climbers show clearly that they are just as capable as men).[64, 124, 179, 294]

Some authors emphasize the problems with mixed-sex expeditions. Women are perceived as unqualified in some accounts.[88, 284, 297] These expeditions occurred in the 1970s, when women were first being included in such trips. Some women were included on expeditions because they were wives (Dianne Roberts on K2[297]) or daughters (Nanda Devi Unsoeld on Nanda Devi[295]). A man with their experience levels wouldn't have been invited on these trips.

Romance is the other problem cited.[284, 295, 376] While romance per se isn't an issue, it does change the dynamics of a trip, as you now have to take into account a couple as opposed to two individuals. As romance blooms, the former goal may pale in comparison, leading to a loss of team strength. Living in a tent isn't very private, so everyone (including the staff) knows what's going on. In Nepal, it's considered to be bad karma to fornicate on the mountain, so realize that you may be jeopardizing the support of your staff if you're violating their idea of proper conduct. However, many a romance has succesfully bloomed at altitude. As long as the team can still function properly, there shouldn't be any problem.

Craig[88] discussed the difficulties of mixed-sex climbing teams and suggested (partly in jest) that all-male and all-female teams might be the solution. Forty years ago there weren't any coed college dorms, women didn't face danger in the armed forces, and equal rights for women were just a dream. I would hope that today our male psyches have advanced to the point where women and men can work together on the high peaks. I've certainly seen it happen on many occasions, but there are still potential problems depending on the nationality of the people involved. Trekking/backpacking/hiking trips are a very different matter, and I've never noticed any gender issues on such trips that weren't directly related to physical capabilities of the individuals involved.

INTERACTIONS WITH TEAMS OR INDIVIDUALS FROM OTHER CULTURES

Other teams on the trek or on the mountain may become trusted friends or despised enemies. Usually, the greater the differences in the nationality and culture, the more difficult it can be to empathize:

> You've got to be really careful climbing with people you don't know... and Americans....I mean they are different. (Dick Renshaw, quoted in Venables 2000, p. 5)

> They swing on, and use, our ropes and kick off rocks all the time. As if the mountains weren't dangerous enough, you have to see a cavorting Italian to understand the real meaning of danger. (Burgess and Burgess 1994, p. 458)

> They [French and Russians] pulled it off [the summit of K2] only by climbing in conditions that we Americans thought insanely dangerous. (Viesturs 2006)

> [The Taiwanese] were climbing in a peculiar style, really close together... which meant it was nearly impossible to pass them. We spent a lot of time waiting for them to move up the ropes. (Stuart Hutchinson, quoted in Krakauer 1997, p. 176)

> [N]ever camp below the French. They will shit on you from a great height. (Brian Blessed, quoted in Dickinson 1997, p. 47)

The last comment is from a British comedian/climber. These examples suggest some cultural differences in concepts of danger and safety that are supported by data. For example, Germans had proportionally more accidents on Denali than any other nationality between 1973 and 1982.[362] European climbers are used to the Alps, which are very "urban" mountains with many climbers, a sophisticated rescue system, and, unfortunately, a high death rate. American and Canadian climbers are used to fewer crowds, less reliable rescue, and the corresponding need for a more safety-conscious attitude. European trekkers/hikers similarly have a more urban view of their environment. Much like Americans tolerate high death rates on the highways, European climbers seem to tolerate high death rates in the mountains.

A key issue on the big mountains is the use of fixed ropes. Usually ropes are installed by the first team on the hill, and it's been common in recent years for these teams to request (or demand) payment from other teams to use the ropes. The problem is that the ropes in many cases are poorly placed, poorly anchored, and of poor material. Chances are your team will be adding rope and anchors as the climb progresses, so you're going to be spending money anyway. In some cases it is possible to agree, prior to fixing ropes, to shared contributions from various teams. Your best bet is to stay off the standard routes—it will be a lot quieter, safer, and saner.

On the mountain you may find yourself combining forces with climbers from other teams to work the route or attempt the summit. This can work well or turn into a disaster, as it did on K2 in 1986.[90, 100] Conflicting goals, language difficulties, personal ambition, and altitude can be potent ingredients for trouble:

> [R]ivalry and discord could create a modern day Tower of Babel and the whole random collection of men and women striving for K2's summit might defeat themselves without any help at all from the mountain. (Curran 1987, p. 123)

Most summited later than expected in 1986, the mountain and weather intervened, and five died.

Hikers, backpackers, and trekkers are not immune to these issues. In the United States or Canada, you won't run into a large number of "foreigners," but most of the trekking you do will be in association with groups from other cultures.

LEADERSHIP

Altitude affects judgment and therefore decision making. At the same time, an expedition or long trek requires many, many decisions be made in the course of a day that will affect the success of the endeavor. Many expeditions have been doomed to failure not through technical difficulty, weather, or bad luck, but through poor decision making and leadership. Decision making is covered in Chapter 11. As with much at high altitude, these aspects of your activity require more care than at sea level.

The type of trip you're on will determine the leadership model used. A group of climbers might share the decision making. A guided trip will be led by the guide, though some guides may ask for more input from clients than other guides. A large, self-organized trip may have an official leader who makes all decisions, or some decisions may be made as a group.

Leadership styles have changed over the years. Early mountaineering expeditions were organized along strictly military lines, with members swearing an oath of allegiance to the leader (e.g. Herzog[153]). The 1939 K2 expedition combined a leader who was a German-born American and an American team:

> *Fritz [Wiessner] also adhered to an authoritarian leadership model, whereas the Americans had a tradition of independence, even of rebellion. They were accustomed to reaching major decisions via general discussion and participation by all. ...* (Kauffman and Putnam 1992, p. 157)

Twenty-five years later:

> *Only an American expedition would attempt to vote itself to the top of Everest.* (Hornbein 1966, p. 102)

And another 25 years later:

> *[T]he team's interpretation of this role [leader] was more of general servant than generalissimo.* (Saunders 1991)

In the mountains of Asia, the bureaucracy still assumes that expeditions follow the old-school model of a united team under the authority of a leader who makes all the decisions. This is often far from the truth. The leader needs to act like a leader in front of the locals, while privately hashing out the decisions with the team. Al Burgess recounts an incident on a trek to K2 in which leader Al Rouse made a decision that angered other members. Burgess speculates that Rouse might have done so to avoid losing face in front of the porters:

> *In that part of the world [Pakistan], strength and decisiveness are highly prized, and a leader always leads from the front.* (Burgess and Burgess 1994, p. 333)

The American K2 expeditions in 1975[297] and 1978[284] provide painful clinics in team dysfunction. Jim Curran analyzed these expeditions and concluded:

> *Whittaker's leadership on both expeditions was flawed on the psychology front and his basic man-management was at times naive.* (Curran 1995, p. 141)

During the American expedition to Nanda Devi in 1978, Marty Hoey almost died of altitude illness as the team argued about the proper course of action, and Nanda Devi Unsoeld did die high on the mountain. While the cause of her death is unknown, there were serious disagreements over the wisdom of Devi's attempting the summit with a hernia and other medical problems:

> *No one of us expected our differences of opinion to lead to death.* (Roskelley 1987, p. 213)

LOCAL CULTURES

Travel abroad, as described by H. W. Tilman in the 1930s, involves visiting a "country of great loveliness, inhabited by peoples [who] are always interesting and sometimes charming" (Tilman, p. 156[344]). In his review of the history of K2, Jim Curran described Dr. William Hunter Workman and his wife, Fanny Bullock Workman, who visited the Karakoram in the 1890s, as follows:

> It is tempting to see them as the forerunners of the archetypal tourist: impatient, critical, often at odds with their porters and local inhabitants, self-important and at times unscrupulous. (Curran 1995, p. 156)

While I've seen few truly unscrupulous tourists, the rest of the description fits far too many Western travelers, regardless of their country of origin. If you travel abroad, the customs will be different, the language will be different, and the people will respond differently than they would at home. Get used to it.

Put yourself in the shoes of your porters or local guides. Ang Rita Sherpa, who made 10 ascents of Everest, gave his views to Goran Kropp:

> "I've helped many people reach the summit," he said in broken English and, I noted, with a trace of bitterness. "I've done the hard part, carrying the loads up, and they have all become rich and famous. People climb the mountain with oxygen and guides and go back home and make lots of money. I climb without oxygen or anything, and I have to live in a stone house. What do you think about that?" (Kropp 1997, p. 120)

As a visitor in another country and culture, you are living in residents' reality. This may include different sex roles, different religions, and different assumptions about politeness, hygiene, and time. Our Western construct of the importance of time has no meaning in many countries, much to the consternation of many a Western traveler. As Rudyard Kipling wrote:

> And the end of the fight is a tombstone white
> with the name of the late deceased
> and this epitaph drear, "A fool lies here
> who tried to hurry the East."
>
> In the East, there is always something new to learn about patience. (Messner 1977, p. 107)

Aleister Crowley made a number of very perceptive observations (embedded among some outrageous ideas) about travel in India/Pakistan during his trip to K2 in 1902:

Other cultures require us to accept different ways of doing things. Prayer wheel, Nepal.

> *[The traveler] has to be uniformly calm, cheerful, just, perspicacious, indulgent and inexorable. He must decline to be swindled out of the fraction of a farthing. If he once gives way, he is done for.... The traveler must always remember that his method of striking a match is accurately reported for hundreds of miles in every direction.* (Crowley 1969, p. 283)

The first sentence should guide your interactions in another country. The second is equally true; news travels faster than an eagle, so it's hard to outrun any mistakes you make.

Theft

Expeditions have reported thefts for decades (e.g. Smythe,[326] Bauer,[32] Tasker,[338] Child,[81] Kauffman and Putnam,[182] Kukuczka,[193] Burgess and Burgess,[67] Dickinson[99]). These can be minor thefts, such as a hat or gloves taken from an unlocked bag, or major thefts, such as a loss of boots, tents, or whole loads. Removing swag from the mountain is common after expeditions (this is considered legitimate), but there have been other instances of camps still in use being looted or removed completely.[90] In 2005 Balti locals removed fixed ropes on Broad Peak while a climber was still on the mountain; he had a dicey descent down wet, loose rock and crappy snow.

Don't be too quick to blame the locals, however. Numerous "modern" European climbers will use the tents and supplies of others without asking. In one case, a Spanish group was angry because they were turned back by avalanche danger, and in their disgust, they kicked a load containing the camp of another team right off the mountain.[355]

Anytime your gear is left unattended, it should be in locked bags. Most thefts are crimes of opportunity; an unlocked bag will be opened, and anything easy to remove can be pulled out. If there are multiple groups milling around a camping area, keep your gear inside your tent and your tent zipped up when you're away. Experienced climbers often use plastic barrels to ship and transport their gear. These are less useful for trekkers, as they generally get into their bags on a daily basis.

In summary, theft is an issue that you don't leave behind when you leave the cities. Don't be paranoid, and don't be an easy target. Remember that you're more likely to encounter locals like Tilman's Sherpa, who saved money by boiling his shirt to make tea.[346]

Gender Issues

Whether through religion or culture, women are not treated the same as men in many countries. You can avoid these countries, fit in with their culture, or do what you want and face the consequences. Travel in Pakistan and other Islamic countries can be difficult for women, but some women are able to overcome the built-in difficulties and have a good time. Female trip leaders can face extra challenges, as local men may not offer appropriate respect (see Blum,[47] p. 153ff).

On expeditions, women seem to have as much (or more) trouble with male climbers as with locals.[179, 349] Men aren't immune to abuse. Sherpanis and other female Tibetan porters can be quite dominating, and they seem to enjoy making fun of males on the team.

Communication Issues

I was going to title this section "Language Issues," but the issue of communication encompasses much more than language. Even if you speak the same language, communication can be difficult due to regional dialects, cultural/ethnic differences, and gender differences (as all spouses know).

I have a friend who enjoys visiting Southeast Asia on a regular basis. He doesn't know more than a word or two of the local languages, yet he gets along wonderfully. Most of us are more comfortable if we learn at least a few simple words or phrases. The glut of travel guides out there ensures your access to a basic vocabulary. Most major languages can be learned from audio CDs or tapes.

These resources will usually provide standard pronunciations. If you listen carefully to everyday spoken English, it's very clear that we don't correctly pronounce a good number of words, and it's the same in any country. If at all possible, find a native speaker to help you learn useful pronunciations.

In many countries, there are many local languages and a single national language, which allows intercommunication among all groups. There is often a "colonial" language, a Western language such as English, French, or Spanish, depending on the history of the country. Finally, English is spoken to some extent in most countries today, especially by individuals in business, government, and the tourist industry.

Your true local, like a porter, will speak his or her local language, may speak some of the national language, and possibly may know a word or two of English, so learning the national language won't necessarily let you speak to everyone you meet. If you want to talk to locals on the trek to Everest Base Camp, you need to speak Sherpa/Tibetan (not Nepali). To speak to porters on the way to K2 Base Camp in Pakistan, you need to learn Balti (not the national language, Urdu).

Whatever you learn, pay close attention to pronunciation. Many words sound similar, and many languages use sounds that are unusual in English. Cherie Bremer-Kamp (1987) greeted local men in Nepal by using the normal Nepali greeting, but they responded by laughing or running away. It turns out that her Australian accent twisted the words from meaning "How's it going?" to "Do you have an erection?"

A basic vocabulary—*hello/goodbye, yes/no, stop/go (taxi), left/right, where's the toilet, too expensive, good job,* and *please/thank you*—can be a great help. Americans especially lay the "thank you" thing on a bit thickly, in part because we can't say anything else. In many cultures "thank you" is used only on special occasions; a smile will often suffice.

In many cases you will be accompanied by a guide or other staff member who will serve as a translator. This works well in most cases, but, especially if you are involved in an argument, don't assume that he or she is translating accurately.

When speaking English, there's no need to speak louder—people aren't deaf. Slow

Your porters may be as young as 13 years old.

down just a bit. Enunciate. Simplify. Heck, I couldn't understand a couple of Valley girls/boys I've traveled with because theytalkwithoutpunctuationoranybreaksbetween-thetorrentofwords. Hard, isn't it? Add a hint of space between each word, keep the verbs simple ("Tomorrow I will go to Camp One," not "Tomorrow I'm heading up to the next camp"). Mix in any local words you know. Help your staff learn better English if you have time; it's the gift that keeps on giving.

Body language and visual signals can be dangerous. A shake of the head may mean yes, and a nod may mean no. Assume that any signal with your hands is profane. Because we can't always speak to others, we're left with body language (which is dicey), so, again, a smile goes a long way.

Other Advice

Clothing is a signal of your economic class in many countries, whether you like it or not. Joe Tasker summarized the situation nicely:

> The [W]esterner who through choice abandons his potential wealth and voy-
> ages like one from the lower classes is looked down upon and is not taken seri-
> ously. (Tasker 1982, p. 49)

This is an important issue if you have to get luggage out of customs, obtain government permission to enter a restricted area, or ask any official for any favor. Ladies, if you wear your normal summer wardrobe in certain countries, don't be surprised if you get propositioned (or worse) by the local men. Islamic countries especially require long sleeves, long pants, and probably a head scarf. Any less and you will be considered a "loose woman" who is looking to share herself indiscriminately.

Avoid giving away candy; the short-term gratitude gives way to long-term tooth decay. Both Nepali and Pakistani children have learned to beg for pens or pencils ("Dot-pen!" is the cry of the children along a trekking route). If you want to give to the children, donate directly to the local schoolmaster, who can ensure that the needy (and not the persistent) children benefit. Rewarding children for begging won't help them at all.

KEY CONCEPTS

1. Interpersonal relationships can have a dramatic impact on the quality of a trip to alttude.
2. Understand the nature of the leadership on your trip and the way in which partipants were chosen.
3. The more serious and technical the trip, the more important experience is.
4. Understand the culture you're traveling in and the people you're traveling with.

Extreme Altitude

Wyss-Dunant[387] defined the reactions of the body to different altitudes. Of most interest is his definition of the "lethal zone," starting at about 7,800 m (25,500 ft), in which it is possible for humans to live for only a few days. Wyss-Dunant goes on to define the "ultimate zone," starting at 8,600 m (28,215 ft), as "a physiological boundary which only a few particularly gifted and well-equipped explorers may overstep" (p. 114). Messner and others have renamed this the Death Zone, and while there is no formal definition of the lower limit, I prefer 7,800 m to the often-cited 8,000 m, as I think it is more physiologically relevant. The term ultimate zone hasn't been used in the literature, but I agree with the concept that there are only a limited number of climbers who can function above 8,500 m without supplemental oxygen.

BASIC QUESTIONS

How Long Can You Stay in the Death Zone?

Not very long. High camps on Everest, K2, and Kangchenjunga are all at 7,900 m or higher, and the goal of most climbers is to depart for a summit attempt the morning after arrival at that camp. Diemberger[100] concludes that a person has three days, possibly four, to complete an ascent and descend safely. However, Willi Bauer, the 45-year-old Austrian with whom Diemberger survived the 1986 K2 disaster, spent 10 days at 8,000 m or above.[90]

There is disagreement as to the value of a rest day at these altitudes. In most cases, such a rest only exacerbates the existing fatigue because of the inability of many climbers to properly hydrate during the rest day. The weather and the terrain will have much to do with your decision.

What Factors Influence Your Ability to Function in the Death Zone?

The factors that influence performance in the Death Zone are no different from those that determine performance elsewhere. The difference is that there are far fewer people who are physiologically capable of adequate performance as you move from 7,800 to 8,848 m.

Climbing the Ice Building couloir on Kangchenjunga with millions of tons of ice hanging overhead.

There is very little scientific research from extreme altitudes, which makes it difficult to decide just what the key issues are. West[367] determined that changing the barometric pressure would have a greater impact on the ability of a climber to reach the summit of Everest without supplemental oxygen than an equivalent change in any physiological variable. In fact, if Everest were located at the latitude of Denali, it couldn't be climbed without supplemental oxygen. Because most ascents in the Death Zone occur during good weather (high pressure), climbers have unwittingly chosen the optimal barometric pressure for their attempts.

There are physiological factors that can be manipulated to some extent prior to an ascent into the Death Zone. Hemoglobin content of the blood will increase as the result of the increase in red cell production. Hemoglobin concentration in the blood will increase for at least six weeks after reaching altitude and is independent of altitude above about 5,500 m.[360] Similarly, ventilatory acclimatization may not be complete at 36 days.[360] Therefore, allowing adequate time for acclimatization is a key factor for ascents of the higher 8,000 m peaks.

The final factor that can be controlled is an adjustment of the blood acid–base balance. Simply put, descending as low as possible for a few days prior to a summit attempt may place the body in a better position to transport oxygen at the highest elevations.[360] Boukreev[57] was a strong proponent of this tactic. Other physiological factors influencing performance (cardiac output, membrane diffusing capacity) can't be modified by the climber.

At 7,800 m on Broad Peak, Pakistan: one of the doorways into the Death Zone.

Supplemental Oxygen

Supplemental oxygen was first used in 1921 on Everest by the British. It was used on the first ascents of many of the 8,000 m peaks and is still commonly used on Everest, though not as often on other peaks. Much of the information I summarize below comes from Hultgren.[172]

Supplemental oxygen doesn't return your body to sea-level performance. In fact, the climbing rates summarized in Hultgren[172] and in Table 13 (see Chapter 12) show no real differences in ascent rates between those accomplished with and without supplemental oxygen. The best climbers can climb faster without oxygen than most people can climb while using oxygen. However, supplemental oxygen reduces the ventilation rate (breathing rate) and cardiac output, but nobody has determined if the energy saved in this way compensates for the energy spent hauling the oxygen gear. Breathing oxygen while sleeping reduces periodic breathing and leads to better sleep.

The system in widespread use today utilizes Poisk cylinders (NPO Poisk Ltd.), a regulator, and a mask. A Poisk 3 L bottle filled with oxygen to 260 bar (at 20°C) weighs 2.7 kg. The bottle will last about six hours at a flow rate of 2 L/min. Two or three bottles will usually be required for a summit climb of Everest (12 to 18 hours). It is essential to get Poisk bottles that are factory-filled and not refills from India or elsewhere. Anyone can order bottles directly from the factory these days; check the Poisk Web site.

Make sure your mask fits properly and comfortably. I would buy a new mask in advance and practice wearing it while exercising, preferably in the cold. The mask should fit as well as your boots fit, and minor problems with either can lead to failure in the climb. There are a number of technical details that you should go over when you've got the gear in front of you. If necessary, make some "cheat sheets" with instructions for using the gear and a table showing the relationship between bottle pressure and time remaining at your flow rate. Only familiarity with the equipment will save your climb (or your life) if something goes wrong up high.

There are other systems out there (UK, Summit), but the consensus is that the Poisk system is still superior. The Summit system has promise, but technical problems with the electronics ruined a number of climbs in the first year or two it was on the market. Until the problems are fixed, stick with the simpler Poisk setup.

Is Oxygen Ethical?

This argument has been ongoing since the first use of "English air".[292] Originally, scientists believed that it was impossible to reach the summit of Everest without supplemental oxygen. A significant exception was Alexander Kellas, who wrote a manuscript entitled "A Consideration of the Possibility of Ascending Mount Everest" in 1920 (which was finally published in 2001). After a careful consideration of the physiological issues, Kellas concluded:

Mount Everest could be ascended by a man of excellent physical and mental constitution in first rate training, without adventitious aids if the physical difficulties of the mountain are not too great… (Kellas 2001, p. 407)

Habeler and Messner confirmed this prediction 58 years later.

Climbers using oxygen have a far higher success rate on Everest[382] and a much lower chance of death during descent from the summits of Everest and K2.[168, 170] This implies that supplemental oxygen allows climbers to surpass their physiological limits and reach summits that their bodies couldn't reach on their own. Since clothing isn't considered to be unethical in low-temperature environments, how can supplementary oxygen be considered unethical in low-oxygen environments?

The opposing view states that, because these peaks can be climbed without supplemental oxygen, then they should be climbed without it. Even modern oxygen gear is heavy and requires high-altitude porters to carry it, exposing them to additional danger. The cylinders are left behind, turning the upper reaches of the peaks into garbage dumps. Supplemental oxygen is expensive, so the amount you use is dictated by your ability to pay.

To me, the biggest ethical issue is that supplemental oxygen does entice you into situations where you will endanger your life and the lives of others if your equipment fails:

It is possible to see client climbers who have used a constant supply of oxygen on their ascents debilitated totally if the supply is interrupted, gasping and incapacitated like fish out of water. (Boukreev 1997, p. 40)

Today, most of the supplemental oxygen is being used by climbers who do not have the physical training, mental training, and climbing experience needed to succeed on the highest peaks. Commercial expeditions promise that almost anyone can get to the summit of Everest, and they use oxygen to fulfill that promise. After the 1996 Everest tragedy, Anatoli Boukreev concluded:

Accessibility is an illusion. Money will not save you here, a guide cannot save you here, supplemental oxygen will not guarantee your life in this extreme [environment]. (Boukreev 1997, p. 43)

I realize that the general public isn't interested in how you climb Everest; they don't care about oxygen, fixed ropes, Sherpas, or whatever other "aids" you are using to get up the mountain. The public only cares whether or not you tag the top. But from the climber's perspective, those issues do matter.

In my opinion, supplemental oxygen is part of the medical kit but not part of the climbing kit. Oxygen should be used to allow a safe descent, not to permit the unqualified (by genetics or by experience) person to ascend. That being said, climbing has always been a sport where you are allowed some latitude in style. If you use oxygen on an expedition, make sure that there is a plan for collecting your used cylinders (especially high on the mountain) and that all of the gear is actually carried completely out of the mountains. And don't brag about how easy the climb was after you get home.

STYLE AND ETHICS ON 8,000 M PEAKS

A number of issues arise when climbing on the world's highest peaks in the 21st century. I'll include a number of somewhat lower but popular peaks such as Denali, Aconcagua, and even Mount Rainier in this discussion.

Crowding

The mountain is no longer the biggest obstacle to a safe and successful ascent. Excess humanity means that there's a race for campsites, bottlenecks on the route, dangerous stress on fixed ropes and anchors, more pollution and garbage, more rockfall, more noise, competition for porters, higher prices, and more social problems.

Crowding contributed directly to deaths on K2 in 1986 when there was an inadequate supply of tents at 7,900 m,[100] and crowding affected the decision-making processes of several teams on Everest in 1996.[191] In 1996 an Adventure Consultants Sherpa fell 40 m into a crevasse after he carried up a duffel bag to claim the best campsite at Camp II, even before the climbing team had arrived at Base Camp.[63] At its worst, crowding reinforces a "safety in numbers" myth that may be unspoken but is assumed subconsciously.

You can avoid crowded routes entirely, but that's impractical on many of the highest peaks. Once you've committed to a crowded route, there are several proactive steps you can take. Talk to the other teams on the route to coordinate the use of campsites and the placement and maintenance of any fixed ropes. Time your ascents to be first on the ropes. And realize that Europeans are used to the crowded Alps and generally are more lackadaisical about rock- and icefall than most North Americans would prefer.

Fixed Ropes

Fixed ropes are common on high peaks. Most climbers are ascending expedition-style, taking multiple trips up and down between camps. The ropes allow individual movement with large packs and provide less-qualified climbers with an additional margin of safety on easier ground. In the old days ropes were only placed on difficult sections, but the presence of so many unqualified people in the mountains has led to much more fixed rope on easier sections of the routes.[57]

Fixed ropes must be maintained, and I've been astounded how so many people will blithely ascend obviously dangerous ropes. It's important that ropes are installed correctly. Always leave several meters of slack in each rope length to allow for shrinkage and repair. The slack should be tied up, out of the way, for future use. Regular climbing ropes will shrink quite a bit over time. I descended some fixed ropes on Broad Peak that were installed by Austrian guides, and the ropes were literally as tight as a guitar string. Needless to say, you couldn't get a descender on them. I only traveled on them once.

A conga line of climbers is not an unusual sight on the West Buttress of Denali.

All ropes must be joined together with just enough slack in the ropes to allow comfortable use. Each anchor is then backed up by the anchors above. The top anchor must be as solid as possible. All ropes must be tied together, not joined with carabiners (they'll get stolen). Any spots that might be abraded by rock should be covered with layers of duct tape or padded in any way possible. Use a hammer to break away sharp rock or ice.

Fixed ropes get knicked all the time by rockfall, icefall, and crampons. It's important to take these weak spots out of the rope by tying an overhand or figure-8 knot in the rope that captures the weak spot in the loop. If there is not enough slack in the rope, you can rig up a temporary patch with a Prusik loop. The higher you go up the hill, the worse the ropes will be. A bad rope will be just as likely to break at 8,300 m as at 5,300 m, but at 8,300 m you're less likely to have enough energy to worry about it.

Anchors always need inspection and often need to be replaced, especially in snow and ice. As you're ascending, it's not unusual to get to a snow/ice anchor and find a picket or screw dangling loose. You might say, "Whew, I'm glad the ropes are tied together, so I'll just keep going." Instead, fix anchors as you go and don't be afraid to berate the lazy fools

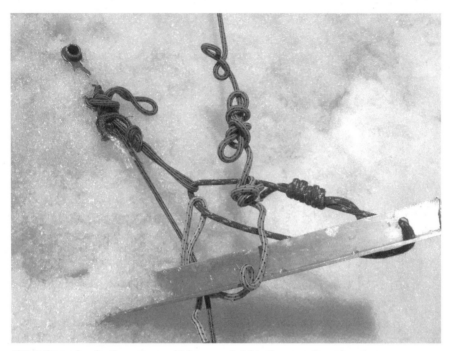
This is the anchor for the rope on which you and eight other people are hanging.

climbing ahead of you for not fixing things. I find that more climbers are willing to fix an anchor they're about to rappel from, but it isn't hard to understand why.

Ignoring fixed ropes is very difficult to do. There's a trail and a reasonably safe belay, so it takes a rare climber indeed to walk a few meters off to the side in order to complete an ascent independently. As a result, some alpinists feel that it is unethical to string a line of fixed ropes up an 8,000 m peak.[229] Others have left no question as to their feelings about fixed ropes:

> Climbing fixed ropes is the worst kind of masturbation. A thousand metres at a time, sometimes two or three days on a fucking fixed rope. Clip on and shove, and shove, shove, shove. It makes me puke. (Gogna Barbacetto, quoted in Messner 1977, p. 48)

Parasitism

Just as an intestinal parasite can flourish while being supported by its host, a parasite climber can rely on the ropes, camps, trail, and overall effort of others to support him while he provides no benefit to those other climbers in return. This style was defined by Reinhold Messner:

> [A]nybody who wants to climb an eight-thousander should be responsible for preparing his own route.... But if the route has already been prepared...it could induce the less experienced, the weaker climbers, up into the death zone too. That this happens on the backs of others is of little concern. As a "parasite," you need exert yourself less to climb high. (Messner 1999a)

> When a person claims to have climbed Nanga Parbat "super-alpine-style" after he has used the chain of camps and ropes of other climbers in the Diamar face, I call his style "super-parasite." (Messner 1999c, p. 10)

In today's reality we can't have the mountains to ourselves, so we are all parasites in a sense, feeding off each other's footsteps, ropes, and campsites. Messner was lucky to have experienced the 8,000 m peaks in the period before the current crowds; I would defy him to repeat his accomplishments today without relying to some extent on other climbers. Indeed, the modern solo climber spends more time dodging others than in surmounting the mountain:

> So far my solo attempt on Everest had turned into an attempt at being solo. (Bettembourg and Brame 1981, p. 264)

The modern solo climber on a standard route can't claim a true solo ascent, but he can lessen his parasite status by sharing in both the expense and effort of maintaining the route. This may mean buying a share of the fixed ropes, carrying loads of ropes up the hill for fixing, or replacing worn ropes or poor anchors; there are many ways to contribute. Unless you are trumpeting your accomplishments in the press, in the long run nobody will care if you're a parasite or not because there are simply too many other parasites out there for you to stand out. I feel much better as a climber when I have contributed to the actual climbing on a route. Goran Kropp[192] accomplished a nearly pure solo on a crowded Everest in 1996.

Speed Climbing

In an attempt to redefine the high-altitude game, it is fashionable to climb the high peaks as quickly as possible. This is more akin to a foot race on a prepared course than a true climb. Speed is without a doubt a useful commodity in the mountains, and speed ascents are a way to provide some uncertainty in a situation where fixed ropes, a known route, and a high chance of rescue exist. The skills involved in a speed ascent are very different from the skills involved in establishing a new route on a high peak, and we must be careful not to equate the two.

Rescue at Extreme Altitude

There has been much discussion of the rescue ethic in the Death Zone. Does a climber have the right to expect a rescue at these altitudes? Do other climbers have the obligation to help with a rescue at these heights? Climbers have asked these questions for years, and the answers are still not clear.

On the first ascent of Lhotse in 1956, the expedition leader contemplated the consequences of a high-altitude accident:

> It was only much later that I realised that to carry down a single seriously injured man would have demanded the last ounce of effort of every man we had on the mountain. (Eggler 1957, p. 188)

At these extreme altitudes, fatigue rules. During a summit attempt on the north side of Everest in 1996, some climbers walked past other climbers who were in distress:

> [Twenty-one-year-old Japanese Eisuke] Shigekawa explained, "We were too tired to help. Above 8,000 meters is not a place where people can afford morality." (Krakauer 1997, p. 241)

A rescue at 7,000+ m requires far more manpower than an equivalent rescue at lower altitude. As a result, a person who can't walk at these high elevations is unlikely to be rescued unless the descent is straight down a fixed rope on a snow slope.

There is an expectation among some clients that their guides are required to rescue them. This is not just the attitude of the rich, inexperienced clients; star climber Chantal Maudit needed rescues at extreme altitude on both K2 and Everest. Ed Viesturs was helping with her rescue from 8,700 m on Everest and wrote:

> At one point, though, I heard [Chantal Maudit] say to Rob [Hall], "I signed up for your trip. You're responsible for me, Rob. You have to get me down." (Viesturs 2006)

This is a dangerous attitude.

A tremendous outcry arose in 2006 over the failure of some Everest climbers to rescue others who were in distress high on the mountain. The resulting furor led to pronouncements from the likes of Sir Edmund Hillary, who hasn't been high for decades. In the old days, there was one (or at most a couple) of teams on the same mountain. These climbers were experienced and working together to reach a common goal. If an accident occurred, the team would commit all available resources to a rescue because of their interdependence as teammates.

Today's high peaks are much different. You will likely be climbing amid a couple of dozen other teams on popular peaks. Climbers are not usually selected by experience, but by ability to pay. Especially on Everest, the support structures (supplemental oxygen, high-altitude porters) are weak or absent on the bargain-basement expeditions.[177] Frankly, there are lots of people on the hill who you don't know or don't respect, so you don't care about them as individuals. And you know what? They feel the same about you. Layer the language and cultural differences on top of this, and there's no wonder that there are differences in attitudes toward rescue.

I'll Rescue You If You'll Rescue Me

This is the unspoken compact that must exist if extreme-altitude rescues are to be assumed. This means that everyone on the peak must be willing to forfeit their financial investment ($5,000 to $50,000) and abort their summit plans for anybody else on the mountain. One could argue that a life is priceless and there should be no question of what amounts to spending tens of thousands of dollars on another person. But decisions are made every day that trade money for lives (lower tax rates mean lower highway safety means more deaths); it's just that these decisions are less personal.

It also means that each potential victim (you) must have the ability to aid in the rescue of any other victim. Only a fraction of the climbers on any peak these days are qualified to be there, let alone to help with a rescue. These climbers may have proxies (high-altitude porters), but there are ethical issues involved in ordering others to put themselves in harm's way.

Rescue at extreme altitude is often self-rescue. One of the most famous self-rescue attempts happened on K2 in 1953, when Art Gilkey developed deep venous thrombosis at 8,000 m. During the rescue attempt, the whole party nearly perished in a fall, held only by the belay of Pete Schoening. Gilkey and his stretcher were carried away in an avalanche that night; otherwise, the remaining climbers would likely have perished in the rescue attempt.[165] That same year on Everest, the English writer/climber Wilfred Noyce voiced a question that most climbers have asked themselves:

> Would one climber be justified in leaving another if that other were doomed?
> (Noyce 1954, p. 179)

If we fast-forward to 1996, guide Rob Hall apparently refused to leave client Doug Hansen on the South Summit of Everest, and both of them died. In retrospect this might be interpreted as a bad decision, but decision making at these extreme altitudes is very difficult under the best of circumstances.

Practical Advice

Any traveler to the highest altitudes needs to develop a personal ethic that is discussed with fellow travelers. Here are my feelings on the subject:

- If you choose to climb a route occupied by many people (possibly of dubious competence), you accept the fact that you may have to participate in a rescue.
- You can't count on other teams to provide help if you need a rescue, even if you would help them.

- It is unethical to continue an ascent if you encounter a climber who is in need of assistance and whom you can effectively help.
- Rescue from extreme altitudes cannot be expected under any circumstances.
- Rescue from extreme altitudes should be attempted with the usual caveat: Never create more casualties.
- Causing your own death by staying with another person who will die anyway only creates more pain and suffering.

Here are the thoughts of several top high-altitude climbers. These statements may seem rather extreme, but remember that these elite climbers are talking about the ascent of any of the world's highest peaks:

> Anyway, at this kind of altitude—it was the highest place I'd ever been—each person has total responsibility for himself. (Burgess and Burgess 1994, p. 399)

> If anyone should get into difficulty, the other would have to try at all costs to find safety for himself alone. (Habeler 1978, p. 176)

> Money and oxygen make it possible to ascend into a zone where it is easy to die, to a place where no one can rescue you if suddenly your own strength is insufficient. The myth of safety is a delusion for dilettantes. (Boukreev 2001, p. 231)

> Please calculate your strength against the difficulties to the top. If you miscalculate, naturally you could die. But the responsibility for the decision lies in yourselves. You are leading climbers. You are responsible for your judgment. If, for example, I should become exhausted at 8500 metres, you need not help me. It will have been my responsibility to have climbed to such an altitude. I should have descended sooner. Nobody can take care of others at high altitude anyway without an oxygen cylinder.... The summit bid, I think, is just like the duelling (sic) of the ancient Samurai. If you are inferior, even though only a slightest inferiority, you should put yourself to the sword. (Masatuga Konishi, quoted in Curran 1995, p. 176)

While the analogy to falling on your sword may seem a bit over the top to the non-Samurai among us, the general concept is bulletproof. You are responsible for yourself. Period.

FAMILY, FRIENDS, AND "WHY?"

Climbing the world's highest peaks is a very risky business; roughly 1 of every 25 climbers (3.8%) has died after descending from the summit of an 8,000 m peak.[170] The overall death rates are lower, approximately 2% on Everest.[169] In any view, these numbers are extremely high, and it's therefore important to ask two questions: Why should we participate in this risky activity? and Is it fair to family and friends? These questions are dealt with in depth by Coffey,[85] and her book is required reading for any aspirant visitor to the Death Zone. Here I will touch only briefly on these issues.

The "why" question has been debated for decades. A commonly voiced viewpoint is that high-altitude climbing is addictive:

> We are all bitten by the same virus. (Ernest Hofstetter, quoted in Sayre 1964, p. 49)

> Like the desire for drink or drugs, the craving for mountains is not easily over-come. (Tilman 1946, p. 277)

The expression "feeding the rat" is part of the climber's lexicon.[2] The rat lives in the climber's belly, and each trip feeds it, makes it stronger, and increases the rat's appetite for further adventure. Sounds like addiction, doesn't it? In addition, it's been shown that the preparation and anticipation of these experiences are very important aspects of the pleasure response in the brain.[306]

Escapism is another theme:

> The world of very-high-altitude climbing belongs only to those who are doing it. [Wife] Lorna no longer existed in the same way; neither did [brother] Al. For the time being, all the bonds that held us to normal life had been severed. What a wild idea: to let the normal world die away and then return to it at a later time. (Adrian Burgess, quoted in Burgess and Burgess 1994, p. 393)

> There is an unthinking simplicity in something so hard [elite cycling], which is why there's probably some truth to the idea that all world-class athletes are actually running away from something. (Armstrong 2001, p. 85)

> The prospect of what is euphemistically termed "settling down," like mud to the bottom of the pond, might perhaps be faced when it became inevitable, but not yet awhile. (Tilman 1946, p. 277)

By the way, Tilman died at age 79 while sailing to the Antarctic; he clearly never felt the inevitability of settling down. The Armstrong quote draws parallels to other elite athletic activities.

A related rationale is the desire to prove oneself against an inanimate adversary:

> I have come here where other yardsticks apply, where a man is still a man, where one is reduced to what is fundamental and quite elementary. Only then am I at one with myself. (Reinhold Messner, quoted in Habeler 1978, p. 194)

A restless urge to come to grips with the mountain, and myself, pulled me on. After three years of civilized living I needed proof of my ability to tolerate such an environment once again, and I needed time for introspection to try to understand an urge that mixed so much sadness with expectancy. (Hornbein 1966, p. 29)

Every year you need to flush out your system and do a bit of suffering... because there's always a question of how you would perform. (Mo Anthoine, quoted in Alvarez 2001, p. 141)

Finally, there are some nonexplanations that, to the participants in these activities, are often as valid as any other explanation:

We are all different, and some of us have wilder dreams than others. That's the way I see it, and I don't know why my dreams look the way they do. Do you? (Kropp 1997, p. 198)

The short answer is "If you have to ask, you'll never know." (Viesturs 2006)

There is no answer in this book to the endless question about the point of expeditions to the Himalayan giants. I never found the need to explain this. I went to the mountains and climbed them. That is all. (Kukuczka 1992, p. x)

I highly recommend reading Coffey[85] for more in-depth coverage of the "why" question.

A dedication to high-altitude climbing often leads to problems with relationships. In many expedition accounts, the climber eagerly returns home at long last only to be dumped by his significant other. Climbers often feel guilty about leaving home while they are on expeditions, then feel guilty dreaming about the mountains while they're at home (e.g. Habeler,[142] Bettembourg and Brame,[42] Rose and Douglas,[294] Viesturs[355]).

For those spouses who stick with their climber, there is generally an understanding of the climber's need to continue with these adventures. Scott Fischer's wife said the following after his death on Everest in 1996:

I fell in love with a climber. ... To ask him to stop would be like asking him not to breathe. (Jeannie Price, quoted in Kropp 1997, p. 83)

Friends of the spouses of climbers often take a dim view of climbing, as evidenced by this exchange:

"Are you the man who's going off to climb mountains?" [the wife's friend] *demanded. And then, without waiting for an answer, she continued, "Well, I think it's absolutely irresponsible. You have no right to leave your wife and chil-*

dren, and go running off on such a harebrained adventure. Why don't men ever grow up?" (Sayre 1964, p. 32)

The children of climbers often endure long-term psychological issues as a result of the absence of the climbing parent.[85]

The typical climber often makes a statement like this in his defense (I certainly have):

[W]hilst we can never eliminate risk in mountaineering, we can certainly reduce it to an acceptable level by choosing objectives carefully and exercising good judgment and caution on the mountains. (Fowler 2005)

This sounds good, but it's really just a platitude. Even the safest route has dangers, and frankly, most dead climbers thought that they were doing these things. Other people suffer when we go to the mountains, even if we always return. For a more complete appreciation of this suffering, read Coffey.[85] After that, if you still feel it's worthwhile, go ahead and climb. At its root, climbing is a selfish behavior, and don't try to pass it off as anything else.

MENTAL OUTLOOK AT EXTREME ALTITUDE

The successful extreme-altitude climber is usually a bit different than your normal person:

Some people find that they can't cope with things being so uncomfortable day after day. It just gets them down. And that, in fact, is how the average person reacts. Unfortunately, climbing is so élitist that when somebody reacts normally the others say, "He doesn't go well at altitude." But the truth is, people who do go well at altitude are a bit freaky. (Mo Anthione, quoted in Alvarez 2001, p. 74)

My companions have never really been able to get undiluted pleasure from being with me. They couldn't possibly; I admit it freely. (Buhl 1956, p. 28)

High-altitude mountaineers appear to be more stoic than the average person;[255] they tend to be more patient and indifferent to pain and suffering. They share with polar explorers and space travelers a high movitation to achieve and an introverted but socially adept personality. [261, 304]

I've already touched on the idea that top climbers are often prima donnas. But maybe David Roberts better expresses their personalities as exhibiting the "coldness of competence".[289] On his way to the summit of Everest without supplemental oxygen, Stephan Venables wrote:

I knew that at this altitude [8,100 m]...a streak of egotism was essential for anyone to reach the top. (Venables 2000, p. 161)

The well-read climber keeps abreast of current events even while on expeditions.

During an attempt on the unclimbed South Face of Lhotse in 1975, the team discussed the "next step" in high-altitude climbing:

> *I don't say it will happen right away. But sometime in the future an eight-thousander will be climbed alpine-style by a party of two. It will need real men to do it, not pant-wetters who cry "Mama mia" as soon as the wind gets up.*
> (Ignazio Piuss, quoted in Messner 1977, p. 47)

On a trip to the Mexican volcanoes, a teammate noted that the three of us got along so well because "deep down, we each know that we're better than the other two."

I don't believe that you need to feel superior to the others on the mountain, but you need to be absolutely committed to the success of your venture and certain of your ability to succeed:

> *During the last few years Helmut has had a great deal of bad luck. Perhaps the reason for this lies in the fact that he doesn't want success strongly enough. He is not a fanatic, but is rather a moderate in pursuing his goals. This makes him*

a good teacher and a good guide—but it also makes him a loser on the mountain. (Habeler 1978, p. 86)

It seemed that each of the people who began with many doubts or hesitations failed to fulfill his ambitions. I went down the list: Craig had been skeptical of his own ability at the outset; Skip had been the last person invited to join the team, and considered himself in a weak position; Bill had made a hard decision whether to come at all. Chris was looking for an escape, for a vacation from his personal problems, more than for the trial of a difficult ascent. (Ridgeway 1980, p. 296)

As Ed Webster thought about why his team had this confidence, he came up with this answer:

Why did we have such confidence? I looked for an answer. A common thread was woven through each of our climbing careers. Robert, Paul, Stephen and I had all habitually climbed very dangerous routes alone. (Webster 2000, p. 369)

Himalayan superstar Jerzy Kukuczka not only climbed high but also climbed very difficult routes in super-alpine style. As he talked about his projected new route on the South Face of K2 to some younger guide, he realized that he was in a different realm altogether:

I was walking along beside some of the top young Swiss guides, but my words could have been spoken into an empty room. They think differently. To reach the summit anyhow will be enough, then back home as fast as possible...he must not risk too much. An adventure, yes. Risk, no. (Kukuczka 1992, p. 138)

KEY CONCEPTS

1. Extreme altitude (the Death Zone) spans altitudes from 7,800 to 8,848 m.

2. It's not possible for the body to adjust to the extreme hypoxia encountered here; only a few days may be spent above 7,800 m, during which time physical deterioration occurs.

3. Supplemental oxygen can be used to overcome the performance limitations of hypoxia, but there are ethical and logistical problems with its use.

4. Death rates are higher when descending from the summits of the highest peaks when oxygen is not used.

5. The biggest problems in the Death Zone are crowding and parasitism, which is the use of fixed ropes, camps, and tracks by people who do not help establish and maintain them.

6. Rescue in the Death Zone should not be assumed. Too many parties are incapable of self-rescue and instead rely on others. There are several ethical issues surrounding rescue in the Death Zone.

7. Climbers who are successful at extreme altitudes often have certain personality traits: stoicism, introversion, a strong will to succeed, and high levels of confidence.

CHAPTER ELEVEN

Decision Making
and Accidents

Life requires a constant stream of decisions. Travel at altitude means making decisions that relate directly to hypoxia and decisions that are independent of altitude. An example of the first type would be a decision about your rate of ascent each day. The second type would be choosing a location to cross a stream (drowning at sea level is no different from drowning at 3,000 m). I'll be using Fig. 21 (see Chapter 3) to structure this discussion.

DECISION-MAKING ISSUES
Direct Effects of Hypoxia

Hypoxia not only affects your physical performance but also affects your judgment (refer back to Fig. 21). While there are a number of studies examining the effects of hypoxia on mental state, it's not possible (or ethical) to test judgment in real-life situations at altitude. Luckily, the mountaineering literature is loaded with many examples of judgment at altitude. At extreme altitudes, the emotions disappear, and things that should matter (like survival) can cease to be important:

> "It was insane," [Jean] Troillet said, twirling his forefinger beside his head for emphasis, as if any was really needed. "Up there, you know, at those altitudes you do not think very well." (Webster 2000, p. 195)

> At 8000 metres...one moves as if in a perpetual mist, one registers things in a hazy way, confusion reigns in one's head. (Kukuczka 1992, p. 113)

> For those who wish to achieve complete philosophical detachment, there is perhaps something to recommend life at high altitudes. The mind appears to

be quite incapable of strong emotion of any sort.... [I] was blissfully resigned to whatever the fates chose to do with me. (Shipton 1943, p. 392)

I could sense a weary fatalism taking hold of me. (Tasker 1982, p. 206)

This phenomenon is not as pronounced below 7,000 m, but if you're not acclimatized, you have to assume that hypoxia may be blunting brain function. Cold and dehydration can also affect emotions and judgment, and there may be ethnic variation in the response to altitude stress.[317]

Emotional Infrastructure

Your judgment will be influenced by a range of internal and external factors. Curran[90] points out that successful boldness begats more boldness, and successful caution begats more caution. He later noted that several of the survivors of the 1986 K2 season failed to learn the lessons of that summer and ended up dying under conditions similar to those who died in 1986.[91] The same pattern can be seen at lower elevations.[4]

It's important to understand your motivations and to make sure you're not skewing your judgment to reach a goal, especially if that goal is a prized summit that seems just barely within reach:

> *In mountaineering you often see people tantalized by the chance to step out-side the limits of their own normal self-image. It is heady stuff, and small con-siderations like safety, group ethics, and loyalties can pale by comparison. It's a time to be wary.* (Burgess and Palmer 1983)

During the tragic international mountaineering camp in the Pamirs in 1974, an entire party of female Soviet climbers perished on Pik Lenin. While other climbers managed to descend from the summit as a massive storm hit, the Soviets refused to split their party. Their leader stated, "We are strong. We are Soviet women. We will camp here and go down in the morning." Bob Craig summarized the problem this way:

> *[T]he psychological force of their commitment to demonstrate that Soviet women were a strong and perhaps a special breed...robbed them of the flexi-bility that is so vital in making prudent decisions on high mountains.* (Craig 1977, p. 217)

Another example comes from Everest in 1996. In spite of his tight control over clients and elaborate rules for movement on the mountain, Rob Hall and three others of his team died. Jon Krakauer offered this explanation:

Hubris probably had something to do with it. Hall had become so adept at running climbers of all abilities up and down Everest that he got a little cocky, perhaps. (Krakauer 1997, p. 272)

Competition with others can lead to poor decisions. Competition between guiding companies was a root cause of the 1996 Everest disaster.[191] Benoit Chamoux was competing with Erhard Loretan to become the next person to climb all of the 8,000 m peaks (Loretan didn't care who was next). Chamoux died while chasing Loretan up Kangchenjunga, failing both in his self-imposed competition and in his bid to stay alive.

Every time you make a decision, you are weighing the costs and benefits of each possible alternative. These costs and benefits are determined by your personal emotional filters. Don't let these filters skew reality and make a risky course of action seem more reasonable than it actually is.

Is it safe to cross the stream?

Indirect Stresses

Distractions such as homesickness, poor interpersonal relationships on the team, troubles with high-altitude porters, and family problems will prevent you from making the best possible decision. Martin Boysen felt that his friend Nick Escourt's death on K2 wasn't a random accident:

> *He had his guard down. . . . He shouldn't have been on the mountain. You just don't go on a big climb if there are any doubts.* (Martin Boysen, quoted in Ridgeway 1980, p. 63)

Jim Curran[90] analyzed the accidents on K2 during the deadly summer of 1986 and summarized the indirect factors that may have contributed to the death of his close friend Al Rouse. Rouse was the leader of a British expedition to the Northwest Ridge that got nowhere. After waiting out bad weather, he teamed up with the Polish female climber Mrufka Wolf to climb the standard Abruzzi Ridge and make the first British ascent of K2:

> *Al might well have been distracted by many intruding external pressures like the responsibility of looking after Mrufka [Wolf], the language difficulties, the problems of being on the Abruzzi in the first place, the disappointment of failing on the North-West Ridge, the despair of returning home unsuccessful.* (Curran 1987, p. 177)

On her fatal trip to K2, Alison Hargreaves was quite homesick and just wanted to get the climb over with and go home.[294] That, combined with a strong drive to reach the summit and pressure from the media, forced her hand; she reached the top but not the bottom. The best advice comes from Ed Viesturs:

> *You've got to be 100 percent there. If you're only slightly not there on a big mountain, it can cause you to fail or get in trouble.* (Viesturs 2006)

Group Dynamics

Poor decision making may not be caused by an individual, but a dangerous "groupthink" can develop when people get together. Describing the sociology of the doomed 1995 K2 summit team that included Alison Hargreaves, fellow climber Peter Hillary made the following observation a few days after the accident:

> *Summit fever had developed in that group. There was a chemistry in there that meant they were going for the summit no matter what. . . . They were all driving each other on. These people came together and because of the place and the atmosphere and their personalities, they became blinkered and simply focused on the top.* (Rose and Douglas 2000, p. 273)

Weeks of bad weather make it tough to stay positive.

Often a decision isn't yours to make on your own. This is where a team of mixed nationalities/languages can be difficult to manage. Different values concerning safety, ethics, and success can lead to conflicting opinions. There is no simple solution—the structure of your group, the leadership scheme, and all of the other issues addressed in Chapter 9 will all influence your group's decision-making process.

Danger versus Effort

In the mountains there are often decisions that pit danger versus effort: Do we cross the river or walk several miles to a bridge? Do we climb up this easy avalanche gully or take a safer but longer ridge? These decisions involve, in the words of Alex MacIntyre, "gambling time and effort against the prospects of eternity".[316] Experience pays big dividends here, but don't defer automatically to experience. Our original route to Camp I on Kangchenjunga led beneath a rampart of tottering seracs (ice cliffs). Even though I was a rookie, I realized that there had to be a better route. Others had the same feeling, so after a couple of trips up this death route, we moved to a safer line.

Keep in mind that the best decision will depend on the situation. For example, suppose you're driving and the signals at a train crossing start flashing. You see the train approaching fast, and you tell your passenger, "I think I can make it in time. Let's try!" Your passenger would rightly consider you to be an idiot. However, if you were being chased by a carload of gun-toting evildoers intent on killing you, then trying to beat the train would be the better decision. Sometimes the choice isn't between a good and bad option, it's between bad options, and you have to choose the best of the worst.

Intuition

Intuition has no scientific basis, but you won't find a good climber who won't listen to that little birdie singing in his ear. Just before a major avalanche, avalanche forecaster Pete Lev had these feelings:

> I was distressed. Something was wrong. All that I knew (or thought I knew) about avalanches seemed to contradict the possibility of immediate danger. But the atmosphere was absolutely heavy with impending disaster. (Peter Lev, quoted in Craig 1977, p. 94)

As the IMAX film team retreated while others climbed to their eventual deaths on Everest in 1996, IMAX leader Dave Breashears pondered the situation:

> So many decisions in the mountains rely on the subtleties of intuition. How do you say to someone, "It just doesn't seem right"? That would fly in the face of [another climber's] decision to continue on up. (Breashears 1999, p. 255)

Listen to the voice, but it should only speak on certain occasions. If it speaks too often, it is fear.

> Such a huge and wild situation is all too conducive to self-doubt. Self-doubt magnified beyond all proportion can drive you completely from the mountain. It is the reasonable elimination of this doubt that makes you a better climber. Self-doubt along with fear [is] necessary. But can you control them both? (Haston 1972, p. 1)

Those "No Fear" decals that you see are obviously placed by people who've never really been afraid. Fear is an important component of the decision-making process that must be carefully consulted but sometimes ignored:

> The fool is not the person who goes up there in full knowledge that this kind of climbing is hazardous, but the one who does not want to know about death, who shuts his eyes to the fact that even he could be killed. (Messner 1989, p. 138)

Practical Advice

Learn to make little decisions before you have to make big decisions. Experience allows you not only to perform well physically but to perform well mentally. If you're unable to evaluate the risks and benefits of the various options, how can you make the correct decision? At the same time it's important to realize that you are responsible for yourself. If you think your group is making a poor decision, you must speak out, regardless of your level of experience. If you're new at the game, watch and listen carefully. If the leader makes a good decision, understand the reasoning behind it.

Are you tired, cold, hypoxic, and/or sick? Maybe there is a better person to make the decision. High-altitude climbers often rely on a radio link to Base Camp to help with decisions if needed. Unfortunately, the climber still has to have the will to carry out the decision (refer back to Fig. 21). Rob Hall was urged by radio to descend from the South Summit of Everest in 1996, but he just sat there and died.

ACCIDENTS AND TRAGEDY

Bad things happen to good people; a bump or a bruise, major trauma, permanent injury, or death can be the result. At moderate altitudes the dangers arise more from the environment you're in than from the direct effects of altitude. At extreme altitudes, hypoxia can more easily lead directly to injury and death. We use the word *accident* to describe the outcome, but these are seldom accidental in the true sense of the word.

Causes of Accidents

There are two types of dangers encountered in the mountains: **objective dangers** and **subjective dangers**.[264] Objective dangers are physical dangers, while subjective dangers are within the climber himself (Table 11). Objective dangers are the same for all, while subjective dangers will differ for each person. Almost all accidents are a result of the interaction between the subjective and objective hazards. For example, a slight change in the orientation of a snow slope led to an avalanche and deaths on Haramosh in 1957.[19] Was this acci-

The Gilkey Memorial at the base of K2 is a somber reminder of the dangers of high mountains.

dent caused by the objective danger (avalanche) or the subjective danger (inability to judge snow conditions)? It was caused by both.

Huey and Eguskitza[169] summarized a variety of previous studies and unpublished data to look at the relationship between altitude and risk of death. The risk of death for trekkers increases at higher altitudes, but the higher altitudes are also associated with less access to high-quality medical care. In any case, the highest death rates currently are in Nepal, with 10.6 deaths per million visitor-days, or about 1 death per 100,000 visitor-days.[320]

Similar results are found for mountaineering. Death rates on Everest are 10 times higher than on Mount Rainier, and death rates on K2 are 20 times higher.[170] The difference between overall death rates on Everest (2%) and K2 (4%) is due to the higher technical difficulty of K2. A large number of mountaineering accidents happen on descent. Huey et al.[170] examined death rates on descent of climbers who had summited an 8,000 m peak without supplemental oxygen. The overall death rate was 3.8%, but there was a strong relationship between altitude and descent death rate. Certain peaks (Annapurna, K2) had a higher death rate than predicted from their altitude, and other peaks (Lhotse, Cho Oyo) had lower death rates than predicted. These deviations make sense given the objective dangers and difficulty of these peaks. The use of supplemental oxygen is correlated with a much lower risk of death during descent from the summits of K2 and Everest.[168, 170]

The big holes in these data sets are the trekking peaks Kilimanjaro (Africa) and Aconcagua (South America). Both peaks are nontechnical volcanoes that are the highest points on their continents. As a result, they attract thousands of inexperienced climbers each year who generally attempt the summits without adequate acclimatization. Accurate statistics on deaths are not released by the governments, likely due to the financial bene-

Table 11

Examples of Objective and Subjective Hazards at Altitude

Objective Hazards	Subjective Hazards
Quality of rock, ice, snow	Lack of experience
Weather	Inadequate technical ability
Rockfall	Poor judgment
Avalanches	Fatigue
Cornices	Unappropriate psychological makeup
Snow bridges	Other stresses (refer back to Fig. 21)
Other people creating rockfall, etc.	

Source: Summarized from Paulcke and Dumler.[264]

fits of tourism to these countries. So don't be fooled into thinking that 8,000 m sets the lower limit on real risk.

How Accidents Happen

Risk will not be a simple function of altitude for either hikers or climbers. Instead, risk will be a function of both objective and subjective hazards. The main contributors to risk will be altitude, technical difficulty, objective dangers (Table 11), motivation toward achieving the goal, and experience level/technical ability relative to the goal. Given this list, you can see why an inexperienced climber who is highly motivated to buy his way up an 8,000 m peak is a potentially dangerous companion. Here are examples of the types of hazards that can lead to tragedy.

Inadequate Equipment

Inadequate equipment is a subjective danger because it indicates either inexperience or an inability to match your goal to your resources. The Soviet women who died in the 1974 Pamirs disaster were using tents with no zippers and four wooden poles,[88] hardly the proper gear for surviving a storm at high altitude. A very common mistake is to not bring enough bamboo wands, which are used to mark the way on snowfields.[377] Himalayan superstar Jerzy Kukuczka died when a second-hand rope broke near the summit of Lhotse.

Passion

Passion is necessary, but overwhelming passion and ambition can lead to poor judgment:

> [Willo Welzenbach's] irresistible desire to fulfill his dream of attempting Nanga Parbat had overcome all scruples about joining the party. (Roberts 1980, p. 241)

> [Rob Slater] had told friends in his hometown of Boulder, Colorado, that he would reach the summit [of K2] or die. (Rose and Douglas 2000, p. 244)

> I've put too much of myself into [Everest] to quit now, without giving it everything I've got. (Doug Hansen, quoted in Krakauer 1997, p. 148)

> There is no escape from a passion like climbing, even though it may be the path to death. (Wanda Rutkiewicz, quoted in Jordan 2005, p. 28)

All of these individuals died on the peaks mentioned except for Wanda Rutkiewicz, who died later on Kangchenjunga after refusing to heed the advice of other climbers to descend. A more measured view is provided by Bill Tilman:

> [W]e should not forget that mountaineering, even on Everest, is not war but a form of amusement whose saner devotees are not willing to be killed rather and accept defeat. (Tilman 1948, p. 468)

Fatigue

Both Krakauer[191] and DeWalt[58] noted that Scott Fischer (Everest 1996) had to make several unexpected special trips up and down the mountain to manage clients who were having problems. Fischer apparently had other health problems as well. The combination of high-altitude deterioration, a preexisting medical condition, and physical and mental fatigue was a deadly mixture. John Noel (of the 1924 Everest expedition) wrote the following of the famous George Mallory before he died on the climb:

> I had an opportunity of observing Mallory closely...and I formed the positive opinion that physically he had become an unfit man.... It was his spirit that was sending him again to the attack.... He was throwing his last ounce of strength into this fight. (Noel 1927)

Exhaustion has been blamed for the death of many climbers, including several on K2 in 1986[90] and Gunther Messner on Nanga Parbat in 1970.[230] Most climbers who die on K2 or Everest either fall or "disappear," implying that they were under severe physiological stress.[170] Under normal conditions, true exhaustion is a sign that the person has attempted something that he or she is not capable of doing. Simply put, the individual's will is stronger than his or her body:

> Unfortunately, the sort of individual who is programmed to ignore personal distress and keep pushing for the top is frequently programmed to disregard signs of grave and imminent danger as well. (Krakauer 1997, p. 177)

Exhaustion can lead to a loss of the fear needed to survive:

> But when you are actually there [at altitude], dead tired and hungry, the dangers barely impress you. It takes energy to be afraid, or indeed to have any emotion, and often there just isn't that much energy around. So a brave man may frequently be merely a tired one. (Sayre 1964, p. 131)

Fear is necessary for self-preservation, and when you are no longer afraid, you are no longer making good decisions.

> My mental fatigue is now greater than the bodily. It is so pleasant to sit doing nothing—and therefore so dangerous. Death through exhaustion is—like death through freezing—a pleasant one. (Messner 1989, p. 248)

At some point a line is crossed where survival is unlikely. The fate of many exhausted climbers is typified by this summary of the 1996 Everest disaster:

They had reached an impasse, stopped, and sat down. Awake, conscious, they had been unable to help themselves. Unable to move. (Breashears 1999, p. 286)

Poor Decision Making

Even without exhaustion, accidents can happen due to poor decisions. Suffice it to say that almost every "accident" has an identifiable cause: Poor decisions were made at some point.

Luck and Fate

There is a strong, almost mystical theme that runs throughout the mountaineering literature concerning luck and fate. Here are two typical examples:

> *Those who have mastered the rules of the "game"—for want of a better word—stand the best chance of surviving: yet without good fortune, nobody can make it. Fate is a vital ingredient.* (Diemberger 1991, p. 420)

> *Everyone has luck, but only up to a point.* (Messner 1989, p. 201)

The 1969 American Dhaulagiri expedition was "unlucky" because they "happened" to be in the "wrong place at the wrong time," and seven climbers died in an avalanche that was started by a freak icefall.[150] In reality, they knew that there was a chance of avalanche, but the chance was considered to be very low. "Good luck" means you got away with a bad decision. Some routes are inherently dangerous; in that case, your bad decision was choosing that route!

Minimize your need for luck by proper preparation and decision making. Good decisions only come from accepting reality.

When Accidents Happen

Just as this book isn't a medical guide, it can't instill the skills needed to respond to the myriad possible accident scenarios. Keep in mind the words of Rob Taylor, who broke his leg on a difficult ice climb on Kilimanjaro and had to wait many days for his (generally untrained) rescuers to arrive:

> *As with many erring people when confronted with a fellow human in suffering, the urge to help is mistaken for the ability to do so.* (Taylor 1981, p. 182)

Everyone should have at least a basic idea of what they would do in case of an accident. Here are some ideas:

- Get some basic training. Any traveler to altitude should know cardiopulmonary resuscitation (CPR) and first aid. Learn how to administer intramuscular and subcutaneous injections; you may not be carrying injectables, but the victim might have them.

- Don't create more victims. This is the first rule of rescue. Evaluate the dangers of the accident site before you go rushing in to help.
- Establish a clear command structure. Wilderness accidents require the victim to be stabilized and then transported to a location that allows for mechanical transport (automobile, helicopter). All aspects of the rescue must be coordinated to minimize the time the victim must spend between the accident and the hospital.
- Understand the psychology of accidents. The best description that I've seen is found in Wilkerson.[378] Be ready for irrational victims, irrational partners, and postaccident stress in rescuers.
- Learn how to behave around helicopters.

After an Accident

There's nothing better than hearing the chopper door shut and the pilot throttle up. Debriefing after an accident allows the rescuers to examine both the causes of the accident and the conduct of the rescue. However, not all individuals involved in a rescue will benefit from this process, so don't force the issue.

Somebody in the victim's party should keep track of any records generated during the rescue, as these might be useful if there are insurance claims filed by the victim. Get the names and contact information of key participants in the rescue.

Death

Most travelers will never encounter death in the mountains. But death happens. Coffey[85] is by far the best treatment of the subject. The immediate emotions of the survivors can vary. After descending from the summit of Everest and learning of the deaths of several climbers the same day, Krakauer[191] wrote that he "retreated into a weird, almost robotic state of detachment" (p. 245). My own experience is similar. After climbing to 8,000 m on Kangchenjunga, we watched as our summit team began their descent. As we brewed up to prepare for their arrival, one climber arrived and reported the fall and death of the other climber. I didn't really feel much of anything due to the stupor of extreme altitude.

Most people will have a variety of feelings in response to death; note the different stages of grief:

> My dear Hermann! His parents—his poor mother—his father! Our own parents! Those at home! (Bauer 1937, p. 141)

> Experience did not help decide how to behave after a death. (Tasker 1982, p. 155)

> There was nothing left to do but for the survivors to get drunk together. (Scott and MacIntyre 1984, p. 208)

I kept wanting to play the record backwards—to change the summit teams, the lead climbers, the mountain; to change ever having wanted to climb an 8,000m peak. But the record would not reverse. (Blum 1998, p. 220)

What more could I have done that day to help my friends? Is it wrong that I lived, that I did not die with them? (Boukreev 2001, p. 101)

Survivor guilt is common and can blossom into full-blown post-traumatic stress syndrome. Those who are troubled by their experiences in an accident should seek professional help sooner rather than later.

Your Responsibilities

Your responsibilities will vary depending on your location. All deaths need to be reported to the appropriate authorities. In most countries the body will need to be recovered. In more remote areas in less-developed countries, the body will be buried or disposed of in the local manner. On a high peak in a remote region, the body may have to be left in place. In some cases there is no body to recover (crevasse fall or avalanche), or the body recovery would put rescuers in danger. In those situations there is nothing to be done.

Always obtain photographs of the body. These are necessary in some countries to establish the fact and cause of death. Of course, you never want to send such information over the Internet or transfer it in any electronic format—provide hard copies to the required officials. Collect any identification, cameras, and mementos from the body for the next of kin. Use the movie feature on your digital camera to interview witnesses, to record the surroundings and weather conditions, and to record the state of any equipment that may have contributed to the accident.

If the body is to be recovered, wrap it up in a sleeping bag and tarp/tent with a pad underneath. This will make it much easier to handle (both physically and psychologically). If the body needs to be left unattended for some time, protect it from scavengers by covering it with equipment, snow, or rocks. If the body is to be committed to the mountain, the traditional burial place is a crevasse or under a large pile of rocks.

After a Death

Any death will cancel most shorter trips. Longer expeditions or treks to remote locations may continue or be canceled depending on the wishes of the other members. The literature is replete with such discussions, and the results go both ways:

For me, personally, the prosecution of our attack on Kangchenjunga was a foregone conclusion. (Bauer 1937, p. 148)

We all felt an obligation to continue. (Craig 1977, p. 166)

John was saying that, in his view, it was vital to cancel the expedition as a whole, otherwise the sponsors and the media would consider it a humiliating rout. (Burgess and Palmer 1983, p. 113)

Goran Kropp[192] not only wondered if he should continue up Everest after the 1996 deaths, but also asked, "But what would people say about me if I climbed past those who had frozen to death?" There are no right answers to these questions. Coffey[85] examines the effects of death in the mountains on family and friends and provides some much-needed insight into this long-ignored topic.

KEY CONCEPTS

1. Hypoxia directly affects the brain, and thus judgment. Judgment is also affected by a variety of psychological factors and external distractions, such as homesickness.
2. Objective (external, physical) dangers and subjective (internal, judgment-related) dangers both contribute to every accident.
3. Prior training and preparation will help minimize death and injury in the case of an accident.

Preparing for
Altitude

While proper preparation doesn't guarantee a successful trip to altitude, it certainly improves your chances. As usual, a day hike will require little or no preparation, while the hardest climbs in the Death Zone may take years of preparation. The value of a specific training regimen for climbers was demonstrated by Reinhold Messner in the 1960s and 1970s with the first one-day ascent of the North Face of Les Droites, first alpine-style ascent of an 8,000 m peak (Hidden Peak, with Peter Habeler), first ascent of Everest without supplemental oxygen (again, with Peter Habeler), and the first pure solo ascent of Everest. While few of us can aspire to such performances, proper training can give us a better chance of reaching our goals. Anatoli Boukreev succinctly lists the essential features of training for any athletic endeavor:

> If there is a mountaineer who can climb the highest peaks the way I do without preparation, I envy that man. For twenty years I have strictly adhered to a self-devised formula of exercise and rest, always seeking to proportion my level of readiness to the level of the approaching goal. (Boukreev 2001, p. 62)

Note that he strictly adhered to his training routine, and his routine was self-devised; he gives exercise and rest equal value and orients his preparation to his goal. Remember that preparation for altitude may also involve significant logistics and planning. This book is not designed to cover all of those issues in detail, but I'll make comments where appropriate.

Slogging up the snow at 6,700 m on Broad Peak will make you wish that you had trained more effectively.

LIMITS TO PERFORMANCE

This may be a good time to go back and review the factors that determine performance and the concepts of fatigue and will (Chapter 3). Take a look back at Fig. 18 and Fig. 21 while you're at it. Fig. 18 shows that your maximum performance for any task can be reached only if you are optimally trained, your mental state is optimal, and the physical environment is optimal for you. The environment at altitude is *not* optimal. Hypoxia limits potential performance, as does cold, heat, humidity, and a host of other factors. So we need to think of an individual's maximal possible performance at a given altitude, which will be then determined by physical and mental optimality. For example, it's been estimated that it is physically possible for an acclimatized individual to ascend at a rate of 100 vertical meters per hour without supplemental oxygen near the summit of Everest, which matches the observed ascent rates of the best climbers.[360]

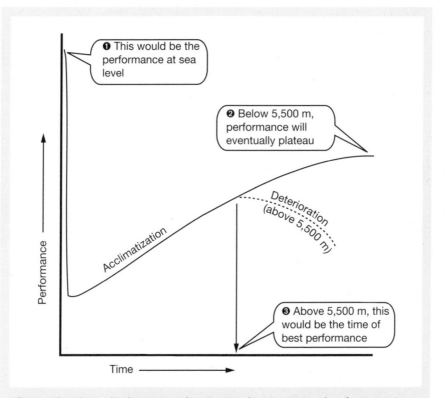

Fig. 31. The relationship between acclimatization, deterioration, and performance. Performance is seriously reduced upon arrival at altitude. Below 5,500 m, acclimatization leads to improved performance over time. Above 5,500 m, high-altitude deterioration will eventually exceed acclimatization, and performance will decline; the optimal time of acclimatization is shown by the arrow. The rate of acclimatization, rate of deterioration, and optimal time for a maximal performance will vary among individuals and for each individual on different trips.

Table 12

Different Responses to Training*

Character	Average Change	Minimum	Maximum	Source
Increase in $\dot{V}O_2$max after 20 weeks (of training)	12%	0%	41%	(Prud'homme et al. 1984)
Increase in $\dot{V}O_2$max after 36 weeks	24%	0%	58%	(Kohrt et al. 1991)
Increase in $\dot{V}O_2$max after 26 weeks	17%	–5%	56%	(Skinner et al. 2001)
Change in systolic blood pressure after 20 weeks	~0 mm Hg	–21.7 mm Hg	+26.2 mm Hg	(Rice et al. 2002)

* All values represent the improvement in subjects' performances relative to performance before training.

At altitude there are two additional complicating factors. First, acclimatization will improve performance as time progresses. A hike that takes four hours on your first day at altitude may take less than two hours after acclimatization. At altitudes over 5,500 m, high-altitude deterioration sets in, and after a few days your performance will begin to deteriorate (Fig. 31). Second, at these high altitudes, there is often a narrow window of opportunity during which the balance between performance and deterioration leads to the best possible performance.

You might be saying, "Wait a minute. I just want to go for a pleasant hike, not set some new speed record for the ascent of Mount Whatnot," and you're absolutely right. Most of your performances at altitude are not going to be a quest for athletic perfection. However, there is usually some minimally acceptable performance, even for a day hike; getting back to the car before dark might be your measure of success. In more extreme situations, failing to attain the minimum acceptable performance might lead to injury or even death. Proper physical and mental training will optimize your personal performance and lead to more of a cushion between you and failure.

RESPONSE TO TRAINING

Fig. 18 shows that you can attain a level of performance as determined by your particular genetic makeup and the environment you have experienced. With traits like strength, aerobic capacity, body fat, and muscular endurance, there's good news and bad news. The

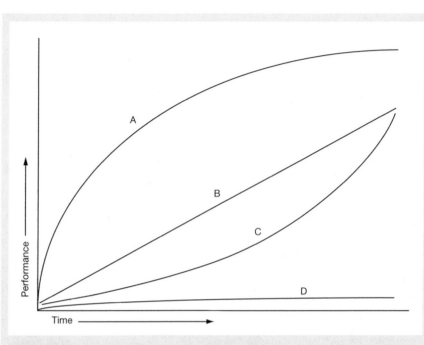

Fig. 32. Individuals respond to training in different ways. (A) A high responder showing early, rapid gains in performance, (B) an average responder showing a continuous gain in performance, (C) the same as (B) but showing a slower initial gain, and (D) a nonresponder. Performance will eventually level off for all individuals. A single individual could show all of these patterns, depending on the trait being trained.

good news is that these characters can often be improved through training. The bad news is that some people may not be able to improve through training.

How can this be? When researchers put people on standardized exercise programs for 15 to 20 weeks and then measure their response to training, an important finding emerges—there's a lot of genetic variation in the response to training (Table 12). A significant number of people turn out to be either **high responders** or **low responders** to training. Approximately 5% of us are low responders (who improve in fitness less than 5% after training), and about 5% of us are high responders (who improve in fitness more than 60% after training); everyone else falls somewhere in between. So some folks can train and train and never get stronger or faster (blame your parents, or your genes, once again). To complicate the situation even further, the same person can be a high responder for one trait but a low responder for another trait.

Finally, you can respond to training slowly or quickly. One person may improve by 5% after 10 weeks of training, while another person may take 15 weeks to attain the same improvement. These findings are summarized in Fig. 32. While a typical person can increase their $\dot{V}O_2$max by about 15% with training, some people can't improve at all, and some can improve nearly 60%. These are not mixtures of athletes and couch potatoes; these are *all* couch potatoes.[*]

What does all of this mean for your training program?

1. Everyone is different (due to both genetics and environment) and has different capabilities to perform.

2. There's no way in advance to predict your ability to respond to training for a particular characteristic.

3. Only experience can allow you to learn your unique capabilities and limitations.

DEVELOPING A TRAINING PROGRAM

Many people search the magazines and the Internet for the Ultimate Workout Plan—the one with a weekly schedule that says if it's Tuesday, you have to go to the weight room. They faithfully follow the plan for four months, get to Denali with their chain-smoking partners…and become the boat anchor that drags the team to failure. What happened? Why didn't that magic schedule work?

While using a one-size-fits-all training plan is better than having no plan at all, there's a basic flaw with all of them: They're not designed for *you*. Tuning your training program to fit your body is the gift that keeps on giving.

Be forewarned: Developing a personalized training program will take effort on your part, and you'll have to do some additional research to come up with an optimal plan. There certainly are specialized fitness experts out there who can help you determine your strengths and weaknesses, and if you can afford it, that's a great approach. Most of us can't, so I'll provide some guidelines to help you decide how and what you should be training.

Determine Your Goals

The purpose of your training plan is to get you from where you are today, physically speaking, to where you want to be. So the first step is to ask yourself what you want to accomplish as the result of your training. Are you training for a once-in-a-lifetime trip or for long-term performance? Are you doing day hikes, going trekking at moderate elevations, doing an expeditionary climb of an 8,000 m peak, or attempting a highly technical climb on a 6,000 m peak? See Chapter 13 for some additional comments on goal setting.

Whether your overall goal is to hike to the top of Mount Elbert, complete the Annapurna trek, or climb the Cassin Ridge on Denali in two days, you need to translate it into measurable training goals. The systems you'll be training are described below, but at this point the main considerations are daily vertical ascent and descent rates, amount of weight to be carried, and technical difficulty of your travel (Table 13). These training goals should be in the same "units" as your training methods. For example, stair climbers (e.g., Stairmaster and

---

[*] Keep in mind that VO_2max isn't correlated with success at altitude, but it is correlated with endurance performance at sea level.

You must train the mind as well as the body. These men enjoyed a one-hour run at –6°F (–19C).

Stepmill) are a favorite training device for climbers. Progress toward a climb rate of 1,500 ft/hr while wearing a 40 lb pack and plastic boots can be easily evaluated.

Keep in mind that your strength/speed in the gym is much greater than most of us will achieve in the hills. If you're new to training and aren't sure what your specific training goals should be, ask more experienced friends. Most people will have to go through a couple of training cycles to determine realistic target goals.

Determine Your Weakest Link

A critical task is to figure out what your physical and mental capabilities are today, which is a lot harder than it sounds. There are four "systems" that need to be considered. Methods for assessing each system are discussed in dozens of books; only a few of the simpler methods are noted here.

Musculoskeletal System

This includes assessments of strength, muscular endurance, flexibility, and muscular imbalance. Many people see strength as the beginning and end of all training; nothing could be further from the truth. Even if strength was the only element of training, different types of altitude travel will require different muscles to do different things. Consider the following training advice from two well-respected top climbers: "No serious climber would ever want to do any exercises designed to increase leg muscle mass"[163] and "Do squats (the king of exercises)".[351] Both recommendations are perfectly valid, depending on your goals (sport rock climbing versus alpine climbing).

Table 13

Examples of Ascent Rates from the Literature*

Climbers	Load (lbs)	Load (kg)	Supplemental Oxygen?	Starting Elevation (m)	Rate (m/hr)	Comment	Source
a. Low-altitude training							
P. Habeler	0	0	No	1,000	1,567.5	Training (1,000 m in 35 minutes)	Habeler (1978)
G. Bettembourg	0	0	No	1,400	1,123.7	Training (1,220 m in 1:05 on snow)	Bettembourg (1981)
b. No supplemental oxygen							
F. Luchsinger and E. Reiss	15	7	No	5,370	182.9	Snow and ice	Eggler (1957
R. Messner and P. Habeler	33	15	No	5,800	120.0	Unroped but technical climbing with packs	Messner (1977
R. Messner and P. Habeler	11	5	No	7,500	200.0	Summit day on Gasherbrum I	Messner (1999)
R. Messner and P. Habeler	11	5	No	8,700	100.0	Near summit of Everest	Messner (1999)
E. Shipton and F. Smythe	15	7	No	7,010	164.6	Rate during summit attempt	Smythe (1937)
E. Shipton and F. Smythe	10	5	No	7,020	300.0	Ascent from the North Col of Everest	Smythe (1937)
c. With supplemental oxygen							
Various	50	23	Yes	6,500	103.6	Kangchenjunga 1955	Evans (1956)
Various	42	19	Yes	6,500	137.2	"	Evans (1956)

Climbers	Load (lbs)	Load (kg)	Supplemental Oxygen?	Starting Elevation (m)	Rate (m/hr)	Comment	Source
Various	40	18	Yes	7,163	91.4	"	Evans (1956)
Various	30	14	Yes	7,711	97.5	"	Evans (1956)
d. From a single, fast climber							
A. Boukreev	44	20	No	Up to 7,000 m	300	Averaged over multiple ascents	Boukreev (2001)
A. Boukreev	26	12	No	7,000–8,000 m	200	"	Boukreev (2001)
A. Boukreev	11	5	No	8 000+ m	100	"	Boukreev (2001)
e. Miscellaneous ascents to over 8,000 m							
H. Buhl	8	4	No	6,815	77.1	Used stimulants on a 17-hour solo first ascent	Messner (2002)
A. Compagnoni and L. Lacedelli (1954)	33	15	Yes	8,346	97.5	Claimed they did it without oxygen but carried the bottles to the top	Bonatti (2001)
G. Mallory, T. Summervell, E. Norton (1922)	?	?	No	7,000	135.0		Rodway (2007)
G. Finch and G. Bruce (1922)	?	?	Yes	7,000	203.0	Oxygen apparatus weighed 16.5 kg	Rodway (2007)
P. Habeler	13	6	No	8.848	900.0	Descent from the summit of Everest, one hour to South Col	Habeler (1978)

* All rates are expressed as meters of ascent per hour. Loads were estimated in a number of cases.

The best way to evaluate this system is to hire a trainer with considerable experience with climbers or trekkers. A less expensive but less accurate way is to engage in the activity of your choice until you're nearly exhausted (but not injured), then go to the weight room 24 to 48 hours afterwards and do a wide variety of exercises using very light weights to see which exercises tweak your sore muscles. Maximum strength of a particular muscle group can be assessed using a single repetition/maximum lift test (see books or the Web for techniques, and don't even think about doing this without a spotter).

Muscular endurance is a key issue in most trips to altitude, where exercise usually lasts for several hours at a stretch. Unless you live near suitable terrain, this can be difficult to mimic, although putting on a pack with a normal load and hiking all day is a good test for trekkers, even on flat terrain at low altitude.

Flexibility is a tricky issue. My opinion is that flexibility is good and that it allows your body to operate more economically. Rather than trying to assess flexibility, I suggest that you work to improve your flexibility unless you're already a human pretzel.

Muscular imbalance is a crucial issue for some of us, though we may never know it. If you do a pull-up, the latissimus dorsi and teres major are the muscles that do the vast majority of the work. But the rotator cuff muscles, chest muscles, and back muscles are just as important, as they stabilize the humerus in the shoulder socket and hold the shoulder blade stable so that leverage can be applied by the larger muscles. These smaller muscles are hard to train adequately and can be injured when the larger muscles are relatively stronger. Major muscle groups must be balanced as well. This doesn't mean that opposing muscle groups must be the same strength. Without expert help, imbalance issues are difficult to diagnose and treat.

Cardiovascular System

I've discussed this system in Chapter 2; it includes your lungs, heart, and blood vessels. For under $100, you can find a sports physiologist who can determine your maximum heart rate, $\dot{V}O_2$max, and anaerobic threshold (how closely your body can operate to $\dot{V}O_2$max for extended periods of time).

For zero dollars, you can go to an outdoor track and estimate $\dot{V}O_2$max using any number of methods, such as the Cooper 12-minute fitness test. Find a 400 m track (almost all colleges and high schools have one). Warm up thoroughly by jogging at an easy pace for 15 to 20 minutes, then run for 12 minutes as fast as possible, but at a constant pace. Have a friend along to time you and count laps; if you do this right, you'll be too fried to count accurately. Calculate your $\dot{V}O_2$max as

$$\dot{V}O_2\text{max (mL } O_2/\text{kg body weight/minute)} = (0.0225 \times \text{meters}) - 11.29$$

For example, if you run 3,000 m in 12 minutes, your $\dot{V}O_2$max is 56.2 mL/kg/min. While this test is pretty accurate, $\dot{V}O_2$max depends on your motivation. It's worth it to try it once, wait a week, then do it again. Use the higher number as your baseline. Other, similar tests are available.

Maximum heart rate can be estimated using the same test. Again, your motivation will determine the accuracy of your results. The only way to accurately measure your heart rate is with a heart-rate monitor. Be sure to buy one that will record average and maximum heart rates, as well as heart rates for each lap. Don't try to use some formula to estimate your maximum heart rate; any training article that uses these outdated formulas is far behind the times and should be ignored.

Metabolic/Physiological System

Your body requires fuel (in the form of carbohydrates, fats, or proteins) and oxygen to release the energy needed to do muscular work. These systems respond to training, but there is no easy way to assess your current status or your response to training. Plus, there is considerable genetic variation among individuals in the amounts of fat and carbohydrate used during exercise (Fig. 2).[132] During longer bouts of sustained exercise, an apparent lack of strength and endurance may actually be an undertrained metabolic system that is unable to deliver energy to your muscle cells. These metabolic pathways are trained in concert with your cardiovascular training program.

Psychological System

Do you have nerves of steel or of rubber? Your mental state can be assessed and you can train it, but it is probably the most neglected system of all. Elite athletes in all sports struggle with the psychological aspects of performance, so there is a rich literature that awaits your research. Numerous tools are available, but you get what you pay for in this instance.

You're a trekker, so you don't have to worry about this stuff, right? Sorry, but psychological issues have ruined many a trek. The day-to-day stresses of travel in a strange land with strangers can add up, and there are dangerous situations (e.g., crossing bad bridges) that will require your keeping your cool. You still need to frankly assess your ability to cope with those issues (refer back to Fig. 21).

To summarize, the hard-core or elite athletes will find it worthwhile to engage the services of trainers, sports physiologists, and sports psychologists to help them plan a training program. Most of us can get a baseline on these systems using simple tests, then use those same tests to gauge our progress in the future.

Construct Your Training Program

You now know your training goals and your current level of performance in the systems described above. The third step is to determine how to train these systems to meet your goals. The training activities you choose will depend on where you live, what equipment you have available, and your personal needs. I'll make a few specific suggestions later in this chapter, but your job is to consult the abundant literature on training and pick those activities that train your weak spots and also fit these training program principles:

- Design a program that will peacefully coexist with your family, job, and other commitments. Avoid overscheduling yourself, and don't worry too much about the day-to-day order in which you do things. Unless you are a sponsored athlete, it's hard to train as long and often as you might like.
- Realize that training takes time. A minimum of 15 weeks is required to see any significant improvement in most systems; 5 to 6 months is a more typical length for a full training period. It will take several years and multiple extended training periods to reach your maximum potential for alpine/high-altitude climbing.
- Emphasize those systems that need the most improvement. If an aspiring alpinist can crank off 25 pull-ups but can't run 2 miles, where should she spend her time? Generally, we dislike training our weaknesses, so if you don't like it, do it (but be careful with past injuries).
- Schedule rest days into your program. Get the amount of rest that *your* body needs. Some folks can train every day for a month; others need a day off after a couple of hard workouts, so listen to your body.
- Only train one system in a particular workout. Successful cardiovascular/metabolic training requires long, low-intensity muscular workouts that may seem rather worthless in terms of strength training but that provide valuable training for the metabolic systems. Similarly, muscular strength and muscular endurance should be trained during different workouts.
- Periodize your training during the year, and take longer rest periods (up to several weeks) after particularly stressful training/climbing periods.
- Be realistic. If you can gain 1,500 ft per hour on the stair machine today, it's unlikely that you will be able to do 4,000 ft per hour after 15 weeks. At some point you may realize that your physical abilities aren't adequate to meet your goals. It's better to realize that now than to be featured in *Accidents in North American Mountaineering*.[4]

Training

I'll discuss some details in a moment; at this point I'll urge you to record your progress. Only by keeping good records will you know if you are making gains. Use a heart-rate monitor for aerobic training, record the elevation gained during your step machine workout, and so on. Record the weather. Record your injuries. Record your mood. Over the years this information will be an invaluable resource as you fine-tune your training strategies.

Debriefing

After you get back from The Big Trip, immediately evaluate the success of your training program. Sore quads from punching downhill? Stiff back from carrying a pack? Still not enough endurance to lock off and place gear? Couldn't keep up with the rest of the trekkers? Discard and add training elements to address the most obvious areas that need improvement.

PRACTICAL ADVICE FOR TRAINING

Training can consume a lot of time, so wasting time while training makes sense only for the unemployed. By wasting time I don't mean spending too much time between sets in the weight room, I mean training using poor technique, using the wrong machines, or using the wrong strategy. Here I want to concentrate on the issue of technique and toss in some other tips.

Where to Train?

The days of the cramped, hot, smelly weight room, dominated by muscleheads, are long gone. As you decide where to do your indoor training, keep the following in mind:

- Is the temperature comfortable, especially if you plan to use cardio machines to do aerobic workouts?
- Are there fans available to help cool you during cardio workouts?
- Is there enough space for you to work out comfortably?
- Is there enough equipment for the typical number of users?
- Are the cardio machines well maintained?
- Is the noise level low enough to listen to music with headphones?

If you don't have hills, find the longest staircase you can for training.

Some of you may set up a workout area in your home or apartment. This allows you to work out 24/7, cuts down on commute time, and ensures that the equipment is clean and well maintained, but it does limit the number of specific exercises that you can do in most cases. Using a health club provides more options (and is the only practical solution) in most cases. Visit the facility at the times you intend to use it to check for crowds.

General Pitfalls

The biggest issue in training is "too heavy/too fast." This primarily afflicts the young of the species. Guys tend to be macho with weights, sacrificing technique for heavy lifts. Both sexes tend to have lousy technique on cardio machines, sacrificing technique for a flurry of leg movement. Slow down, lighten up, and quit trying to impress somebody else. I work out in college facilities, and I estimate that 60% to 70% of those users fall into this trap.

The other main issue is maintaining focus. You can't do a good workout while you're reading, listening to music, and talking on the phone. Frankly, I think it's best not to work out with more than one or two friends; the chitchat and groupthink detracts from your focus. On the other hand, don't be an iPod zombie, avoiding all social contact with your fellow exercisers.

Strength Training

Strength training usually involves the use of body weight, barbells, dumbbells, or machines. Some simple weight-training rules: Don't drop the weights to demonstrate how strong you are by the big crash they make. Put the plates and dumbbells away when you're finished. Don't lift in front of the dumbbell racks and block other users' access. Don't occupy a machine for 10 minutes while you chat with friends and make others delay their workout. Do use the mirrors (if available) to help maintain proper form.

Learn proper technique from a book[95] or a personal trainer. Watching others is a particularly poor way to learn proper technique. Since most of us have a dominant, stronger arm, I prefer dumbbell workouts for the upper body rather than barbell or machine exercise. Dumbbells also allow your arms to pronate (twist) naturally as they move, which prevents elbow tendinitis.

There are many approaches to structuring workouts. The simplest is to pick a weight and do three sets of eight repetitions of each exercise (or 3 × 12 on the legs). Other approaches include high repetitions (15 to 30) with a lower weight, or a progressive set (sets of 8-6-4-3-2-1-4) with increased weight as the reps decrease. I recommend starting any program with very light weights and high reps. This allows you to focus on technique, and the high reps will help recruit more muscle fibers (refer back to Fig. 16).

As you move to higher weights, it is possible to undertrain the accessory muscles that help to stabilize and control movement. Technical climbers especially need to make sure they do exercises that properly train the rotator cuff muscles and upper back muscles.

Machines vary a lot in their usefulness. Some machines can be adjusted to fit you, others can't. Machines are generally designed to isolate specific muscles, which is good if those muscles are hard to train. I use machines only when dumbbells or barbells won't work. I haven't used the home machines that depend on rubber bands or flexible rods for resistance, but you'll not see these in a health club.

If a health club is not an option, it's quite feasible to set up a home gym at a low cost. A pair of dumbbells with removable plates, an exercise ball, a pull-up bar, and a dip bar will allow you to do a wide range of exercises. Exercise balls are useful for developing core strength and for developing those accessory muscles. Old-fashioned calisthenics (push-ups, pull-ups, squat thrusts) are great exercises that need only a bit of floor space. Don't feel limited by a lack of equipment; you can't spend your way to fitness.

Aerobic Training

This is a bit of a misnomer because you are training all of the major systems—muscular, cardiovascular, metabolic, and psychological. As noted above, certain exercises will mimic travel at altitude, and these should be included in healthy amounts in your program. I much prefer outdoor aerobic workouts, and if you're so inclined, then it's likely that you'll be doing a lot of running or cycling. Minute for minute, running gives you the most concentrated exercise you can get anywhere, anytime (Nordic skiing is seldom possible year-round). Cycling gives your quads good training for uphill walking. The truly blessed live near the mountains and can train daily on the real thing.

Many live in a situation that doesn't allow for regular outdoor workouts, so we're back to the health club. The biggest problem with machine-based aerobic workouts is cheating, primarily on elliptical trainers and stair machines. Aside from a bicycle, your hands should only be used for support on an escalator-style step machine. These are quite easy to stumble on as your attention wanders. But never lean on your arms on any machine other than a cycle! By hanging on a machine, you are taking weight off your legs, and that calorie counter on the machine is seriously overestimating your energy consumption. If you can't do the workout without hanging on, slow down. If the pace seems too slow, increase the resistance. At most, place a couple of fingers on the bars for stability. Reading while on a machine makes you hang on and disrupts your biomechanics, so avoid it (except on a recumbent bike).

I don't recommend using aerobic machines that also include arm motion. These arm bars almost never fit your biomechanics and lead to strange upper-body motions. Your head is the leader for whole-body posture, so keep your head up and maintain an erect, natural posture.

If you plan to travel with a pack, it's essential to do some training with one. Wearing a pack changes the angle of the back and head,[13] increases quadriceps and calf involvement,[188] and significantly alters the biomechanics of walking.[197] Shoulders and upper back bear about 70% of the vertical force exerted by the pack,[196] so training these muscles is crucial to performance at altitude.

Don't just throw a 40 lb/20 kg pack on and chug away. Start light, just as if you are doing a weight routine. There tend to be weaknesses in our back muscles that are magni-

An escalator-style machine is the top choice for indoor aerobic training.

fied by a pack; these back muscles need to be trained first, before working on the larger leg muscles that will be stressed by a larger pack. I like to use 20 lb bags of nonclay cat litter in the pack, as they ride well and have a reasonable density.

On the escalator-style stair machine or a treadmill, ankle weights are an important training aid for the climber. The old adage that "one pound on the legs equals five on the back" is accurate. The added weight of mountaineering boots and crampons can easily be 5 to 6 lb (2.2 to 2.7 kg) on each leg. Strap-on weights for each ankle will allow you to replicate the muscular effort of heavy footwear. Just for grins, wear your boots on the machine one day. It's a good demonstration of biomechanics. The stride changes necessary to hike in heavy boots impose a fatigue due to changes in muscle use.

Training the Ventilatory Muscles

Travel at high altitude requires deep and rapid breathing. Cibella et al.[82] measured ventilation during maximum exercise at sea level and after one month of acclimatization at 5,050 m. More air was moved and more calories were consumed by respiratory muscles at altitude (129 vs. 40 cal/min). The actual work of breathing (calories consumed per liter of air moved) is the same at sea level and at altitude.[82] They estimated that maximal ventilation requires 5% of the oxygen taken in at sea level and 26% of the oxygen taken in a altitude. This number will only increase as one goes higher.

Hypoxia reduces the oxygen available to the diaphragm muscles, hastens diaphragm fatigue, and places an additional load on the other ventilatory muscles.[141] Since breathing has high priority, ventilation may divert scarce oxygen supplies from other muscles to the diaphragm and rib cage muscles. In addition, the perception of ventilatory distress is greater at altitude, increasing the likelihood of central (brain) fatigue.[178] There are no gender differences in inspiratory muscle fatigue.[260]

The diaphragm and rib cage muscles need to be strong at altitude. They can be trained,[221] and training leads to improvements in lung capacity and exercise capacity,[110] so you need to include training sessions specifically targeted to respiratory training. There is some suggestion that aerobic endurance training (long, slow workouts) actually detrains the ventilatory muscles, so ventilatory training is best done as several 2.5- to 5.0-minute sprints while running, biking, or hill climbing. For example, start with four repetitions of 800 m sprints on a track, separated by a 400 m jog, and gradually increase the number to eight repetitions over time. You can do the same on a bike, by power hiking up a steep hill, or on a step machine. Pace yourself so that all repetitions can be completed in the same amount of time. By the time you finish your last repetition, you should be suffering but still in control of your form.

Various devices are sold that allow you to train your breathing muscles by restricting inspiration and/or expiration. Although these can't hurt, I still think that more extended bouts of ventilatory exercise are more effective, as they serve a dual purpose (cardiovascular and ventilatory training). An unpublished study has demonstrated that training with a device can work if the rate of ventilation is increased as well as the resistance to ventilation. Sit-ups and biceps curls have been shown to increase diaphragm muscle thickness, so they serve as a form of ventilatory training.[97] Ilg[173] discusses proper breathing techniques for aerobic athletes and will be useful for the altitude athlete. Various forms of yoga also develop proper breathing techniques. And don't forget that wearing a pack affects lung function,[72] so do some ventilatory training while wearing a pack.

Overtraining

Overtraining is a danger for the fanatic. Training can become an addiction and an end unto itself. Watch for signs of overtraining: increased resting heart rate, a "rundown" feeling, and illness. Mental distress over missing a workout is another warning sign. See Noakes[249] for more information on overtraining.

If you have periodized your training to peak at the time of your trip,[351] you should reach your peak physical condition just before your trip. Those with extreme talent need not worry about such details:

> [Peaking] didn't sit very comfortably in the usual Fowler regime of five days behind the desk and occasional climbing weekends. In fact, I have always tended to look on mountaineering as an excellent way to keep fit rather than something to get fit for. (Fowler 2005, p. 193)

I know people who can step out of the house and perform at their top level. But I know a lot more people (myself included) who would fail miserably using that strategy.

PRETRIP BODY WEIGHT MANAGEMENT

For almost all travelers, weight management means keeping your body weight down. Excess fat is just dead weight to be carried around, creating additional stress on your muscles and cardiovascular systems at altitude. Even 5 lb/2 kg can make a difference in how fatigued you are after a day's walk or climb. If you want to lose weight, you need (as always) to figure out what works best for you, and by all means avoid rapid weight loss. This can make you weak, compromise your immune system, and generally increase the risk of problems on your trip. If you have followed the training advice and matched your ability to your planned travel, then you won't have a problem.

The visitor to extreme altitude has a different problem. Weight loss can be severe after extended stays at high altitude. On Kangchenjunga I went from about 185 to 160 lb. Your body consumes both fats and protein (muscle) at higher altitudes, probably due to digestive malfunction (Chapter 7), so it's best to start the climb a bit heavy. This was recognized over a century ago by Aleister Crowley:

> I had realized from the first that the proper preparation for a journey of this sort is to get as fat as possible before starting, and stay as fat as possible as long as possible. (Crowley 1969, p. 299)

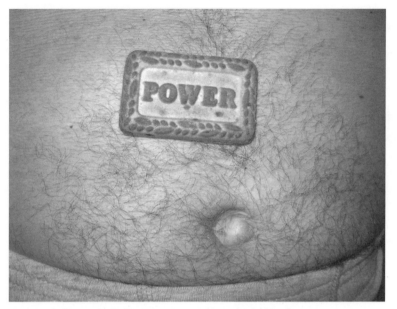

A power belly may be better than six-pack abs at high altitudes.

One of the greatest Himalayan climbers of all time, Jerzy Kukuczka, endured the disdain of some now-forgotten guide:

> *"So you are this Kukuczka? You don't look like a mountaineer."*
>
> *The Swiss guide was not so much looking into my eyes, as rather lower, to just below the belt where I display a rather unsportsmanlike girth. ... We can have a chat at 8000 metres, I murmured to myself. (Kukuczka 1992, p. 133)*

Jim Curran[90] speculated that the "greyhound-thin" Al Rouse was not suited to survive the many days he spent at 8,000 m on K2, while the somewhat portly Kurt Diemberger and Willi Bauer had the energy reserves needed to stay alive during the same ordeal. However, the presence of extra body fat doesn't stop the loss of muscle tissue.[61]

Before any 8,000 m expedition, I try to put on an extra 5 to 10 lb (2 to 4 kg) in the three weeks before the trip. In my younger days I couldn't have done that, but it's worth a try, especially if you have very low body fat. For the older folks, I'm sorry to report that the last fat that's used will be the waist/abdominal fat that you probably would love to lose.

KEY CONCEPTS

1. Any trip to altitude will have a definition of success that will require a certain level of physical and mental performance.
2. People differ in their ability to respond to training (get stronger/faster).
3. Each person must develop a training program that fits his or her training goals and current state of fitness.
4. The cardiovascular, musculoskeletal, metabolic, and psychological systems must all be trained for optimal performance.
5. Learn to train properly to maximize performance and minimize time spent training.

Before, During, and After Your Trip

Throughout this book I've emphasized that a successful trip to altitude will require more than just proper physiological acclimatization. In this chapter I've assembled a number of suggestions that may help you have a more successful trip. Some of these tips apply to any trip, some apply only to certain kinds of trips.

BEFORE YOUR TRIP
Planning
While the highly experienced traveler may disdain planning,[344] most of us will benefit from careful thought about our proposed adventure. As you develop experience, it will become simpler and simpler to put a trip together.

Many a trip has been doomed from the beginning as a consequence of poor goal setting. Overconfidence in one's abilities is a congenital weakness in our species, at least while having a beer:

> From the safety of the pub, we could climb any mountain. (Saunders 1991, p. 58)

Whether you're taking a day hike or attempting the North Face of Jannu,

> [t]he first thing is to know yourself, to establish, or at least assess, your own limitations, then you must see to it that your level of performance matches the difficulty and danger of the proposed climb. (Buhl 1956, p. 146)

Recall that this was the first step of your training program. This issue needs to be revisited prior to your departure; if your training leaves you still not strong enough, or techni-

Climbers wait for planes at Kahiltna International Airport (Denali). Mount Hunter is in the background.

cally competent enough, to accomplish your goals, then it only makes sense to change your itinerary. The difficulty is to gauge your capabilities at altitude from your sea-level performance. This is not too difficult for travel below 6,000 m. Predicting your potential performance from 6,000 to 7,000 m is more difficult, and for travel between 7,500 and 8,850 m, there are too many variables to allow a prediction. Only experience will help you here.

Too much planning can also be problematic. Some people plan their trips years in advance and are then disappointed when conditions aren't appropriate for travel to that area. Be flexible.

Once your overall goal is chosen, establish your personal goals. I suggest three goals, in the following order:

1. Come home safe and sound.
2. Make new friends, and don't turn friends into enemies.
3. Climb the peak/do the trek/complete the hike.

Organizing the Trip

This can be fun or frustrating and usually ends up being both. Planning a weekend trip may just involve deciding who drives and who brings the tent. Planning a major trek or expedition may involve months of work and thousands of details. While most of us pay for our own trips, begging for money (fundraising) has been the lot of the high-altitude climber for decades.[83, 355] The stress of organizing can be the first step toward a later disaster. For example, Maurice Barrard was exhausted from the stress of organizing and fundraising for the 1986 K2 expedition on which he and his wife, Liliane, died on descent.[179]

Your baggage must withstand the rigors of your transport system.

Technical difficulty and altitude are not a good mix for the inexperienced. North Face of Kangchenjunga, 7,000 m.

The more complex the trip, the more important it is to have adequate help with planning. Including team members in the planning and organization will build confidence among members and keep the leader from going too crazy. When working with trekking agents or other overseas contacts, make no assumptions and ask many questions. If you're working with a reputable agency, you should be in good shape. No matter how well you plan, there are always surprises.

As you pack for a big trip, keep a very detailed list of what's in each piece of luggage. This can help you find things later, and it can help if you have lost luggage. Keep two versions of this list: a version with actual values of each checked item (and year purchased) for insurance reasons and a version with reduced values in case overseas customs officials try to charge you import fees. I also take digital photos of each piece of luggage and then record the baggage tag numbers for each piece. Luggage regularly gets lost, and it's easier to show a photo to the airline staff than to describe the bag in another language. All bags should be locked with Transportation Security Administration–approved locks.

Anticipate that your bags will be searched and don't pack bags to the bursting point. Always put any electronic gear, batteries, and water bottles at the top of a bag that's easy to open and close. Don't ship a liquid-fuel stove that isn't new unless you disassemble it, run it through the dishwasher, and air-dry it for a couple of days. Fuel bottles should be treated the same way and then filled with food (e.g., M&Ms). Even so, your stove/bottles may be confiscated. Of course, you should *never* ship compressed gas of any kind, as you could easily kill everyone on the plane! On international trips I stencil or decal each piece with my info and the name and address of the trekking agent. Take extra decals for the return flight. And duct tape. Lots of duct tape. And a couple of felt-tip permanent markers.

DURING THE TRIP

It's always a relief to get into the car or plane. The planning is over, the packing is done, and the long-awaited adventure has finally begun. In the old days, travel to foreign lands took place by ship. This allowed the traveler to slowly ease into the new lifestyle.[51] However, the need to leave in late January for a May trip to Nepal would seriously limit most travelers. Today's long-distance travel always takes place by airplane, which is seldom a relaxing experience. Everyone has to develop a strategy for minimizing stress during travel.

Major travel can result in jet lag. This is independent of travel fatigue, which can occur even if no time zones are crossed. Jet lag is a result of the discord that arises between the day–night cycle at the destination and the internal body rhythms that are tuned to the day–night cycle at the origin of travel. Jet lag can take many days to subside (up to 9 days for 12 hours of time change), and eastward journeys require more recovery than westward journeys.[361]

A variety of strategies for minimizing jet lag are presented by Waterhouse et al.[361] Most adventure travelers don't need to perform at peak levels immediately upon arrival, so a rigorous jet-lag abatement program isn't crucial. However, there are a couple of things that can help. I try to begin shifting my sleep patterns a couple of days before departure, then avoid sleeping during the destination daytime while traveling. Exposure to bright light at the correct time can help;[361] normal artificial lighting may not be strong enough. The standard advice to be active during the day upon arrival is only correct in certain circumstances. Melatonin might (or might not) help you reset your internal clock.

Clearing customs isn't the hassle it used to be in most countries. Read up on the latest from the Internet discussion boards, then plan accordingly. Some great (though dated) advice is found in Burgess and Burgess (p. 245 ff).[67] Sometimes essential materials (like two-way radios) have been confiscated by customs,[88] and in some countries bribery is still the accepted lubricant for smooth progress. If you are shipping an entire expedition into the country, your agent should know what to do.

After Arrival

You will often need to buy food and other supplies once you arrive at your destination. This may be done as you're swirling in jet lag, extreme heat, and the sights and smells of an alien culture. One of your first tasks is to get money. While ATM machines are available in most countries, you'll be given bills in large denominations that are really not useful outside North America and Europe. Currency exchanges are often a good deal, but they won't give you small bills either. Large bills ($50 to $100) fetch the best exchange rate. A large bank is usually your best bet for getting the small bills you need in the backcountry. Watch for counterfeit bills if you obtain small bills from a currency exchange.

Once you get your money, keep track of it. The French managed to misplace their entire stash of expedition cash on the way to Makalu in 1956 (they did find it eventually).[120] The Barrards left nearly $23,000 in a Pakistani cab in 1986, further increasing the stress they were experiencing.[179]

In the old days, locally purchased supplies had to be sewn in waterproof sacks or soldered into tins.[32] Today the situation is simpler, but make sure you account for the extra bags and containers you'll need to transport your added supplies. There are never enough ziplock bags, so stuff some extras into the corners of your luggage before you leave home.

Techniques for Backcountry Travel

One way to prepare for climbing a big mountain is to carry a big pack on the approach. Or is it? The 1939 K2 expedition carried small packs on the approach.[30] Shipton[318] recommended carrying nothing to conserve strength for the mountain. Haston (p. 142)[152] concurs, stating that "the best thing is to take a light pack with essentials and wander along enjoying the scenery." Others feel that a heavier pack is better. The American Gasherbrum I expedition carried 40 to 50 lb on the approach,[83] and the kings of machismo, the 1975 American K2 expedition, carried 50 to 60 lb while racing their way up the Baltoro Glacier.[297]

Unless you are a photographer, there is no reason to carry more than 20 lb (9 kg) on a trek or approach. It's fine to train (pretrip) with a heavier pack, but there's really no advan-

Good advice for pit toilet rookies: "Finish up carefull your toilet filings to make sure that your fill an excriment in the hole." Barafu Camp (4,600 m), Kilimanjaro.

tage to lugging a heavy load when you don't have to. If you're backpacking or carrying loads to a higher camp, the pack should weigh no more than 25% of your body weight if you want to use energy most efficiently.[29]

The Importance of Rhythm in Movement

Economy of movement leads to the efficient use of energy. Many authors emphasize the importance of rhythm:

> The man who wears himself out on a mountain is he who has never learnt to walk properly.... [R]hythm is an attitude of mind rather than any conscious physical control.... (Smythe 1937, p. 616)

> The great secret is to get the rhythm. Once that is right, you can plod on for hours. (Venables 2000, p. 132)

> The basis of all mountaineering is the conservation of energy by the three fundamental principles—rhythmic movement, balance and precise placing of the feet. (Shipton 1943, p. 385)

This slower, constant rhythm may take a good deal of concentration to attain.[100, 325] The pace achieved during rhythmic movement will vary from person to person; this can be a problem on a roped team moving together, such as on a glacier. You have to defer to the slowest climber, which can be frustrating to all involved. A trip up Kilimanjaro can be excruciating for a trained climber, simply because the guides insist on an incredibly slow pace that is appropriate for a novice but not for somebody who is trained and experienced at altitude. However, your natural pace while carrying a load won't necessarily be the optimal pace,[114] so be open to suggestions by more experienced individuals.

What do you do with your brain as you're moving slowly up the trail? There are number of strategies, and the simplest is to count steps. Mo Anthoine would determine the number of steps between camps and use that to occupy his mind:

> On Everest, I was counting on really a grand scale....I knew how many steps I'd done and how many I still had to do. I used to do mental arithmetic. I'd work out what fraction I'd done, then I'd turn it into a percentage....When I'm not counting, I time myself....Both are ways of finding out if I am performing properly. (Mo Anthoine, quoted in Alvarez 2001, p. 135)

Roger Baxter-Jones suggests some variations to the basic counting theme:

> Himalayan climbing is about putting one foot in front of another and breathing whilst doing so. Keep doing this and you'll make it. Like Doug [Scott] I play breathing games, changing rhythms, counting steps, directing the inhalation to wherever the strain is. Silly mind games help too, such as imagining you are moving the mountain down with your feet as you stay at the same height. (Roger Baxter-Jones, quoted in Scott and MacIntyre 1984, p. 190)

Music is an increasingly popular tool for occupying the mind during travel. Alpinists such as Marc Twight[350] used music during difficult solo ascents, and iPods and their brethren are common sights on the trail and on the mountain. Keep in mind that a device using a hard drive won't function above about 4,000 to 5,000 m; only solid-state devices can be used at higher altitudes (the same goes for your computer). While music has its advantages, you may not hear that troupe of monkeys in the forest, the birds as they fly over, the shout of your partner warning you of rockfall, the approach of an avalanche...You get the idea.

If you are moving over terrain that doesn't allow for a constant rhythm to be established, you need to be able to shift gears to adjust the rhythm to the landscape. Keep in mind that "rhythm" doesn't necessarily mean "slow." Occasionally safety will require fast movement: Crossing a rock slide area on a trail, passing beneath a serac on a climb, and climbing up a rockfall-prone couloir all require speed. You will need to conserve enough energy beforehand and then pace yourself properly so that you can reach a safe location as quickly as possible.

Just as the trek or climb is broken down into daily stages, the daily movement needs to be broken down into intermediate stages. The fatigue of altitude can discourage almost anyone climbing or hiking to a seemingly far-off point, so the key is not to worry about your end goal and set an intermediate goal: the next big rock on the trail, that patch of green in the distance, or the top of the hour on your watch. Technical climbers have it easier, as each ropelength is a discrete and measurable unit of progress. At low altitudes your intermediate stages might take a couple of hours to complete; at 8,000 m your goals may only be 10 to 20 minutes apart.[66]

Trekking poles are a useful accessory, especially if you're carrying a load. Poles reduce impact forces on joints, especially when carrying a pack downhill.[49] Use poles that can be adjusted easily for length, and be careful using them on tricky terrain (such as a boulderfield). When climbing moderate snow unroped, a ski pole and a regular-length ice axe provide security when moving both up and down. Those short ice tools make you look like a stud until you're bent over double trying to use one on a low-angle snowslope.

Typical Ascent Rates during Climbs

Your speed during an ascent can be a useful tool for gauging your acclimatization and your performance relative to teammates. Table 13 provides some examples of climb rates at different elevations, with different loads, and with or without supplemental oxygen. At low elevations during training, it's possible to attain very high rates of elevation gain (Table 13.A). On a real climb with a typical load, ascent rates vary between 100 and 300 m/hr at elevations between 5,000 and 7,000 m. Using supplementary oxygen doesn't seem to help below 7,000 m (Table 13.C). Above 8,000 m, the rate of climb is at most 100 m/hr without oxygen, which agrees with the predicted theoretical maximum.[360]

Anatoli Boukreev was quite fast (Table 13.D). You won't reach these rates unless you are a world-class athlete, but they do give you a yardstick for comparison. Boukreev stated that he could descend at twice the speed of ascent; most of us will be able to do better than that since we climb up more slowly. Peter Habeler's descent from the summit of Everest after the first ascent without oxygen is of particular note. He descended 900 m (3,000 ft) in one hour, a testament to his training regimen and strength of will.

Getting Up in the Morning

Many of us can't reconcile the early-morning starts inherent in the mountains:

> The early start is one of the most horrible aspects of mountaineering. If all the solemn oaths—made with stars as their witnesses—were kept, the sport of mountaineering would vanish within a fortnight. (Clinch 1982, p. 115)

Beginnings are delicate things, and I think this applies to the beginning of each day. There are morning people and not-morning people; I'm not a morning person, so I feel your pain if you're a reluctant riser, and I offer some suggestions. In some cases you won't have a choice of a wakeup time: The porters will sometimes take the tent down while you're still in it. A civilized trek in Nepal might include bed tea, delivered to your tent door, as an inducement to get up and about.

Organization is the key to an easy start to the day. I learned this long ago from Fletcher,[117] who advocated a backpacking system that allows you to cook breakfast without ever leaving your sleeping bag. This philosophy can be extended to trips where you have a cook and to climbs where you're cooking with snow. First, do as much packing as possible in the evening. Organize your clothing for the next day and stack it up in the order you'll need it in the morning. In cold situations you'll likely want to prewarm your clothing, so make sure you can reach it from your sleeping bag. Pack up as much gear as possible before going to sleep.

Make sure you get enough sleep by going to bed early enough. Use earplugs if necessary, listen to music, or read a bit if your tentmate doesn't mind. If you have to cook for yourself, have the pot full of water just outside the tent (covered, with the lid weighted down). The stove, utensils, and cooking supplies should be within easy reach. My goal is to be able to have the water heating up without doing more than sticking my arms out of my sleeping bag for a couple of minutes. Once the stove is going, you can slowly begin to dress inside your sleeping bag. With luck, you're dressed and the water's hot at the same time, allowing you to emerge into the cool air while you're getting your first hot drink. This process can take hours at the highest altitudes. Modify this approach as needed to deal with bears, pack rats, or other critters.

If you're trekking, it's a good idea to immediately pack your gear so that porters can make up their loads; your leader will instruct you. On a trek it's useful to keep your sleeping kit together in one bag so you can quickly pack in the morning.

Another tip comes from Bob Bates:

> If the camp is to be moved, the next step is the deflating of the air mattresses. This is done simply by unscrewing the valve. It is the finest way for a man of weak character to get himself out of bed…the rocks beneath the tent floor, gently at first, then more forcefully, prod him into action. (Bates et al. 1939, p. 240)

If all else fails, this can be a useful way to get your sluggish tentmate to start moving in the morning.

Enforced Inactivity

Climbing expeditions often include periods of inactivity as a result of bad weather or the need to acclimatize. While a break is sometimes welcome, too much rest isn't a good thing:

Bed tea is a delightful practice on the trek in Nepal.

The first and greatest [hardship] was malaise, which was mostly due to lack of food and exercise. The latter complaint seems rather ridiculous; but it is an absolute fact. (Crowley 1969, p. 318)

[I]t was evident that two days and nights in our sleeping bags had taken more out of us than a hard day's work. (Tilman 1937, p. 240)

These anecdotal observations are backed up by Saltin et al.,[303] who examined the effects of 20 days of bed rest on cardiovascular traits. $\dot{V}O_2$max, stroke volume, and cardiac output decreased dramatically. Average heart rate during submaximal exercise ($\dot{V}O_2 = 1.5$ L/min) increased from 129 to 164 beats per minute. While these changes can be reversed with training, this potential physical deterioration due to inactivity must be prevented through regular activity. Shovel out tents, build a new latrine, hike to a lower camp, build cairns...do something! It's easy to imagine how high-altitude deterioration, inactivity deterioriation, and psychological deterioration due to boredom could combine to doom a trip to certain failure. While high-altitude deterioration is inevitable, the other two issues can be controlled.

Digital music and books can help pass the time.

Dealing with Altitude, Stress, and Emotional Issues

Altitude tends to magnify any personal emotional issues you have and any frictions with other teammates (Chapter 9). On short trips it's possible to sweep these issues aside and still reach your hiking or climbing goals. On longer, higher trips these issues can lead to a general deterioration in spirit and result in mild depression:

> *Depression is one of the subtle ways by which the mountain fights us. It is one of her defenses that she makes us sick, tired, listless, quarrelsome with our companions and disinclined to mentally continue the fight. She exhausts our minds quite as much as she exhausts our bodies.* (Noel 1927, p. 133)

On any trip you need to monitor your companions and yourself for altitude illness, and I think it's quite appropriate to monitor your emotional states with the same care. Review Chapters 9 and 11 for more examples and ideas for dealing with these issues.

AFTER THE TRIP

Any experience that pulls you out of your normal life for a period of time, focuses your efforts on a definable goal, and then tosses you back into "real life" will undoubtedly have psychological consequences. Coffey[85] provides a more complete discussion of this topic that should be read by both the traveler and the spouse/family prior to departure.

It's very common to be mildly depressed after returning from a long trip. All of a sudden you're thrust back into a reality that contrasts greatly with the alternate reality that you just left:

> *Since the descent I have been infinitely melancholy.* (Messner 1989, p. 253)

> *Whenever I got trapped indoors for too long, lapsing into the funk that Paula calls my "wilted flower" state, she'd send me out into the yard.* (Viesturs 2006)

> *Historians tell us that Frank Smythe only began to function properly above 20,000 feet. This adds up to a pretty considerable handicap, when you consider how much of his life must have been spent at lower altitudes.* (Patey 1971, p. 238)

Patey was writing somewhat in jest, but there's a crucial truth there. It's not hard to see why working in the yard might not compare to a life-or-death situation in the Death Zone. It might help if we think of the brain as a malleable object. The stresses of a high-altitude expedition (or the battlefield, or solo ocean racing) may change the growth and firing patterns of neurons or the release of neurotransmitters to accommodate the intensity and stress of the situation. After returning from your trip, the brain may take some time to reset to a more mild set of stresses. In addition, you've removed the exhilaration that "feeds the rat"; in this case the depression may be a symptom of withdrawal because you're not getting your fix.[306] After military training, anger and fatigue levels remained high for nearly 90 days,[18] and a major trek or expedition might leave you unsettled for a period of months as your brain reprograms for life in a different environment.

In most cases, these issues fade away, and you are left with the positives: the new friends, the shared victories, the newly gained confidence, to name a few. Similar positive outcomes are expressed by polar explorers.[261]

There is considerable disagreement about the severity and longevity, and indeed the existence of mental impairment after exposure to high altitudes. For example, climbers showed decreased memory, reaction time, and ability to concentrate 75 days after their first ascent of a peak 5,900 m or higher.[78] Regard et al.[275] studied eight climbers who had ascended to 8,500 m or higher without oxygen; at least one had spent 358 hours above 8,000 m. All subjects had been below 5,000 m for at least two months. The researchers found that the high-altitude climbers varied more than the matched control group and that the climbers exhibited slightly reduced concentration, short-term memory, and conceptual ability. There was no correlation between length of exposure to extreme altitudes and impairment. Having a high hypoxic ventilatory response (refer back to Fig. 5) may lead to more mental impairment.[162] Only 1 of 13 climbers who ascended Everest without supplemental oxygen had normal brain magnetic resonance imaging (MRI) scans, and a significant fraction of others ascending lower peaks had abnormal MRI scans as well.[116] Other studies have shown no long-term consequences of altitude (e.g. Anooshiravani et al.).[7] At sea level, stress itself can cause structural changes in the structure of the brain.[306]

I usually feel a bit "fuzzy" if I've spent several days above 7,000 m. A more sinister anecdotal observation of one of the climbers studied by Regard etal.[275] suggests that there might be long-term consequences if you make too many visits to the Death Zone:

> Reinhold Messner has scaled all fourteen 8,000-meter peaks in the world without using supplemental oxygen. The sad thing is, you can tell. His personality has gotten strange, and the thin air has probably damaged his brain. People say that he is like an old boxer who's taken too many punches. (Kropp 1997, p. 199)

Physical Issues

It's likely that you'll return from a trek or climb to a sub-7,000 m peak feeling tired and a couple of pounds lighter. If you've been in the Death Zone, had dysentery, and been traveling for two to three months, your own spouse may have a hard time recognizing you upon your return. The literature is filled with accounts of weight loss on expeditions. I probably lost 12 kg (25 lb) on Kangchenjunga, much of it muscle; losses of 8 to 12 kg are not unusual.[99, 191, 225] Needless to say, you will be craving protein to allow your muscles to rebuild after such an experience.*

You'll suffer a decrease in athletic performance until the muscle mass is regained. This weight/muscle loss is one reason why it's difficult to climb multiple high peaks in a short time unless you're blessed with good conditions and fine weather. Not everyone suffers decreases in performance after a climb to extreme altitude. After returning to India from 8,200 m on Everest in 1938, Tilman[345] completed a 38-mile walk with two climbs from 2,000 to 14,000 ft in under 16 hours because he was "pressed for time."

If you're used to training hard, now is not the time to start again. Give your body time to recover under an easy exercise regime. This is also good time to assess your weaknesses and start to remodel your body by selective exercise.

---

* If you head for the nearest steak house after getting back to cities such as Kathmandu, make sure you get your steak cooked well done. The last thing you need is some tropical parasitic disease due to undercooked meat.

Immune System

We are still learning how the immune system is affected by altitude,[223] exercise,[249] and the combination of the two.[220] Altitude does not seriously impair the immune system,[223] or does it?[187] Many of the stresses that occur at altitude (refer back to Fig. 21) may affect the immune system,[223, 306] making it difficult to determine exactly what is messing with your immune response.

It's not unusual to get sick after a big trip. While this is usually something as simple as a head cold, you have to watch carefully and make sure a simple illness isn't the harbinger of a more serious issue. If you've been traveling in an exotic locale, it's quite possible to exhibit symptoms of an infection acquired abroad several weeks after your return. Be a bit of a hypochondriac after your trip; that bowel discomfort could indicate a tapeworm. Most medical labs won't expect to see anything exotic in your stool sample, so don't assume they're right when they say you're clean. I've taken meds to deal with parasites even though they weren't found by the lab. As long as the medication doesn't have severe side effects, prophylaxis might be better than allowing a parasite to get established in your body. A talk with your physician may be in order just to be sure the medications are right for you.

Finally, male reproductive function may be affected after travel to higher altitudes. Climbers who ascended to 6,700 m had lower testosterone levels, fewer sperm, and more abnormal sperm for at least three months after the expedition.[258] All traits returned to normal at some point thereafter. It's unlikely that shorter trips to lower altitude have such an effect, and I'm not aware of any similar studies on women.

Appendix A:
Some Scientific Background

I don't expect everyone reading this book to remember all of the scientific concepts that are needed to understand the biology and chemistry that are discussed. Here you will find some background on the behavior of gases, partial pressures, diffusion, and other biological concepts. Skim through the headings to find the topic you're looking for.

Certain scientific terms come up over and over in this book. Below is a list of the common prefixes and roots and their meanings. Some terms combine the prefixes and roots, such as isocapnic, normoxia, hyberbaric, apnea, and hypoxemia.

PREFIX OR ROOT	MEANING
a-	without; lack of
-baria	barometric pressure
-capnia	carbon dioxide
-cythemia	red blood cell count
dys-	impaired, abnormal, difficult
hyper-	above, higher
hypo-	below, lower
iso-	constant; the same
normo-	ambient environmental level
-oxemia	blood oxygen content
-oxia	oxygen levels (usually atmospheric)
-pnea	breathing (mechanical respiration)
-thermia	temperature
-volemia	blood volume

THE ATMOSPHERE

The atmosphere is a mixture of different gases, liquids, and solids. Recall that any substance can assume any one of these three phases, depending on the temperature. The best example is water: It's a gas above 100°C, a solid below 0°C, and a liquid in between. I'll restrict the discussion to only the mixture of gases, which includes the oxygen and carbon dioxide that are of primary interest.

The atmosphere is 78% nitrogen and 21% oxygen, with the remaining 1% split among carbon dioxide, argon, and other gases. Only oxygen and carbon dioxide are of direct interest in this book. Water vapor is also important, but the amount in the atmosphere varies dramatically from day to day, so I'll not include it at the moment.

The atmosphere is held in place by Earth's gravity—otherwise it would just randomly disperse into space. While any one molecule in the atmosphere is essentially weightless, when you stack them all up, they represent a lot of weight on top of your head (and pushing on your sides). At sea level, we are pressed by the weight of 14.7 lb of atmosphere on every square inch of our body. We don't notice it because our innards are pushed outward with the same exact pressure. If you change elevation quickly in a plane or car, you will sometimes feel pressure in your ears; swallowing or yawning will make them "pop." This is just a pressure difference caused by the rapid elevation change.[*]

Rather than using pounds per square inch, researchers use millimeters of mercury (mm Hg) to represent atmospheric pressure. Keep in mind that standard atmospheric pressure at sea level is 760 mm Hg, and this value decreases to somewhere around 253 mm Hg at the summit of Everest (8,848 m).[368] Why does pressure decrease as altitude increases? Less gas above us, of course. Atmospheric pressure is measured with a barometer, and you hear this value reported as the barometric pressure (in the United States, it's reported in inches of mercury, not millimeters).

Keep in mind that as pressure decreases, the total number of molecules of nitrogen, oxygen, and other gases will decrease. That's because higher pressures will compress the gases, pushing the molecules closer together. So a box of air at sea level has a lot more gas molecules in it than does the same box at the top of Mount Fuji.

What's more, the percentage of nitrogen, oxygen, and other gases in the atmosphere doesn't change as pressure changes. On the beach in Cancun, the atmosphere is 21% oxygen, and at the top of Denali, it's also 21%. But there's a lot less oxygen because the total amount of gas is less. As a result, we can measure barometric pressure and use it to determine the amount of oxygen that will be available.

The Behavior of Gases

Because oxygen and carbon dioxide are of critical interest when we go to altitude, it is important to understand how gases behave when in mixtures and when dissolved in liquids. These behaviors are strictly chemical/physical behaviors and cannot be changed by biological processes.

The air pressure in your car's tires is around 30 pounds of air pressure per square inch (psi). This is the total pressure of the gas in the tire. But that gas is a mixture of nitrogen, oxygen, carbon dioxide, water vapor, and all of the other gases in the atmosphere. How much of the 30 psi is due to nitrogen? To oxygen? To carbon dioxide?

Luckily, it's simple. Dalton's law states that all of the gases in a mixture behave independently, so we can take the fraction of the total mixture that is a certain gas (say, nitrogen) and

---

[*] Babies will often cry during takeoffs and landings because the rapid change in cabin pressure causes discomfort. The crying helps open the eustachian tubes and equalize the pressure.

multiply it by the total pressure to get the partial pressure of the gas. In this example, the gas is 78% nitrogen, so 30 psi × 0.78 = 23.4 psi, the **partial pressure** of nitrogen. If we add all of the partial pressures together, we get the total pressure of a mixture of gases. Partial pressures are written as PO_2, PCO_2, PN_2, and so on. The PO_2 of the atmosphere at sea level would be 760 mm Hg (total pressure) × 21% (fraction of total that's oxygen) = 160 mm Hg. Recall that mm Hg is a unit of pressure, like psi.

Gases are dissolved in the water in our bodies, so the behavior of a gas in a liquid is of major biological importance. Boil a pan of water for 20 minutes. That water now contains virtually no gas molecules because the high water temperature causes gas molecules to leave the water. Now pour the water into an airtight container, leaving no air space at the top, and screw the lid on tight. After the water cools, it still won't have any gases dissolved in it. Open the lid. What will happen, gas-wise?

The gas molecules in the atmosphere will randomly strike the surface of the water, and some of these gas molecules will enter the water. Since 78% of the atmosphere is nitrogen, 78% of the molecules that collide with the surface of the water will be nitrogen. The actual number of nitrogen molecules striking the surface of the water will depend on how dense the atmosphere is; more molecules means more collisions. This means that the partial pressure of a gas is our best measure of the number of collisions with the surface of our water.[*]

The actual amount of a gas that ends up being dissolved in the water depends not only on the number of collisions with the surface of the water but also on the ease with which the gas dissolves into the water. This is called the **solubility** of the gas. It turns out that carbon dioxide is much more soluble in water than is oxygen. If these two gases have the same partial pressure in a gas mixture, they will also have the same partial pressures in liquid solution. However, there will be a higher concentration of carbon dioxide in the water (more carbon dioxide molecules per liter of water) than of oxygen. This can be quite confusing, so a look at Fig. A1 may help.

Just remember that we always talk about the diffusion of gases using partial pressures, and the natural movement of solids and liquids (including water) using concentrations. Gases will always naturally move from an area of higher partial pressure to an area of lower partial pressure; it doesn't matter if the movement is between liquid and liquid, gas and gas, or liquid and gas (see Diffusion, below). Also, the rate of movement is directly related to the difference in partial pressures, so a bigger difference means faster natural movement. Your can of soda foams because carbon dioxide is moving from an area of higher partial pressure (the liquid) to an area of lower partial pressure (the atmosphere).[**]

---

[*] The partial pressures of the gas dissolved in liquid and the gas in the atmosphere are equal when the number of molecules of gas entering the liquid is the same as the number leaving the liquid. If we have a gas such as O_2 that doesn't dissolve easily in water, there will be few molecules entering and few leaving the liquid.

[**] Temperature also affects the solubility of a gas (warm soda foams more than cold soda). Trout live in cold water because there's more O_2 dissolved there than in warm water. In our bodies the temperature is pretty uniform (37°C/98.6°F), so we can ignore temperature for the most part. Other factors (electrolytes) can affect solubility as well.

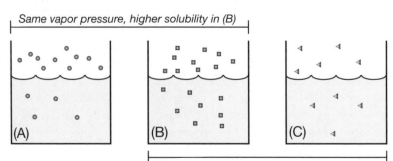

Same vapor pressure, higher solubility in (B)

(A)   (B)   (C)

Higher vapor pressure in (B), same solubility

Fig. A1. The amount of a gas dissolved in solution depends on the amount of gas in the atmosphere (the partial pressure) and the ease with which it dissolves in the water (solubility). A different gas is represented in the three containers. Containers (A) and (B) have the same partial pressures for the gases above the liquid, but the gas in (B) has a higher solubility, so the amount of gas dissolved is greater. The dissolved gases in (A) and (B) have the same partial pressures, however. The gas in (C) has the same solubility as the gas in (B), but its partial pressure is 50% lower. Therefore, the liquid in (C) will contain 50% fewer gas molecules.

BIOLOGICAL CONCEPTS

Homeostasis

Every author uses room temperature as an example of **homeostasis**, so I will too (Fig. A2). In the room there is a thermostat that is set to the desired temperature (the equilibrium temperature). The room temperature is monitored by a sensor (a thermostat). If the room temperature gets too high, the "brains" of the thermostat will send a signal to the air conditioner, which then cools the room. When the room reaches the equilibrium temperature, the air conditioner will shut off. In reality the room will become a little too cool (there is still cold air in the ductwork when the air conditioner shuts down). Thus temperature will actually fluctuate above and below the set point (Fig. A2.B).[*]

Your body works in a similar fashion. Sensors determine the state of a character (e.g., blood sodium concentration), and an interpreter (generally, the brain) decides if the sodium concentration is within normal range. If not, it signals a response to bring the concentration back to normal. Sometimes the body can't respond effectively at the biochemical or physiological levels; try living naked outdoors in the Yukon this winter. In that

---

[*] These oscillations are a result of a time lag in the recognition of a problem and the response by the body. The longer the lag time, the longer the wavelength of the oscillation. Lag times are why you don't (or shouldn't) drive inches behind the bumper of the car in front of you on the freeway. If the other car slows down, you must first recognize the speed change, then apply your brakes, and your car must slow down. All of those take time.

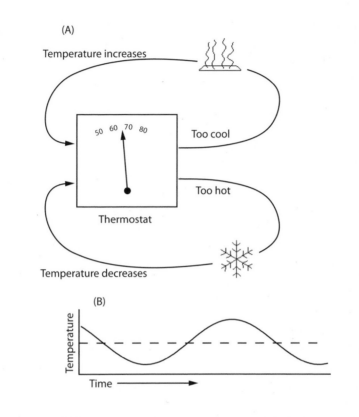

Fig. A2. (A) A mechanical example of homeostasis. If the room gets too hot, the air-conditioning turns on. If the room gets too cold, the furnace comes on. (B) The temperature will fluctuate slightly around the set point due to time lags in the sensory and response components.

circumstance, we might respond behaviorally, by avoiding the Yukon entirely, wearing proper clothing, and/or living in a very warm house.

There is a wide array of sensors in the body, several of which will be mentioned in this book. The response to a stimulus can be carried out by either the nervous system (through an electrical signal) or the endocrine system (through a chemical signal). The nervous and endocrine systems are coupled together in a complex fashion. The interpreter (brain) is responsible for integrating many different inputs and then deciding what the response should be. While I talk about this process as if it's a conscious decision, it is generally not under conscious control.

Getting Work Done in the Body

Every thought, every movement, and every sensation happens because of a series of complex chemical reactions. It's possible to understand the practical bits of the science of altitude without delving into these complexities. There are a couple of concepts that do keep popping up as we talk about different aspects of high-altitude biology, so a more complete understanding of these topics will serve you well.

Virtually every biological process involves (1) moving those molecules from one compartment to another and (2) building molecules or taking them apart.

How Do Substances Move from One Place to Another?

In this book we're most concerned with the movement of oxygen, carbon dioxide, and glucose. How does oxygen get from the atmosphere into your blood? How does glucose get from your blood into a muscle cell? There are four ways that substances can move, and the first, diffusion, is probably the simplest but most difficult to understand.

Diffusion. A woman walks into a closed room, and a few minutes later you smell her perfume. This is an example of diffusion, and a clear understanding of this process will help immensely as we talk about the movement of oxygen through the body.

Imagine this woman putting a dab of perfume behind her ear. All of the perfume molecules are very close to each other, and like all molecules,[*] they are constantly vibrating and randomly banging into each other (and any other molecule in the vicinity). As they do so, the molecules tend to scatter, bouncing farther and farther away from where they started. Eventually, all of the perfume molecules will be randomly distributed in the atmosphere of our closed room.

Think about a pool table. When you hit the balls, they tend to scatter. Technically, they could end up in a nice triangle like the one you started with, but it's extremely, extremely unlikely. Or your bedroom. Left to itself, it seems to get more and more messy and disorganized as clothes move from an area of greater concentration (your drawers) to an area of lesser concentration (your floor).

In biological situations we are usually concerned with movement of a substance from one compartment to another. For example, in Fig. A3.A we have two compartments of equal volume that share a common wall (the dashed line). Think of these as cubes sharing a common wall that our substance (the circles) can pass through. In this case, the concentration of the substance is higher in the left compartment and lower in the right. As these molecules naturally bounce into each other, some will (by purely random chance) move to the other compartment. Eventually, we should find equal numbers of molecules in both compartments (A3.B). Again, this assumes the two compartments are the same size.

---

[*] Molecules above a temperature of absolute zero (0° Kelvin, or −273.15°C or −459.67°F) all vibrate as a result of the heat energy they contain. At absolute zero, all vibration stops, and diffusion would not take place because the molecules wouldn't move on their own.

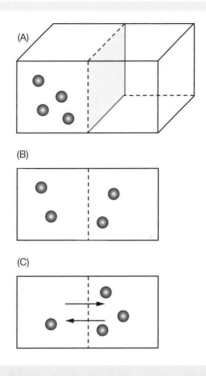

Fig. A3. (A) Here are two containers separated by a common wall. They are filled with water, and a substance (circles) is found in one container. The common wall is leaky and allows the substance (but not the water) to pass through into the adjoining compartment. (B) The molecules naturally vibrate, and this causes them to randomly move; some will bounce into the other container, so that an equilibrium will be reached with equal numbers of molecules in each compartment. (C) The molecules will continue to randomly move back and forth, so that on average the number of molecules will be equal in the two compartments. This is called a dynamic equilibrium.

But remember the molecules are moving randomly. What's to stop them from moving back to the left compartment? Nothing, and they do just that (A3.C). Molecules continue to move randomly back and forth, but on average, an equal number of molecules will be found on both sides of the barrier.* Think of very busy gas station. There will be cars leaving and entering all the time, but the number of cars at the station, on average, will remain constant. Both oxygen and carbon dioxide diffuse through the membranes of the lung and

---

* Technically, we should be talking about concentrations (number of particles per unit volume), but I simplified it by making the compartments the same size. If the compartments are of different sizes, the larger compartment will have proportionally more particles.

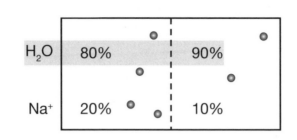

Fig. A4. Osmosis, or diffusion of water. In this example the sodium (Na^+, small circles) can't diffuse through the membrane, but water can. Since the left compartment is 80% water (H_2O) and the right compartment is 90% H_2O, the net movement will be right to left. At equilibrium, both compartments will be 85% H_2O, but they won't have the same total number of molecules. I'll let you figure out how many are in each compartment.

blood vessels. oxygen diffuses into the blood because there's more in the air than in the blood, and carbon dioxide does the reverse.

Water also diffuses; that process is called **osmosis** and works exactly the same as "regular" diffusion. This is a very important process that is critical in almost every biological compartment. In the left compartment of Fig. A4, 80 of 100 molecules, or 80%, are water (Na+ is sodium, and let's assume it doesn't diffuse). On the right, 90% of the molecules are water. So the proportion of water molecules is higher on the right side, and assuming our common wall is permeable to water but not sodium, then the net movement of water will be into the left compartment. At equilibrium we will have 85% water in both compartments (I leave the solution of the number of water molecules in each compartment to you). You can demonstrate osmosis by taking a nice crisp carrot and putting it in a cup of water that has lots of salt in it. Come back later, and you've got a "rubber" carrot because the water that makes the carrot crisp is drawn out by osmosis.

If you're really ambitious, set up two identical carrot/salt water experiments and put one in the refrigerator. If you check them every half hour of so, you'll see that the warm carrot goes limp faster than the cold carrot. This is because warmer molecules vibrate more, bounce more, and therefore diffuse more quickly. That's why you won't smell that dead opossum under your porch in the winter, but as soon as it warms up....

Aside from temperature, what influences the rate of diffusion? When will a substance diffuse more quickly or slowly? Take the model in Fig. A5: two boxes (cells) sharing a common wall, through which diffusion occurs. If we make that common wall bigger, the rate of

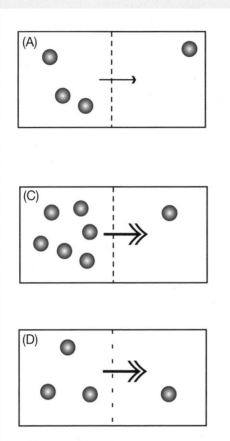

Fig. A5. Diffusion will be faster than (A) if (B) there is more surface area available for diffusion, (C) if there is a greater difference between the concentrations in the two compartments, and (D) if the membrane is easier to diffuse through.

diffusion will increase. We can do that by changing the shape of our cells. So, more surface area means more diffusion. This turns out to be a very critical factor and one that dictates the form of many organs in our body.

Another way to speed up diffusion is to increase the concentration gradient, which is the difference in the concentrations between the two cells. The bigger the difference, the faster the rate of diffusion. Finally, the ease of passage of our substance through the wall joining the boxes (or the membrane adjoining cells) influences diffusion. This could be a simple matter of the thickness of the membrane or the number of layers of membranes, or it could be related to the physical structure of the membrane. If you've ever squeezed your car into a tight parking spot, you know that it's hard to get in and out. The same thing happens in some membranes, where some substances can pass easily and other can pass only with difficulty. These factors influencing diffusion rates are summarized in Fig. A5.

Active transport. Diffusion happens spontaneously. But what if we want to move a substance from an area of lesser concentration to an area of greater concentration—like racking pool balls in a triangle or taking our scattered dirty clothes and putting them into a basket? This requires energy, and in biological systems the process is called **active transport**. If we want to put a lot of glucose in a particular cell, we need to "pump" it in by using energy. If diffusion is equivalent to water flowing downhill, active transport is like pumping water uphill.

Facilitated diffusion. Sometimes substances move across a membrane to an area of lesser concentration but do so by attaching to a carrier molecule. No energy is used (unlike active transport). Think of the diffusing substance as being chaperoned by the carrier molecule; no chaperone, no (or little) diffusion. This may be how oxygen moves into muscle cells, using myoglobin as a carrier molecule.

Convection. The perfume in the first example could have been blown by a breeze to your nose. This is not diffusion. Similarly, gases can dissolve in the blood plasma and be carried by the overall flow of the bloodstream. Strictly speaking, this process is different from diffusion, which is caused by random movement by the molecules themselves; convective movement is caused by outside forces.

How Do Molecules Get Assembled and Taken Apart?

How does a bite of hamburger end up allowing you to move a muscle? A series of chemical reactions occur that take the molecules in the beef protein apart, change their structure, and extract the energy stored in the protein molecules for use in your muscles. Similarly, when your body builds a new muscle cell, it synthesizes new proteins, fats, and other molecules from smaller building blocks. A series of linked chemical reactions is known as a biochemical pathway; in this book we won't consider any complete pathways and will talk in general about only a few pathways. However, a few general comments will be useful for future use.

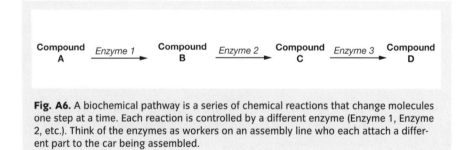

Fig. A6. A biochemical pathway is a series of chemical reactions that change molecules one step at a time. Each reaction is controlled by a different enzyme (Enzyme 1, Enzyme 2, etc.). Think of the enzymes as workers on an assembly line who each attach a different part to the car being assembled.

Fig. A6 shows a fake, very simple biochemical pathway. Molecule A is modified (by either taking something off or adding something, we don't care here) and becomes Molecule B. This reaction is controlled by an **enzyme** (labeled E1), which determines how fast this process will go. Enzymes are **catalysts,** and catalysts speed up chemical reactions. The catalytic converter in your car uses metal catalysts to rapidly break down polluting molecules in the exhaust. Enzymes allow reactions to take place quickly when the reaction would naturally take place very slowly or not at all. For example, two molecules might join easily if they were close together and lined up correctly. An enzyme might position the two molecules in the right relationship for them to bond together easily.

We can think of this pathway as an assembly line, with each worker (enzyme) doing one step in the assembly (or disassembly) of the new molecule. The number of new Molecule D produced each second will be determined by the slowest worker/enzyme. So what's the simplest way to maximize our production of Molecule D? Add more molecules of each type of enzyme (which is equivalent to adding more assembly lines).

Because enzymes are often anchored to membranes within the cell, this means we have to add more membrane (equivalent to adding more factory floor space). A good example of this in the cell is a structure called the mitochondrion, which is the location of cellular energy production (Chapter 7). The mitochondrion has a folded inner membrane, which increases the number of enzymes it can hold and therefore the number of chemical reactions that can take place. On a larger scale, increased surface area via folding is seen in the intestine (to increase absorption), in the brain (to provide more brain capacity), and in the lungs (to increase rates of diffusion of gases).

Appendix B:
Lake Louise Consensus Scoring System for Acute Mountain Sickness (AMS)

This is a useful checklist to use as you spend time at altitude. Keep in mind that this system is for adults. A modified checklist for young children (< 3 years old) is presented in Appendix C. The checklist presented here may underestimate symptoms in children 4–11 years old.[328]

The Lake Louise Scoring System consists of three parts: a self-assessment, completed by the affected individual; a clinical assessment, completed by a physician or other examiner; and a functional assessment, also completed by the individual. The self-assessment is required, while the other parts are optional.

Self-Assessment Score

Score yourself for the five symptoms listed below. Remember that fatigue will be expected after exercise. The sleep question may not be relevant in some situations. Always record the date, time, current altitude, and your recent ascent history when you complete the self-assessment.

Score   **Symptom**

_____ S1. *Headache*
  (0) None at all   (2) Moderate headache
  (1) Mild headache   (3) Severe, incapacitating headache

_____ S2. *Gastrointestinal symptoms*
  (0) Good appetite   (2) Moderate nausea and/or vomiting
  (1) Poor appetite and/or nausea   (3) Severe, incapacitating nausea/vomiting

_____ S3. *Fatigue and/or weakness*
  (0) Not tired or weak   (2) Moderate fatigue/weakness
  (1) Mild fatigue/weakness   (3) Severe fatigue/weakness

_____ S4. *Dizziness or light-headedness*
  (0) None   (2) Moderate
  1) Mild   (3) Severe, incapacitating

_____ S5. *Difficulty sleeping*
  (0) Slept as well as usual   (2) Woke many times, poor night's sleep
  (1) Did not sleep as well as usual (3) Could not sleep at all

_____ Total Self-Assessment Score

Clinical Assessment

The questions below should be answered by a physician or other examiner. Clarifications below are for untrained examiners.

Score   **Symptom**

_____ C1. *Change in mental status*

    (0) No change   (3) Stupor/semi-consciousness
    (1) Lethargy/lassitude[1]   (4) Coma
    (2) Disoriented/confused

_____ C2. *Ataxia (heel/toe walking)[2]*

    (0) None   (3) Falls down
    (1) Balance maneuvers[3]   (4) Unable to stand
    (2) Steps off the line

_____ C3. *Peripheral Edema[4]*

    (0) None   (2) Two or more locations
    (1) One location

_____ Total Clinical Score

[1] Inability to motivate to perform appropriate tasks.
[2] Draw a line 2 to 3 m (6 to 10 ft) long on safe, flat ground that's not too rough. Demonstrate walking by placing heel of front foot against toe of rear foot.
[3] Using arms and body movement to maintain balance.
[4] Swelling of the extremities (e.g. ankles) or around the eyes.

Functional Score

Overall, if you had any of these symptoms, how did they affect your activities?

_____ F1. Effect on activities

    (0) None   (2) Moderate reduction
    (1) Mild reduction   (3) Severe reduction; bed rest

Evaluation

You have AMS if you have a headache and any of the following are true:

- Your total self-assessment score (sum of S1 through S5) is 3 or higher.
- The sum of your total self-assessment score (S1 through S5) and your total clinical assessment score (C1 through C3) is 5 or higher.
- The sum of all scores is 6 or higher.

Other points:

- If you do not have a headache, you almost certainly do not have AMS.
- Scores of 2 or higher on either the mental status or ataxia assessment (question 6 or 7) suggest more severe AMS or high-altitude cerebral edema (HACE).
- Inability to complete the self-assessment suggests severe AMS or HACE.

Appendix C:
Children's Lake Louise
Scoring System for AMS

Since preverbal children (those < 3 years old) can't explain how they feel, Pollard et al.[266] created a version of the Lake Louise AMS scoring system for use by parents, who will know when their child is acting abnormally. Note that this scale is not definitive and should be used as a guideline for diagnosing only AMS and not HAPE or HACE. When in doubt, seek medical assistance.

Score your child for each of the questions below.

Fussiness is crying, tension, or other irritability that you can't explain through normal causes (hunger, pain, fatigue).

_____ A. *Amount of unexplained fussiness when awake during the past 24 hours*
  (0) No fussiness
  (1)
  (2)
  (3) Intermittent fussiness
  (4)
  (5)
  (6) Constant fussiness

_____ B. *Intensity of fussiness when awake*
  (0) No fussiness
  (1)
  2)
  (3) Moderate
  (4)
  (5)
  (6) Very strong

_____ C. *How well has your child eaten today?*
    (0) Normal
    (1) Slightly less than normal
    (2) Much less than normal
    (3) Vomiting or not eating

_____ D. *How playful is your child today?*
    0) Normal
    (1) Playing slightly less
    (2) Playing much less than normal
    (3) Not playing

_____ E. *The ability of your child to sleep today is*
    (0) Normal
    (1) Slightly less or more than normal
    (2) Much less or more than normal
    (3) Not able to sleep

_____ *Fussiness Score.* Add *A* and *B* together

_____ *Activity Score.* Add *C, D,* and *E* together

Is the Fussiness Score 4 or higher? _____

Is the Activity Score 3 or higher? _____

If you answered 'Yes' to both questions, then AMS is the diagnosis.

Appendix D:
Literature Cited

[1] Ainsworth, B. E. 2002. The Compendium of Physical Activities Tracking Guide.
http://prevention.sph.sc.edu/tools/docs/documents_compendium.pdf

[2] Alvarez, A. 2001. Feeding the Rat: A Climber's Life on the Edge. Thunder's Mouth Press, New York.

[3] Amann, M., L. M. Romer, A. W. Subudhi, et al. 2007. Severity of arterial hypoxemia affects the relative contributions of peripheral muscle fatigue to exercise performance. J Physiol 581(Pt 1):389–403.

[4] American Alpine Club. 1952-2006. Accidents in North American Mountaineering. American Alpine Club, Golden, CO.

[5] Anand, I., and Y. Chandrashekhar. 1996. Fluid metabolism at high altitudes. In B. M. Marriott and S. J. Carlson, eds. Nutritional Needs in Cold and in High-Altitude Environments (pp. 331–356). National Academy Press, Washington, DC.

[6] Anand, I. S., Y. Chandrashekhar, S. K. Rao, et al. 1993. Body fluid compartments, renal blood flow, and hormones at 6,000 m in normal subjects. J Appl Physiol 74:1234–1239.

[7] Anooshiravani, M., L. Dumont, C. Mardirosoff, et al. 1999. Brain magnetic resonance imaging (MRI) and neurological changes after a single high altitude climb. Med Sci Sports Exerc 31:969–972.

[8] Arden, N. K., and T. D. Spector. 1997. Genetic influences on muscle strength, lean body mass, and bone mineral density: a twin study. J Bone Miner Res 12:2076–2081.

[9] Armellini, F., M. Zamboni, R. Robbi, et al. 1997. The effects of high altitude trekking on body composition and resting metabolic rate. Horm Metab Res 29:458–461.

[10] Armstrong, L. 2001. It's Not about the Bike: My Journey Back to Life. Berkeley Books, New York.

[11] Armstrong, L. E. 2005. Hydration assessment techniques. Nutr Rev 63:S40–54.

[12] Arzy, S., M. Idel, T. Landis, et al. 2005. Why revelations have occurred on mountains? Linking mystical experiences and cognitive neuroscience. Med Hypotheses 65:841–845.

[13] Attwells, R. L., S. A. Birrell, R. H. Hooper, et al. 2006. Influence of carrying heavy loads on soldiers' posture, movements and gait. Ergonomics 49:1527–1537.

[14] Ayton, J. M. 1993. Polar hands: spontaneous skin fissures closed with cyanoacrylate (histoacryl blue) tissue adhesive in Antarctica. Arctic Med Res 52:127–130.

[15] Backer, H. 2000. Editorial: In search of the perfect water treatment method. Wilderness Environ Med 11:1–4.

[16] Backer, H. 2003. A different experience as a medical advisor for an adventure travel company. High Alt Med Biol 4:255–256.

[17] Baden, D. A., T. L. McLean, R. Tucker, et al. 2005. Effect of anticipation during unknown or unexpected exercise duration on rating of perceived exertion, affect, and physiological function. Br J Sports Med 39:742–746; discussion 742–746.

[18] Bardwell, W. A., W. Y. Ensign, and P. J. Mills. 2005. Negative mood endures after completion of high-altitude military training. Ann Behav Med 29:64–69.

[19] Barker, R. 1959. The Last Blue Mountain. The Mountaineers, Seattle.

[20] Barry, P. W., N. P. Mason, M. Riordan, et al. 1997. Cough frequency and cough receptor sensitivity are increased in man at high altitude. Clin Sci 93:181–186.

[21] Bärtsch, P., D. M. Bailey, M. M. Berger, et al. 2004. Acute mountain sickness: controversies and advances. High Alt Med Biol 5:110–124.

[22] Bärtsch, P., E. Grunig, E. Hohenhaus, et al. 2001. Assessment of high altitude tolerance in healthy individuals. High Alt Med Biol 2:287–296.

[23] Bärtsch, P., H. Mairbaurl, M. Maggiorini, et al. 2005. Physiological aspects of high-altitude pulmonary edema. J Appl Physiol 98:1101–1110.

[24] Basnyat, B., T. A. Cumbo, and R. Edelman. 2000. Acute medical problems in the Himalayas outside the setting of altitude sickness. High Alt Med Biol 1:167–174.

[25] Basnyat, B., J. H. Gertsch, P. S. Holck, et al. 2006. Acetazolamide 125 mg BD is not significantly different from 375 mg BD in the prevention of acute mountain
sickness: the prophylactic acetazolamide dosage comparison for efficacy (PACE) trial. High Alt Med Biol 7:17–27.

[26] Basnyat, B., J. Leomaster, and J. A. Litch. 1999. Everest or bust: a cross sectional, epidemiological survey of acute mountain sickness at 4234m in the Himalaya. Aviat Space Environ Med 70:867–873.

[27] Basnyat, B., and J. A. Litch. 1997. Medical problems of porters and trekkers in the Nepal Himalaya. Wilderness Environ Med 8:78–81.

[28] Basnyat, B., T. Wu, and J. H. Gertsch. 2004. Neurological conditions at altitude that fall outside the usual definition of altitude sickness. High Alt Med Biol 5:171–179.

[29] Bastien, G. J., P. A. Willems, B. Schepens, et al. 2005. Effect of load and speed on the energetic cost of human walking. Eur J Appl Physiol 94:76–83.

[30] Bates, R. H., R. L. Burdsall, W. P. House, et al. 1939. Five Miles High. Lyons Press, New York.

[31] Bauer, A., F. Demetz, D. Bruegger, et al. 2006. Effect of high altitude and exercise on microvascular parameters in acclimatized subjects. Clin Sci (Lond) 110:207–215.

[32] Bauer, P. 1937. Himalayan Campaign: The German Attack on Kangchenjunga. Blackwell, Oxford.

[33] Baumgartner, R. W., A. M. Siegel, and P. H. Hackett. 2007. Going high with preexisting neurological conditions. High Alt Med Biol 8:108–116.

[34] Bean, W. B., and L. W. Eichna. 1943. Performance in relation to environmental temperature: Reactions of normal young men to simulated desert environment. Federation Proceedings 2:144–158.

[35] Beidleman, B. A., S. R. Muza, C. S. Fulco, et al. 2004. Intermittent altitude exposures reduce acute mountain sickness at 4300 m. Clin Sci (Lond) 106:321–328.

[36] Beidleman, B. A., S. R. Muza, C. S. Fulco, et al. 2006. White blood cell and hormonal responses to 4300 m altitude before and after intermittent altitude exposure. Clin Sci (Lond) 111:163–169.

[37] Beidleman, B. A., S. R. Muza, P. B. Rock, et al. 1997. Exercise responses after altitude acclimatization are retained during reintroduction to altitude. Med Sci Sports Exerc 29:1588–1595.

[38] Bemben, M. G., and H. S. Lamont. 2005. Creatine supplementation and exercise performance: recent findings. Sports Med 35:107–125.

[39] Bennington, J. H., and H. C. Heller. 1995. Restoration of brain energy metabolism as the function of sleep. Prog Neurobiol 45:347–360.

[40] Berg, J. M., J. L. Tymoczko, and L. Stryer. 2006. Biochemistry. 6th ed. W.H. Freeman and Company, New York.

[41] Bernardi, L., A. Schneider, L. Pomidori, et al. 2006. Hypoxic ventilatory response in successful extreme altitude climbers. Eur Respir J 27:165–171.

[42] Bettembourg, G., and M. Brame. 1981. The White Death. Reynard House, Seattle, WA.

[43] Bezruchka, S. 2005. Altitude Illness: Prevention and Treatment. 2nd ed. The Mountaineers, Seattle.

[44] Bickler, P. E., J. R. Feiner, and J. W. Severinghaus. 2005. Effects of skin pigmentation on pulse oximeter accuracy at low saturation. Anesthesiol 102:715–719.

[45] Bircher, H. P., U. Eichenberger, M. Maggiorini, et al. 1993. Relationship of mountain sickness to physical fitness and exercise intensity during ascent. J Wilderness Med 5:302–311.

[46] Bitterman, M. E. 1944. Fatigue defined as reduced efficiency. Am J Psychol 57:569–573.

[47] Blum, A. 1998. Annapurna: a Woman's Place. Sierra Club Books, San Francisco.

[48] Blume, F. D., S. J. Boyer, L. E. Braverman, et al. 1984. Impaired osmoregulation at high altitude: studies on Mt Everest. JAMA 252:524–526.

[49] Bohne, M., and J. Abendroth-Smith. 2007. Effects of hiking downhill using trekking poles while carrying external loads. Med Sci Sports Exerc 39:177–183.

[50] Bonatti, W. 2001. The Mountains of My Life. The Modern Library, New York.

[51] Bonington, C. 1973. The Ultimate Challenge. Stein and Day, New York.

[52] Bonington, C. 2001. Annapurna South Face. Thunder's Mouth Press, New York.

[53] Bosco, G., A. Ionadi, S. Panico, et al. 2003. Effects of hypoxia on the circadian patterns in men. High Alt Med Biol 4:305–318.

[54] Bouchard, C. 1993. Heredity and health-related fitness. Phys Activity Fitness Res Dig 1(4). President's Council on Physical Fitness and Sports.

[55] Bouchard, C., and T. Rankinen. 2001. Individual differences in response to regular physical activity. Med Sci Sports Exerc 33:S446–451; discussion S452–443.

[56] Boukreev, A. 1997. The oxygen illusion: perspectives on the business of high-altitude climbing. Am Alpine J 39:37–43.

[57] Boukreev, A. 2001. Above the Clouds. St. Martin's Press, New York.

[58] Boukreev, A., and W. DeWalt. 1997. The Climb. St. Martin's Press, New York.

[59] Boulware, D. R. 2003. Backpacking-induced paresthesias. Wilderness Environ Med 14:161–166.

[60] Boutilier, R. G. 2001. Mechanisms of cell survival in hypoxia and hypothermia. J Exp Biol 204:3171–3181.

[61] Boyer, S. J., and F. D. Blume. 1984. Weight loss and changes in body composition at high altitude. J Appl Physiol 57:1580–1585.

[62] Braun, B., J. T. Mawson, S. R. Muza, et al. 2000. Women at altitude: carbohydrate utilization during exercise at 4,300 m. J Appl Physiol 88:246–256.

[63] Breashears, D. 1999. High Exposure. Simon & Schuster, New York.

[64] Bremer-Kamp, C. 1987. Living on the Edge. Peregrine Smith, Layton, UT.

[65] Brooks, G. A., and G. E. Butterfield. 2001. Metabolic response of lowlanders to high-altitude exposure: malnutrition versus the effect of hypoxia. In T. Hornbein and R. B. Schoene, eds. High Altitude: An Exploration of Human Adaptation (pp. 569–599). Marcel Dekker, New York.

[66] Buhl, H. 1956. Lonely Challenge. E.P. Dutton & Company, New York.

[67] Burgess, A., and A. Burgess. 1994. The Burgess Book of Lies. The Mountaineers, Seattle.

[68] Burgess, A., and J. Palmer. 1983. Everest: The Ultimate Challenge. Beaufort Books, New York.

[69] Burtscher, M. 2004. Endurance performance of the elderly mountaineer: requirements, limitations, testing, and training. Wien Klin Wochenschr 116:703–714.

[70] Burtscher, M., R. Likar, W. Nachbauer, et al. 1998. Aspirin for prophylaxis against headache at high altitudes: randomised, double blind, placebo controlled trial. BMJ 316:1057–1058.

[71] Butterfield, G. 1996. Maintenance of body weight at high altitudes: in search of 500 kcal/day. In B. M. Marriott and S. J. Carlson, eds. Nutritional Needs in Cold and in High-Altitude Environments (pp. 357–378). National Academy Press, Washington, D.C.

[72] Bygrave, S., S. J. Legg, S. Myers, et al. 2004. Effect of backpack fit on lung function. Ergonomics 47:324–329.

[73] Cairns, S. P. 2006. Lactic acid and exercise performance : culprit or friend? Sports Med 36:279–291.

[74] Calbet, J. A., R. Boushel, G. Radegran, et al. 2003. Why is VO2 max after altitude acclimatization still reduced despite normalization of arterial O2 content? Am J Physiol Regul Integr Comp Physiol 284:R304–316.

[75] Carlsson, S., T. Andersson, P. Lichtenstein, et al. 2006. Genetic effects on physical activity: results from the Swedish Twin Registry. Med Sci Sports Exerc 38:1396–1401.

[76] Castellani, J. W., A. J. Young, D. W. Degroot, et al. 2001. Thermoregulation during cold exposure after several days of exhaustive exercise. J Appl Physiol 90:939–946.

[77] Castellani, J. W., A. J. Young, J. E. Kain, et al. 1999. Thermoregulation during cold exposure: effects of prior exercise. J Appl Physiol 87:247–252.

[78] Cavaletti, G., and G. Tredici. 1993. Long-lasting neuropsychological changes after a single high altitude climb. Acta Neurol Scand 87:103–105.

[79] Chapman, R. F., J. Stray-Gundersen, and B. D. Levine. 1998. Individual variation in response to altitude training. J Appl Physiol 85:1448–1456.

[80] Cheuvront, S. N., R. Carter, 3rd, J. W. Castellani, et al. 2005. Hypohydration impairs endurance exercise performance in temperate but not cold air. J Appl Physiol 99:1972–1976.

[81] Child, G. 1988. Thin Air: Encounters in the Himalayas. Peregrine Smith, Layton, UT.

[82] Cibella, F., G. Cuttitta, S. Romano, et al. 1999. Respiratory energetics during exercise at high altitude. J Appl Physiol 86:1785–1792.

[83] Clinch, N. 1982. A Walk in the Sky. The Mountaineers, Seattle.

[84] Cliver, D. O. 2006. Cutting boards in Salmonella cross-contamination. J AOAC Int 89:538–542.

[85] Coffey, M. 2003. Where the Mountain Casts Its Shadow. St. Martin's Press, New York.

[86] Conley, K. E., W. F. Kemper, and G. J. Crowther. 2001. Limits to sustainable muscle performance: interaction between glycolysis and oxidative phosphorylation. J Exp Biol 204:3189–3194.

[87] Coppin, E. G., S. D. Livingstone, and L. A. Kuehn. 1978. Effects on handgrip strength due to arm immersion in a 10 degree C water bath. Aviat Space Environ Med 49:1322–1326.

[88] Craig, R. 1977. Storm and Sorrow in the High Pamirs. Simon & Schuster, New York.

[89] Crowley, A. 1969. The Confessions of Aleister Crowley. Hill & Wang, New York.

[90] Curran, J. 1987. K2: Triumph and Tragedy. Houghton Mifflin Company, Boston.

[91] Curran, J. 1995. K2: The Story of the Savage Mountain. The Mountaineers, Seattle.

[92] Daanen, H. A., and H. J. van Ruiten. 2000. Cold-induced peripheral vasodilation at high altitudes— a field study. High Alt Med Biol 1:323–329.

[93] Dallimore, J., F. J. Cooke, and K. Forbes. 2002. Morbidity on youth expeditions to developing countries. Wilderness Environ Med 13:1–4.

[94] Daries, H. N., T. D. Noakes, and S. C. Dennis. 2000. Effect of fluid intake volume on 2-h running performances in a 25 degrees C environment. Med Sci Sports Exerc 32:1783–1789.

[95] Delavier, F. 2006. Strength Training Anatomy. 2nd ed. Human Kinetics, Champaign, IL.

[96] Dempsey, J. A., and P. D. Wagner. 1999. Exercise-induced arterial hypoxemia. J Appl Physiol 87:1997–2006.

[97] DePalo, V. A., A. L. Parker, F. Al-Bilbeisi, et al. 2004. Respiratory muscle strength training with non-respiratory maneuvers. J Appl Physiol 96:731–734.

[98] Dickinson, J., D. Heath, J. Gosney, et al. 1983. Altitude-related deaths in seven trekkers in the Himalayas. Thorax 38:646–656.

[99] Dickinson, M. 1997. The Other Side of Everest: Climbing the North Face through the Killer Storm. Times Books, New York.

[100] Diemberger, K. 1991/ 1999. The Endless Knot. In The Kurt Diemberger Omnibus (pp. 321–590). The Mountaineers, Seattle.

[101] Drummond, E. 1973. Mirror mirror. In K. Wilson, ed. Games Climbers Play (pp. 27-42). Diadem, London.

[102] Dudley, R. 2001. Limits to human locomotor performance: phylogenetic origins and comparative perspectives. J Exp Biol 204:3235–3240.

[103] Duff, J. 1999. Observations while treating altitude illness. Wilderness Environ Med 10:274.

[104] Dunn, K. M., L. F. Cherkas, and T. D. Spector. 2005. Genetic influences on variation in female orgasmic function: a twin study. Biol Lett 1:260–263.

[105] Durrer, B., H. Brugger, and D. Syme. 2003. The medical on-site treatment of hypothermia: ICAR-MEDCOM recommendation. High Alt Med Biol 4:99–103.

[106] Eggler, A. 1957. The Everst-Lhotse Adventure. Harper & Brothers, New York.

[107] Eichna, L. W., W. B. Bean, W. F. Ashe, et al. 1945. Performance in relation to environmental temperature: reactions of normal young men to hot humid (simulated jungle) environment. Bull Johns Hopkins Hosp 76:25–58.

[108] Enander, A. 1984. Performance and sensory aspects of work in cold environments: a review. Ergonomics 27:365–378.

[109] Endoh, T., T. Nakajima, M. Sakamoto, et al. 2005. Effects of muscle damage induced by eccentric exercise on muscle fatigue. Med Sci Sports Exerc 37:1151–1156.

[110] Enright, S. J., V. B. Unnithan, C. Heward, et al. 2006. Effect of high-intensity inspiratory muscle training on lung volumes, diaphragm thickness, and exercise capacity in subjects who are healthy. Phys Ther 86:345–354.

[111] Evans, C. 1956. Kangchenjunga: The Untrodden Peak. Hodder & Stoughton, London.

[112] Falk, B., O. Bar-Or, J. Smolander, et al. 1994. Response to rest and exercise in the cold: effects of age and aerobic fitness. J Appl Physiol 76:72–78.

[113] Fallowfield, J. L., C. Williams, J. Booth, et al. 1996. Effect of water ingestion on endurance capacity during prolonged running. J Sports Sci 14:497–502.

[114] Falola, J. M., N. Delpech, and J. Brisswalter. 2000. Optimization characteristics of walking with and without a load on the trunk of the body. Percept Mot Skills 91:261–272.

[115] Fanshawe, A., and S. Venables. 1995. Himalaya Alpine Style. The Mountaineers, Seattle.

[116] Fayed, N., P. J. Modrego, and H. Morales. 2006. Evidence of brain damage after high-altitude climbing by means of magnetic resonance imaging. Am J Med 119:168 e161–166.

[117] Fletcher, C. 1972. The Complete Walker. Alfred A. Knopf, New York.

[118] Forster, P. 1984. Reproducibility of individual response to exposure to high altitude. BMJ 289:1269.

[119] Fowler, M. 2005. On Thin Ice. Baton Wicks, London.

[120] Franco, J. 1957. Makalu. Alden Press, London.

[121] Franklin, B. A., P. Hogan, K. Bonzheim, et al. 1995. Cardiac demands of heavy snow shoveling. JAMA 273:880–882.

[122] Freund, B., and M. Sawka. 1996. Influence of cold stress on human fluid balance. In B. M. Marriott and S. J. Carlson, eds. Nutritional Needs in Cold and in High-Altitude Environments (pp. 161–179). National Academy Press, Washington, D.C.

[123] Gaillard, S., P. Dellasanta, L. Loutan, et al. 2004. Awareness, prevalence, medication use, and risk factors of acute mountain sickness in tourists trekking around the Annapurnas in Nepal: a 12-year follow-up. High Alt Med Biol 5:410–419.

[124] Gammelgaard, L. 1999. Climbing High. Seal Press, Seattle.

[125] Garcia, N., S. R. Hopkins, and F. L. Powell. 2000. Intermittent vs continuous hypoxia: effects on ventilation and erythropoiesis in humans. Wilderness Environ Med 11:172–179.

[126] Garner, S. H., J. R. Sutton, R. L. Burse, et al. 1990. Operation Everest II: neuromuscular performance under conditions of extreme simulated altitude. J Appl Physiol 68:1167–1172.

[127] Garske, L. A., M. G. Brown, and S. C. Morrison. 2003. Acetazolamide reduces exercise capacity and increases leg fatigue under hypoxic conditions. J Appl Physiol 94:991–996.

[128] Ge, R. L., S. Witkowski, Y. Zhang, et al. 2002. Determinants of erythropoietin release in response to short-term hypobaric hypoxia. J Appl Physiol 92:2361–2367.

[129] Gertsch, J. H., T. B. Seto, J. Mor, et al. 2002. Ginkgo biloba for the prevention of severe acute mountain sickness (AMS) starting one day before rapid ascent. High Alt Med Biol 3:29–37.

[130] Ghofrani, H. A., F. Reichenberger, M. G. Kohstall, et al. 2004. Sildenafil increased exercise capacity during hypoxia at low altitudes and at Mount Everest base camp: a randomized, double-blind, placebo-controlled crossover trial. Ann Intern Med 141:169–177.

[131] Gladden, L. B. 2004. Lactate metabolism: a new paradigm for the third millennium. J Physiol 558:5–30.

[132] Goedecke, J. H., A. St Clair Gibson, L. Grobler, et al. 2000. Determinants of the variability in respiratory exchange ratio at rest and during exercise in trained athletes. Am J Physiol Endocrinol Metabol 279:E1325–1334.

[133] Gonzales, J. U., and B. W. Scheuermann. 2006. Gender differences in the fatigability of the inspiratory muscles. Med Sci Sports Exerc 38:472–479.

[134] Gonzalez-Alonso, J., J. A. Calbet, and B. Nielsen. 1999a. Metabolic and thermodynamic responses to dehydration-induced reductions in muscle blood flow in exercising humans. J Physiol 520 Pt 2:577–589.

[135] Gonzalez-Alonso, J., R. Mora-Rodriguez, P. R. Below, et al. 1995. Dehydration reduces cardiac output and increases systemic and cutaneous vascular resistance during exercise. J Appl Physiol 79:1487–1496.

[136] Gonzalez-Alonso, J., R. Mora-Rodriguez, and E. F. Coyle. 1999b. Supine exercise restores arterial blood pressure and skin blood flow despite dehydration and hyperthermia. Am J Physiol 277:H576–583.

[137] Gonzalez-Alonso, J., R. Mora-Rodriguez, and E. F. Coyle. 2000. Stroke volume during exercise: interaction of environment and hydration. Am J Physiol Heart Circ Physiol 278:H321–330.

[138] Goodman, T., and B. Basnyat. 2000. A tragic report of probable high-altitude pulmonary edema in the Himalayas: preventative implications. Wilderness Environ Med 11:99–101.

[139] Gore, C. J., and W. G. Hopkins. 2005. Counterpoint: positive effects of intermittent hypoxia (live high:train low) on exercise performance are not mediated primarily by augmented red cell volume. J Appl Physiol 99:2055–2057; discussion 2057–2058.

[140] Grover, R. F., and P. Bärtsch. 2001. Blood. *In* T. Hornbein and R. B. Schoene, eds. High Altitude: An Exploration of Human Adaptation (pp. 493–523). Marcel Dekker, New York.

[141] Gudjonsdottir, M., L. Appendini, P. Baderna, et al. 2001. Diaphragm fatigue during exercise at high altitude: the role of hypoxia and workload. Eur Respir J 17:674–680.

[142] Habeler, P. 1978. The Lonely Victory. Simon & Schuster, New York.

[143] Hackett, P. H., and R. C. Roach. 2004. High altitude cerebral edema. High Alt Med Biol 5:136–146.

[144] Hainsworth, R., M. J. Drinkhill, and M. Rivera-Chira. 2007. The autonomic nervous system at high altitude. Clin Auton Res 17:13–19.

[145] Hamel, P., J. A. Simoneau, G. Lortie, et al. 1986. Heredity and muscle adaptation to endurance training. Med Sci Sports Exerc 18:690–696.

[146] Hanton, S., D. Fletcher, and G. Coughlan. 2005. Stress in elite sport performers: a comparative study of competitive and organizational stressors. J Sports Sci 23:1129–1141.

[147] Hargreaves, J. S. 2006. Laboratory evaluation of the 3-bowl system used for washing-up eating utensils in the field. Wilderness Environ Med 17:94–102.

[148] Harirchi, I., A. Arvin, J. H. Vash, et al. 2005. Frostbite: incidence and predisposing factors in mountaineers. Br J Sports Med 39:898–901; discussion 901.

[149] Hartung, G. H., L. G. Myhre, S. A. Nunneley, et al. 1984. Plasma substrate response in men and women during marathon running. Aviat Space Environ Med 55:128–131.

[150] Harvard, A., and T. Thompson. 1974. Mountain of Storms. Chelsea House, New York.

[151] Hashmi, M. A., M. Rashid, A. Haleem, et al. 1998. Frostbite: epidemiology at high altitude in the Karakoram mountains. Ann R Coll Surg Engl 80:91–95.

[152] Haston, D. 1972. In High Places. Macmillian, New York.

[153] Herzog, M. 1952. Annapurna. E.P. Dutton and Company, New York.

[154] Hillary, E. 1999. View from the Summit. Pocket Books, New York.

[155] Hillebrandt, D. 2002. A year's experience as advisory doctor to a commercial mountaineering expedition company. High Alt Med Biol 3:409–414.

[156] Hopkins, S. R. 2006. Exercise induced arterial hypoxemia: the role of ventilation-perfusion inequality and pulmonary diffusion limitation. Adv Exp Med Biol 588:17–30.

[157] Hoppeler, H., and M. Vogt. 2001. Muscle tissue adaptations to hypoxia. J Exp Biol 204:3133–3139.

[158] Hoppeler, H., M. Vogt, E. R. Weibel, et al. 2003. Response of skeletal muscle mitochondria to hypoxia. Exp Physiol 88:109–119.

[159] Hornbein, T. 1966. Everest: The West Ridge. Ballantine Books, New York.

[160] Hornbein, T., and R. B. Schoene, eds. 2001. High Altitude: An Exploration of Human Adaptation. Marcel Dekker, New York.

[161] Hornbein, T. F. 2001. The high-altitude brain. J Exp Biol 204:3129–3132.

[162] Hornbein, T. F., B. D. Townes, R. B. Schoene, et al. 1989. The cost to the central nervous system of climbing to extremely high altitude. N Engl J Med 321:1714–1719.

[163] Hörst, E. 1996. Flash Training. Chockstone Press, Evergreen, CO.

[164] Houston, C. S. 1985. The physiology of altitude illness: its role in alpine style rush tactics. Am Alpine J 27:158–161.

[165] Houston, C. S., and R. Bates. 1979. The Savage Mountain. The Mountaineers, Seattle.

[166] Hsu, A. R., K. E. Barnholt, N. K. Grundmann, et al. 2006. Sildenafil improves cardiac output and exercise performance during acute hypoxia, but not normoxia. J Appl Physiol 100:2031–2040.

[167] Huerta, C., S. Johansson, M. A. Wallander, et al. 2007. Risk factors and short-term mortality of venous thromboembolism diagnosed in the primary care setting in the United Kingdom. Arch Intern Med 167:935–943.

[168] Huey, R. B., and X. Eguskitza. 2000. Supplemental oxygen and mountaineer death rates on Everest and K2. JAMA 284:181.

[169] Huey, R. B., and X. Eguskitza. 2001. Limits to human performance: elevated risks on high mountains. J Exp Biol 204:3115–3119.

[170] Huey, R. B., X. Eguskitza, and M. Dillon. 2001. Mountaineering in thin air: patterns of death and of weather at high altitude. Adv Exp Med Biol 502:225–236.

[171] Huey, R. B., R. Salisbury, J.-L. Wang, et al. 2007. Effects of age and gender on success and death of mountaineers on Mount Everest. Biol Lett 3:498-500.

[172] Hultgren, H. N. 1997. High Altitude Medicine. Hultgren Publications, Stanford, CA.

[173] Ilg, S. 1999. The Winter Athlete: Secrets of Wholistic Fitness for Outdoor Performance. Johnson Books, Boulder, CO.

[174] Ilgner, A. 2006. The Rock Warrior's Way. Desiderata Institute, La Vergne, TN.

[175] Jain, S. C., J. Bardhan, Y. Swamy, et al. 1980. Body fluid compartments in humans during acute high-altitude exposure. Aviat Space Environ Med 51:234–236.

[176] Jean, D., C. Leal, S. Kriemler, et al. 2005. Medical recommendations for women going to altitude. High Alt Med Biol 6:22–31.

[177] Jenkins, M. 2006. What the pros know. Outside Magazine September:78.

[178] Jones, P., and I. Lee. 1996. Macronutrient requirements for work in cold environments. In B. M. Marriott and S. J. Carlson, eds. Nutritional Needs in Cold and in High-Altitude Environments (pp. 189–202). National Academy Press, Washington, D.C.

[179] Jordan, J. 2005. Savage Summit. HarperCollins, New York.

[180] Kamler, K. 2004. Surviving the Extremes. St. Martin's Press, New York.

[181] Kang, J., E. C. Chaloupka, M. A. Mastrangelo, et al. 2002. Physiological and biomechanical analysis of treadmill walking up various gradients in men and women. Eur J Appl Physiol 86:503–508.

[182] Kauffman, A., and W. Putnam. 1992. K2: The 1939 Tragedy. The Mountaineers, Seattle.

[183] Kayser, B. 2003. Exercise starts and ends in the brain. Eur J Appl Physiol 90:411–419.

[184] Keatisuwan, W., T. Ohnaka, and Y. Tochihara. 1996. Physiological responses of women during exercise under dry-heat condition in winter and summer. Appl Human Sci 15:169–176.

[185] Kellas, A. M. 2001. A consideration of the possibility of ascending Mount Everest. High Alt Med Biol 2:431–461.

[186] Kinoshita, N., H. Yamazaki, S. Onishi, et al. 2000. Physiological profile of middle-aged and older climbers who ascended Gasherbrum II, an 8035-m Himalayan peak. J Gerontol A Biol Sci Med Sci 55:M630–633.

[187] Kleessen, B., W. Schroedl, M. Stueck, et al. 2005. Microbial and immunological responses relative to high-altitude exposure in mountaineers. Med Sci Sports Exerc 37:1313–1318.

[188] Knapik, J., E. Harman, and K. Reynolds. 1996. Load carriage using packs: a review of physiological, biomechanical and medical aspects. Appl Ergon 27:207–216.

[189] Kohrt, W. M., M. T. Malley, A. R. Coggan, et al. 1991. Effects of gender, age, and fitness level on response of VO2max to training in 60–71 yr olds. J Appl Physiol 71:2004–2011.

[190] Komi, P. V., J. H. Viitasalo, M. Havu, et al. 1977. Skeletal muscle fibres and muscle enzyme activities in monozygous and dizygous twins of both sexes. Acta Physiol Scand 100:385–392.

[191] Krakauer, J. 1997. Into Thin Air. Villard, New York.

[192] Kropp, G. 1997. Ultimate High: My Everest Odyssey. Discovery Books, New York.

[193] Kukuczka, J. 1992. My Vertical World. The Mountaineers, Seattle.

[194] Kuntsi, J., H. Rogers, G. Swinard, et al. 2006. Reaction time, inhibition, working memory and "delay aversion" performance: genetic influences and their interpretation. Psychol Med 36:1613–1624.

[195] Kupper, T. E., B. Schraut, B. Rieke, et al. 2006. Drugs and drug administration in extreme environments. J Travel Med 13:35–47.

[196] Lafiandra, M., and E. Harman. 2004. The distribution of forces between the upper and lower back during load carriage. Med Sci Sports Exerc 36:460–467.

[197] LaFiandra, M., R. C. Wagenaar, K. G. Holt, et al. 2003. How do load carriage and walking speed influence trunk coordination and stride parameters? J Biomech 36:87–95.

[198] Lafleur, J., M. Giron, M. Demarco, et al. 2003. Cognitive effects of dexamethasone at high altitude. Wilderness Environ Med 14:20–23.

[199] LeBlanc, J. 1996. Cold exposure, appetite, and energy balance. In B. M. Marriott and S. J. Carlson, eds. Nutritional Needs in Cold and in High-Altitude Environments (pp. 203–214). National Academy Press, Washington, D.C.

[200] Lee, W. W., K. Mayberry, R. Crapo, et al. 2000. The accuracy of pulse oximetry in the emergency department. Am J Emerg Med 18:427–431.

[201] Leigh-Smith, S. 2004. Carbon monoxide poisoning in tents-a review. Wilderness Environ Med 15:157–163.

[202] Lemon, P. W., M. A. Tarnopolsky, J. D. MacDougall, et al. 1992. Protein requirements and muscle mass/strength changes during intensive training in novice bodybuilders. J Appl Physiol 73:767–775.

[203] Leon-Velarde, F., M. Maggiorini, J. T. Reeves, et al. 2005. Consensus statement on chronic and subacute high altitude diseases. High Alt Med Biol 6:147–157.

[204] Lessov-Schlaggar, C. N., Z. Pang, G. E. Swan, et al. 2006. Heritability of cigarette smoking and alcohol use in Chinese male twins: the Qingdao Twin Registry. Int J Epidemiol 35:1278–1285.

[205] Levine, B. D., and J. Stray-Gundersen. 2005. Point: positive effects of intermittent hypoxia (live high:train low) on exercise performance are mediated primarily by augmented red cell volume. J Appl Physiol 99:2053–2055.

[206] Levine, B. D., and J. Stray-Gundersen. 2006. Dose-response of altitude training: how much altitude is enough? Adv Exp Med Biol 588:233–247.

[207] Liffrig, J. R. 2001. Phototrauma prevention. Wilderness Environ Med 12:195–200.

[208] Lindstedt, S. L., and K. E. Conley. 2001. Human aerobic performance: too much ado about limits to VO_2. J Exp Biol 204:3195–3199.

[209] Litch, J. A., and R. A. Bishop. 2000. High altitude global amnesia. Wilderness Exp Med 11:25–28.

[210] Litch, J. A., and R. A. Bishop. 2001. Reascent following resolution of high altitude pulmonary edema (HAPE). High Alt Med Biol 2:53–55.

[211] Lundby, C., M. Sander, G. van Hall, et al. 2006. Maximal exercise and muscle oxygen extraction in acclimatizing lowlanders and high altitude natives. J Physiol 573:535–547.

[212] Lundby, C., and G. van Hall. 2001. Peak heart rates at extreme altitudes. High Alt Med Biol 2:41–45.

[213] Mader, T. H., and G. Tabin. 2003. Going to high altitude with preexisting ocular conditions. High Alt Med Biol 4:419–430.

[214] Maggiorini, M., H. P. Brunner-La Rocca, S. Peth, et al. 2006. Both tadalafil and dexamethasone may reduce the incidence of high-altitude pulmonary edema: a randomized trial. Ann Intern Med 145:497–506.

[215] Major, G. C., and E. Doucet. 2004. Energy intake during a typical Himalayan trek. High Alt Med Biol 5:355–363.

[216] Maraini, F. 1961. Karakoram: The Ascent of Gasherbrum IV. Viking Press, New York.

[217] Marrao, C., P. Tikuisis, A. A. Keefe, et al. 2005. Physical and cognitive performance during long-term cold weather operations. Aviat Space Environ Med 76:744–752.

[218] Mason, N. P., and P. W. Barry. 2007. Altitude-related cough. Pulm Pharmacol Ther 20:388-395.

[219] Maughan, R., and S. Shirreffs. 2004. Exercise in the heat: challenges and opportunities. J Sports Sci 22:917–927.

[220] Mazzeo, R. S. 2005. Altitude, exercise and immune function. Exerc Immunol Rev 11:6–16.

[221] McCool, F. D., J. O. Benditt, P. Conomos, et al. 1997. Variability of diaphragm structure among healthy individuals. Am J Respir Crit Care Med 155:1323–1328.

[222] McLaughlin, J. B., B. D. Gessner, and A. M. Bailey. 2005. Gastroenteritis outbreak among mountaineers climbing the West Buttress route of Denali—Denali National Park, Alaska, June 2002. Wilderness Environ Med 16:92–96.

[223] Meehan, R. T., P. N. Uchakin, and C. F. Sams. 2001. High altitude and human immune responsiveness. In T. Hornbein and R. B. Schoene, eds. High Altitude: An Exploration of Human Adaptation (pp. 645–661). Marcel Dekker, New York.

[224] Meeusen, R., P. Watson, and J. Dvorak. 2006. The brain and fatigue: new opportunities for nutritional interventions? J Sports Sci 24:773–782.

[225] Messner, R. 1977. The Challenge. Oxford University Press, New York.

[226] Messner, R. 1989. The Crystal Horizon. The Mountaineers, Seattle.

[227] Messner, R. 1999a. All 14 Eight-Thousanders. The Mountaineers, Seattle.

[228] Messner, R. 1999b. Free Spirit: A Climber's Life. The Mountaineers, Seattle.

[229] Messner, R. 1999c. To the Top of the World: Challenges in the Himalaya and Karakoram. The Mountaineers, Seattle.

[230] Messner, R. 2002. The Naked Mountain. The Mountaineers, Seattle.

[231] Minetti, A. E. 1995. Optimum gradient of mountain paths. J Appl Physiol 79:1698–1703.

[232] Minetti, A. E., F. Formenti, and L. P. Ardigo. 2006. Himalayan porter's specialization: metabolic power, economy, efficiency and skill. Proc Biol Sci 273:2791–2797.

[233] Minetti, A. E., C. Moia, G. S. Roi, et al. 2002. Energy cost of walking and running at extreme uphill and downhill slopes. J Appl Physiol 93:1039–1046.

[234] Missitzi, J., N. Geladas, and V. Klissouras. 2004. Heritability in neuromuscular coordination: implications for motor control strategies. Med Sci Sports Exerc 36:233–240.

[235] Montain, S. J., S. N. Cheuvront, and M. N. Sawka. 2006. Exercise associated hyponatraemia: quantitative analysis to understand the aetiology. Br J Sports Med 40:98–105; discussion 198–105.

[236] Montain, S. J., and E. F. Coyle. 1992. Influence of graded dehydration on hyperthermia and cardiovascular drift during exercise. J Appl Physiol 73:1340–1350.

[237] Montain, S. J., S. A. Smith, R. P. Mattot, et al. 1998. Hypohydration effects on skeletal muscle performance and metabolism: a 31P-MRS study. J Appl Physiol 84:1889–1894.

[238] Morel, O. E., R. Aubert, J. P. Richalet, et al. 2005. Simulated high altitude selectively decreases protein intake and lean mass gain in rats. Physiol Behav 86:145–153.

[239] Mortenson, G., and D. O. Relin. 2007. Three Cups of Tea: One Man's Mission to Promote Peace…One School at a Time. Penguin Books, New York.

[240] Moudgil, R., E. D. Michelakis, and S. L. Archer. 2005. Hypoxic pulmonary vasoconstriction. J Appl Physiol 98:390–403.

[241] Moul, J. L. 1998. Differences in selected predictors of anterior cruciate ligament tears between male and female NCAA Division I collegiate basketball players. J Athl Training 33:118–121.

[242] Murdoch, D. 1995. Symptoms of infection and altitude illness among hikers in the Mount Everest region of Nepal. Aviat Space Environ Med 66:148-151.

[243] Muza, S. R., A. J. Young, M. N. Sawka, et al. 2004. Ventilation after supplemental oxygen administration at high altitude. Wilderness Environ Med 15:18–24.

[244] Nag, P. K., R. N. Sen, and U. S. Ray. 1978. Optimal rate of work for mountaineers. J Appl Physiol 44:952–955.

[245] National Institutes of Health. 2003. The Seventh Report of the Joint National Committee on Prevention, Detection, Evaluation, and Treatment of High Blood Pressure (03-5233). Washington, D.C.

[246] Nickol, A. H., J. Leverment, P. Richards, et al. 2006. Temazepam at high altitude reduces periodic breathing without impairing next-day performance: a randomized cross-over double-blind study. J Sleep Res 15:445–454.

[247] Niermeyer, S. 2007. Going to high altitude with a newborn infant. High Alt Med Biol 8:117–123.

[248] Nimmo, M. 2004. Exercise in the cold. J Sports Sci 22:898–915; discussion 915–916.

[249] Noakes, T. D. 2003. Lore of Running. 4th ed. Human Kinetics, Champaign, IL.

[250] Noakes, T. D. 2005. Comments on Point:Counterpoint "Positive effects of intermittent hypoxia (live high:train low) on exercise performance are/are not mediated primarily by augmented red cell volume". J Appl Physiol 99:2453.

[251] Noakes, T. D., J. A. Calbet, R. Boushel, et al. 2004. Central regulation of skeletal muscle recruitment explains the reduced maximal cardiac output during exercise in hypoxia. Am J Physiol Regul Integr Comp Physiol 287:R996–999; author reply R999–1002.

[252] Noakes, T. D., J. E. Peltonen, and H. K. Rusko. 2001. Evidence that a central governer regulates exercise performance during hypoxia and hyperoxia. J Exp Biol 204:3225–3234.

[253] Noakes, T. D., K. Sharwood, D. Speedy, et al. 2005. Three independent biological mechanisms cause exercise-associated hyponatremia: evidence from 2,135 weighed competitive athletic performances. Proc Natl Acad Sci U S A 102:18550–18555.

[254] Noel, J. 1927. The Story of Everest. Little, Brown and Company, Boston.

[255] Noel-Jorand, M. C., F. Joulia, and D. Braggard. 2001. Personality factors, stoicism and motivation in subjects under hypoxic stress in extreme environments. Aviat Space Environ Med 72:391–399.

[256] Noyce, W. 1954. South Col: A Personal Story of the Ascent of Everest. William Sloane Associates, New York.

[257] Oelz, O., H. Howald, P. E. di Prampero, et al. 1986. Physiological profile of world-class high-altitude climbers. J Appl Physiol 60:1734–1742.

[258] Okumura, A., H. Fuse, Y. Kawauchi, et al. 2003. Changes in male reproductive function after high altitude mountaineering. High Alt Med Biol 4:349–353.

[259] Olfert, I. M., J. Balouch, A. Kleinsasser, et al. 2004. Does gender affect human pulmonary gas exchange during exercise? J Physiol 557:529–541.

[260] Ozkaplan, A., E. C. Rhodes, A. W. Sheel, et al. 2005. A comparison of inspiratory muscle fatigue following maximal exercise in moderately trained males and females. Eur J Appl Physiol 95:52–56.

[261] Palinkas, L. A., and P. Suedfeld. 2007. Psychological effects of polar expeditions. Lancet. DOI:10.1016/S0140-6736(07)61056-3

[262] Pastene, J., M. Germain, A. M. Allevard, et al. 1996. Water balance during and after marathon running. Eur J Appl Physiol Occup Physiol 73:49–55.

[263] Patey, T. 1971. The art of climbing down gracefully. In One Man's Mountains (pp. 231–240). Victor Gollancz, London.

[264] Paulcke, W., and H. Dumler. 1973. Hazards in Mountaineering. Oxford University Press, New York.

[265] Pedlar, C., G. Whyte, S. Emegbo, et al. 2005. Acute sleep responses in a normobaric hypoxic tent. Med Sci Sports Exerc 37:1075–1079.

[266] Pollard, A. J., S. Niermeyer, P. Barry, et al. 2001. Children at high altitude: an international consensus statement by an ad hoc committee of the International Society for Mountain Medicine, March 12, 2001. High Alt Med Biol 2:389–403.

[267] Powell, F. L., and N. Garcia. 2000. Physiological effects of intermittent hypoxia. High Alt Med Biol 1:125–136.

[268] Pronk, M., I. Tiemessen, M. D. Hupperets, et al. 2003. Persistence of the lactate paradox over 8 weeks at 3,800 m. High Alt Med Biol 4:431–443.

[269] Prud'homme, D., C. Bouchard, C. Leblanc, et al. 1984. Sensitivity of maximal aerobic power to training is genotype-dependent. Med Sci Sports Exerc 16:489–493.

[270] Pugh, L. G. C. E., M. B. Gill, S. Lahiri, et al. 1964. Muscular exercise at great altitudes. J Appl Physiol 19:431–440.

[271] Rai, R. M., M. S. Malhotra, G. P. Dimri, et al. 1975. Utilization of different quantities of fat at high altitude. Am J Clin Nutr 28:242–245.

[272] Raichle, M. E., and T. Hornbein. 2001. The high altitude brain. In T. Hornbein and R. B. Schoene, eds. High Altitude: An Exploration of Human Adaptation (pp. 377–423). Marcel Dekker, New York.

[273] Rankinen, T., M. S. Bray, J. M. Hagberg, et al. 2006. The human gene map for performance and health-related fitness phenotypes: the 2005 update. Med Sci Sports Exerc 38:1863–1888.

[274] Reeves, J. T., and K. R. Stenmark. 2001. The pulmonary circulation at high altitude. In T. Hornbein and R. B. Schoene, eds. High Altitude: An Exploration of Human Adaptation (pp. 293–342). Marcel Dekker, New York.

[275] Regard, M., O. Oelz, P. Brugger, et al. 1989. Persistent cognitive impairment in climbers after repeated exposure to extreme altitude. Neurology 39:210–213.

[276] Reichl, M. 1987. Neuropathy of the feet due to running on cold surfaces. BMJ 294:348–349.

[277] Reynolds, R. D. 2005. Fat desire and fat intake at extreme altitude: observations from the "On Top Everest '89" Nutrition Research Expedition. Wilderness Environ Med 16:232–234.

[278] Reynolds, R. D., J. A. Lickteig, P. A. Deuster, et al. 1999. Energy metabolism increases and regional body fat decreases while regional muscle mass is spared in humans climbing Mt. Everest. J Nutr 129:1307–1314.

[279] Reynolds, R. D., J. A. Lickteig, M. P. Howard, et al. 1998. Intakes of high fat and high carbohydrate foods by humans increased with exposure to increasing altitude during an expedition to Mt. Everest. J Nutr 128:50–55.

[280] Ricart de Mesones, A., J. Turon Sans, M. Misiego, et al. 2002. Neuropathic pain and dysesthesia of the feet after Himalayan expeditions. High Alt Med Biol 3:395–399.

[281] Rice, T., P. An, J. Gagnon, et al. 2002. Heritability of HR and BP response to exercise training in the HERITAGE Family Study. Med Sci Sports Exerc 34:972–979.

[282] Richalet, J. P., P. Gratadour, P. Robach, et al. 2005. Sildenafil inhibits altitude-induced hypoxemia and pulmonary hypertension. Am J Respir Crit Care Med 171:275–281.

[283] Richard, S., D. Orr, and C. Lindholm. 1991. The NOLS Cookery: Experience the Art of Outdoor Cooking. 3rd ed. NOLS/Stackpole Books, Harrisburg, PA.

[284] Ridgeway, R. 1980. The Last Step. The Mountaineers, Seattle.

[285] Roach, R., and B. Kayser. 2001. Exercise and hypoxia: performance, limits, and training. In T. Hornbein and R. B. Schoene, eds. High Altitude: An Exploration of Human Adaptation (pp. 663–705). Marcel Dekker, New York.

[286] Roach, R. C., and P. H. Hackett. 2001. Frontiers of hypoxia research: acute mountain sickness. J Exp Biol 204:3161–3170.

[287] Roach, R. C., D. Maes, D. Sandoval, et al. 2000. Exercise exacerbates acute mountain sickness at simulated high altitude. J Appl Physiol 88:581–585.

[288] Robergs, R. A., F. Ghiasvand, and D. Parker. 2004. Biochemistry of exercise-induced metabolic acidosis. Am J Physiol Regul Integr Comp Physiol 287:R502–516.

[289] Roberts, D. 1986. Moments of Doubt. The Mountaineers, Seattle.

[290] Roberts, D. 2000. True Summit: What Really Happened on the Legendary Ascent of Annapurna. Simon & Schuster, New York.

[291] Roberts, E. 1980. Welzenbach's Climbs. The Mountaineers, Seattle.

[292] Rodway, G. 2007. George Ingle Finch and the Mount Everest expedition of 1922: breaching the 8000-m barrier. High Alt Med Biol 8:68–76.

[293] Roscoe, C., E. Baker, C. Gustafson, et al. 2006. Investigating carbon monoxide exposure on Denali. Wilderness Environ Med 17:75–80.

[294] Rose, D., and E. Douglas. 2000. Regions of the Heart. National Geographic Society, Washington, D.C.

[295] Roskelley, J. 1987. Nanda Devi. Avon Books, New York.

[296] Roskelley, J. 1993. Stories off the Wall. The Mountaineers, Seattle.

[297] Rowell, G. 1977. In the Throne Room of the Mountain Gods. Sierra Club, San Francisco.

[298] Rupert, J. L., and M. S. Koehle. 2006. Evidence for a genetic basis for altitude-related illness. High Alt Med Biol 7:150–167.

[299] Rusko, H. K., H. O. Tikkanen, and J. E. Peltonen. 2004. Altitude and endurance training. J Sports Sci 22:928–944; discussion 945.

[300] Rutkiewicz, W. 1987. The first woman's ascent of K2. In J. Curran, ed. K2: Triumph and Tragedy (pp. 195–200). Houghton Mifflin Company, Boston.

[301] Ryan, T. A. 1944. Varieties of fatigue. Am J Psychol 57:565–569.

[302] Sadnicka, A., R. Walker, and J. Dallimore. 2004. Morbidity and determinants of health on youth expeditions. Wilderness Environ Med 15:181–187.

[303] Saltin, B., G. Blomqvist, J. H. Mitchell, et al. 1968. Response to exercise after bed rest and after training. Circulation 38(5 Suppl):1–78.

[304] Sandal, G. M. 1998. The effects of personality and interpersonal relations on crew performance during space simulation studies. Life Support Biosph Sci 5:461–470.

[305] Santee, W. R., W. F. Allison, L. A. Blanchard, et al. 2001. A proposed model for load carriage on sloped terrain. Aviat Space Environ Med 72:562–566.

[306] Sapolsky, R. M. 2004. Why Zebras Don't Get Ulcers. 3rd ed. Owl Books, New York.

[307] Saunders, V. 1991. Elusive Summits. Sphere Books, London.

[308] Sayre, W. 1964. Four Against Everest. Tower Books, New York.

[309] Schena, F., F. Guerrini, P. Tregnaghi, et al. 1992. Branched-chain amino acid supplementation during trekking at high altitude: the effects on loss of body mass, body composition, and muscle power. Eur J Appl Physiol Occup Physiol 65:394–398.

[310] Schneider, M., D. Bernasch, J. Weymann, et al. 2002. Acute mountain sickness: influence of susceptibility, pre-exposure and ascent rate. Med Sci Sports Exerc 34:1886–1891.

[311] Schoene, R. B. 2001. Fatal high altitude pulmonary edema associated with absence of the left pulmonary artery. High Alt Med Biol 2:405–406.

[312] Schoene, R. B. 2005a. Dexamethasone: by safe means, by fair means. High Alt Med Biol 6:273–275.

[313] Schoene, R. B. 2005b. Limits of respiration at high altitude. Clin Chest Med 26:405–414, vi.

[314] Schoene, R. B., S. Lahiri, and P. H. Hackett. 1984. Relationship of hypoxic ventilatory response to exercise performance on Mount Everest. J Appl Physiol 56:1478–1483.

[315] Schwartz, R. B., D. J. Ledrick, and A. Lindman. 2001. A comparison of carbon monoxide levels during the use of a multi-fuel camp stove. Wilderness Environ Med 12:236–238.

[316] Scott, D., and A. MacIntyre. 1984. The Shishapangma Expedition. The Mountaineers, Seattle.

[317] Sharma, V. M., and M. S. Malhotra. 1976. Ethnic variations in psychological performance under altitude stress. Aviat Space Environ Med 47:248–251.

[318] Shipton, E. 1943/ 1999. Upon that Mountain. In The Six Mountain Travel Books (pp. 305-454). The Mountaineers, Seattle.

[319] Shirreffs, S. M., and R. J. Maughan. 1997. Whole body sweat collection in humans: an improved method with preliminary data on electrolyte content. J Appl Physiol 82:336–341.

[320] Shlim, D. R., and J. Gallie. 1992. The causes of death among trekkers in Nepal. Int J Sports Med 13 Suppl 1:S74–76.

[321] Shlim, D. R., P. Hackett, C. S. Houston, et al. 1995. Diplopia at high altitude. Wilderness Environ Med 6:341–343.

[322] Simon-Schnass, I. 1996. Oxidative stress at high altitudes and effects of vitamin E. In B. M. Marriott and S. J. Carlson, eds. Nutritional Needs in Cold and in High-Altitude Environments (pp. 393–418). National Academy Press, Washington, DC.

[323] Skinner, J. S., A. Jaskolski, A. Jaskolska, et al. 2001. Age, sex, race, initial fitness, and response to training: the HERITAGE Family Study. J Appl Physiol 90:1770–1776.

[324] Smith, C. A., J. A. Dempsey, and T. Hornbein. 2001. Control of breathing at high altitude. In T. Hornbein and R. B. Schoene, eds. High Altitude: An Exploration of Human Adaptation (pp. 139–173). Marcel Dekker, New York.

[325] Smythe, F. 1930/ 2000. The Kangchenjunga Adventure. In Frank Smythe: The Six Alpine/Himalayan Climbing Books (pp. 139–346). The Mountaineers, Seattle.

[326] Smythe, F. 1937/ 2000. Camp 6. In Frank Smythe: The Six Alpine/Himalayan Climbing Books (pp. 515–652). The Mountaineers, Seattle.

[327] Smythe, F. 2000. The Six Alpine/Hymalayan Climbing Books. The Mountaineers, Seattle.

[328] Southard, A., S. Niermeyer, and M. Yaron. 2007. Language used in Lake Louise Scoring System underestimates symptoms of acute mountain sickness in 4- to 11-year-old children. High Alt Med Biol 8:124–130.

[329] Speedy, D. B., T. D. Noakes, and C. Schneider. 2001. Exercise-associated hyponatremia: a review. Emerg Med (Fremantle) 13:17–27.

[330] Sridharan, K., S. Ranganathan, A. K. Mukherjee, et al. 2004. Vitamin status of high altitude (3660 m) acclimatized human subjects during consumption of tinned rations. Wilderness Environ Med 15:95–101.

[331] Stampfer, M. J. 2006. Vitamins and Minerals: What You Need to Know (SR12000). Harvard Medical School, Boston.

[332] Steele, P. 1999. Backcountry Medical Handbook. 2nd ed. The Mountaineers, Seattle.

[333] Strydom, N. B., C. H. Wyndham, C. H. van Graan, et al. 1966. The influence of water restriction on the performance of men during a prolonged march. South African Med J 40:539–544.

[334] Swenson, E. R. 2001. Renal function and fluid homeostasis. In T. Hornbein and R. B. Schoene, eds. High Altitude: An Exploration of Human Adaptation (pp. 525–570). Marcel Dekker, New York.

[335] Syme, D. 2002. Position paper: on-site treatment of frostbite for mountaineers. High Alt Med Biol 3:297–298.

[336] Tanner, D. A., and J. M. Stager. 1998. Partitioned weight loss and body composition changes during a mountaineering expedition: a field study. Wilderness Environ Med 9:143–152.

[337] Tarnopolsky, M. A., S. A. Atkinson, J. D. MacDougall, et al. 1992. Evaluation of protein requirements for trained strength athletes. J Appl Physiol 73:1986–1995.

[338] Tasker, J. 1982. Savage Arena. St. Martin's Press, New York.

[339] Taylor, R. 1981. The Breach. Coward, McCann & Geoghegan, New York.

[340] Thompson, A. E., and J. E. Pope. 2005. Calcium channel blockers for primary Raynaud's phenomenon: a meta-analysis. Rheumatology 44:145–150.

[341] Thrush, D., and M. R. Hodges. 1994. Accuracy of pulse oximetry during hypoxemia. South Med J 87:518–521.

[342] Tikuisis, P. 1995. Predicting survival time for cold exposure. Int J Biometeorol 39:94–102.

[343] Tikuisis, P., I. Jacobs, D. Moroz, et al. 2000. Comparison of thermoregulatory responses between men and women immersed in cold water. J Appl Physiol 89:1403–1411.

[344] Tilman, H. W. 1937/ 2003. The Ascent of Nanda Devi. In The Seven Mountain Travel Books (pp. 149–267). The Mountaineers, Seattle.

[345] Tilman, H. W. 1946/ 2003. When Men and Mountains Meet. In The Seven Mountain Travel Books (pp. 269–421). The Mountaineers, Seattle.

[346] Tilman, H. W. 1948/ 2003. Everest 1938. In The Seven Mountain Travel Books (pp. 423–509). The Mountaineers, Seattle.

[347] Truesdell, A. G., and R. L. Wilson. 2006. Training for medical support of mountain operations. Mil Med 171:463–467.

[348] Tschop, M., C. J. Strasburger, G. Hartmann, et al. 1998. Raised leptin concentrations at high altitude associated with loss of appetite. Lancet 352:1119–1120.

[349] Tullis, J. 1987. Clouds from Both Sides. Sierra Club Books, San Francisco.

[350] Twight, M. 2001. Kiss or Kill. The Mountaineers, Seattle.

[351] Twight, M., and J. Martin. 1999. Extreme Alpinism: Climbing Light, Fast, and High. The Mountaineers, Seattle.

[352] Twombly, S. E., and L. C. Schussman. 1995. Gender differences in injury and illness rates on wilderness backpacking trips. Wilderness Environ Med 4:363–376.

[353] Vander, A., J. Sherman, and D. Luciano. 1998. Human Physiology: The Mechanisms of Body Function. 7th ed. WCB/McGraw-Hill, Boston.

[354] Venables, S. 2000. Everest: Alone at the Summit. Thunder's Mouth Press, New York.

[355] Viesturs, E. 2006. No Shortcuts to the Top. Broadway Books, New York.

[356] Wagner, P. D. 2001. Gas exchange. In T. Hornbein and R. B. Schoene, eds. High Altitude: An Exploration of Human Adaptation (pp. 199–234). Marcel Dekker, New York.

[357] Wang, R. Y., S. C. Tsai, J. J. Chen, et al. 2001. The simulation effects of mountain climbing training on selected endocrine responses. Chin J Physiol 44:13–18.

[358] Wang, W. J., and R. H. Crompton. 2004. The role of load-carrying in the evolution of modern body proportions. J Anat 204:417–430.

[359] Ward, M. P. 1954. High altitude deterioration. Proc R Soc, Series B, London 143:40–42.

[360] Ward, M. P., J. Milledge, and J. B. West. 2000. High Altitude Medicine and Physiology. 3rd ed. Arnold, London.

[361] Waterhouse, J., T. Reilly, and B. Edwards. 2004. The stress of travel. J Sports Sci 22:946–965; discussion 965–946.

[362] Waterman, J. 1983. Surviving Denali: A Study of Accidents on Mount McKinley. A.A.C., New York.

[363] Waugh, R. J. 1977. Penile frostbite: an unforeseen hazard of jogging [letter]. N Engl J Med 296:178.

[364] Weathers, B. 2000. Left for Dead: My Journey Home from Everest. Villard, New York.

[365] Webster, E. 2000. Snow in the Kingdom. Mountain Imagery, Eldorado Springs, CO.

[366] Weil, J. V. 2004. Sleep at high altitude. High Alt Med Biol 5:180–189.

[367] West, J. B. 1983. Climbing Mt. Everest without oxygen: an analysis of maximal exercise during extreme hypoxia. Respir Physiol 52:265–279.

[368] West, J. B. 1999. Barometric pressures on Mt. Everest: new data and physiological significance. J Appl Physiol 86:1062–1066.

[369] West, J. B. 2002. Unexplained severe fatigue and lassitude at high altitude. High Alt Med Biol 3:237–241.

[370] West, J. B. 2003. Acclimatization to high altitude: truths and misconceptions. High Alt Med Biol 4:401–402.

[371] West, J. B. 2004. The physiologic basis of high-altitude diseases. Ann Intern Med 141:789–800.

[372] West, J. B. 2006. Human responses to extreme altitudes. Integr Comp Biol 46:25–34.

[373] West, J. B., S. Lahiri, K. H. Maret, et al. 1983. Barometric pressures at extreme altitudes on Mt. Everest: physiological significance. J Appl Physiol 54:1188–1194.

[374] Westerterp, K. R., and B. Kayser. 2006. Body mass regulation at altitude. Eur J Gastroenterol Hepatol 18:1–3.

[375] Westerterp-Plantenga, M. S., K. R. Westerterp, M. Rubbens, et al. 1999. Appetite at "high altitude" [Operation Everest III (Comex-'97)]: a simulated ascent of Mount Everest. J Appl Physiol 87:391–399.

[376] Wickwire, J., and D. Bullitt. 1988. Addicted to Danger. Pocket Books, New York.

[377] Wilcox, J. 1981. White Winds. Hwong Publishing, Los Alamitos, CA.

[378] Wilkerson, J., ed. 2001. Medicine for Mountaineering and Other Wilderness Activities. 5th ed. The Mountaineers, Seattle.

[379] Willson, J. D., M. L. Ireland, and I. Davis. 2006. Core strength and lower extremity alignment during single leg squats. Med Sci Sports Exerc 38:945–952.

[380] Windsor, J. S., P. Richards, and G. Rodway. 2006. Painful fissures and diabetes mellitus at altitude. Wilderness Environ Med 17:205–206.

[381] Winslow, R. M., M. Samaja, and J. B. West. 1984. Red cell function at extreme altitude on Mount Everest. J Appl Physiol 56:109–116.

[382] Wiseman, C., L. Freer, and E. Hung. 2006. Physical and medical characteristics of successful and unsuccessful summiteers of Mount Everest in 2003. Wilderness Environ Med 17:103–108.

[383] Withey, W. R., J. S. Milledge, E. S. Williams, et al. 1983. Fluid and electrolyte homeostasis during prolonged exercise at altitude. J Appl Physiol 55:409–412.

[384] Wolf, L. 1998. A woman's perspective on Mt. Kilimanjaro. Wilderness Environ Med 9:124.

[385] Wolff, C. B. 2000. Cerebral blood flow and oxygen delivery at high altitude. High Alt Med Biol 1:33–38.

[386] Worme, J. D., J. A. Lickteig, R. D. Reynolds, et al. 1991. Consumption of a dehydrated ration for 31 days at moderate altitudes: energy intakes and physical performance. J Am Diet Assoc 91:1543–1549.

[387] Wyss-Dunant, E. 1953. Acclimatisation. In M. Kurz, ed. The Mountain World (pp. 110–117). Swiss Foundation for Alpine Research/Harper and Brothers, New York.

[388] Yaron, M., S. Niermeyer, K. N. Lindgren, et al. 2002. Evaluation of diagnostic criteria and incidence of acute mountain sickness in preverbal children. Wilderness Environ Med 13:21–26.

[389] Yaron, M., S. Niermeyer, K. N. Lindgren, et al. 2003. Physiologic response to moderate altitude exposure among infants and young children. High Alt Med Biol 4:53–59.

[390] Yoneda, I., and Y. Watanabe. 1997. Comparisons of altitude tolerance and hypoxia symptoms between nonsmokers and habitual smokers. Aviat Space Environ Med 68:807–811.

[391] Young, A., M. Sawka, and K. Pandolf. 1996. The physiology of cold exposure. In B. M. Marriott and S. J. Carlson, eds. Nutritional Needs in Cold and in High-Altitude Environments (pp. 127–147). National Academy Press, Washington, D.C.

[392] Young, A. J., J. W. Castellani, C. O'Brien, et al. 1998. Exertional fatigue, sleep loss, and negative energy balance increase susceptibility to hypothermia. J Appl Physiol 85:1210–1217.

[393] Zaccaria, M., A. Ermolao, P. Bonvicini, et al. 2004. Decreased serum leptin levels during prolonged high altitude exposure. Eur J Appl Physiol 92:249–253.

[394] Zhao, L., N. A. Mason, N. W. Morrell, et al. 2001. Sildenafil inhibits hypoxia-induced pulmonary hypertension. Circulation 104:424–428.

[395] Zilberstein, B., A. G. Quintanilha, M. A. Santos, et al. 2007. Digestive tract microbiota in healthy volunteers. Clinics 62:47–54.

[396] Zoll, J., E. Ponsot, S. Dufour, et al. 2006. Exercise training in normobaric hypoxia in endurance runners. III. Muscular adjustments of selected gene transcripts. J Appl Physiol 100:1258–1266.

Appendix E:
Recommended Reading

CHAPTER 2

Bouchard (1993) provides a readable summary of genetic differences among individuals.

West et al. (1983) describes the various factors that affect barometric pressure.

CHAPTER 3

Noakes (2003) is a general reference on aerobic exercise and mental training.

Roach and Kayser (2001) is a highly technical but good reference on exercise during hypoxia.

Sapolsky (2004) examines the effects of all different kinds of stress on the body and mind.

Twight and Martin (1999) discuss will and passion.

CHAPTER 4

Baumgartner et al. (2007) discusses travel to altitude with preexisting neurological conditions.

Boukreev (2001) is a fine reference covering acclimatization to extreme altitude.

Jean et al. (2005) discusses issues women face at altitude.

Niermeyer (2007) specifically deals with infants at altitude.

Pollard et al. (2001) and Yaron et al. (2002) discuss children at altitude.

CHAPTER 5

Basnyat et al. (2000) discuss nonneurological issues at altitude.

Basnyat et al. (2004) discuss common neurological symptoms at altitude.

Baumgartner et al. (2007) discuss travel at altitude with preexisting neurological conditions.

Bezruchka (2005) is a compact and complete book on diagnosing and treating altitude illness.

Hillebrandt (2002) and Backer (2003) discuss the roles of medical advisers to commercial trekking agencies.

Kamler (2004) is an excellent first-person account of a doctor working in the wilderness and contains a lot of easily understood science.

Steele (1999) is a lightweight guide for general wilderness first aid.

Truesdell and Wilson (2006) discuss physician training for mountain medicine.

West (2004) provides a succinct explanation of the science of high-altitude illnesses.

CHAPTER 6

Basnyat et al. (2000) summarizes a variety of acute medical issues (mostly neurological) that are seen at altitude.

Schoene (2005b) provides a good summary of the effects of altitude on respiration.

CHAPTER 7

Bemben and Lamont (2005) review creatine supplementation.

Butterfield (1996) provides a good summary of appetite and digestion issues.

Noakes (2003) spends much time discussing heat and dehydration at sea level.

Stampfer (2006) edited a useful guide to vitamins and minerals.

Twight (1999) dispenses excellent food and hydration advice that can be used by any traveler to altitude, though his emphasis is on alpine climbing.

www.cdc.gov is a useful source of information on disease organisms, hygiene, and water purification.

www.ciwec-clinic.com is the best Web site for information on traveler's diarrhea.

CHAPTER 8

Maughan and Shirreffs (2004) provide an overview of the effect of heat on exercise. Wilkerson (2001) covers all of the topics in this chapter.

www.cosmeticsdatabase.com has analyses of the effectiveness and safety of various sunscreens.

www.ikar-cisa.org provides protocols for the treatment of both heat and cold injuries in wilderness situations.

CHAPTER 9

Jordan (2005) and Rose and Douglas (2000) provide a number examples of the hardships women face as travelers and high-altitude climbers.

Mortenson and Oliver (2007) demonstrates the joys and challenges of building schools for girls in Pakistan and Afganistan.

Rowell (1977) and Ridgeway (1980) illustrate how (and sometimes why) everything can go wrong due to relationship problems.

CHAPTER 10

It's hard to pick favorites here, so any of the cited books in this chapter would be good. I especially like Kukuczka (1992), Webster (2000), and anything by Tilman, Messner, or Boukreev.

CHAPTER 11

Coffey (2003) is the best resource covering the aftermath of tragedy in the mountains.

Waterman (1983) and American Alpine Club (1952-2006) are two fine resources for the study of accidents at altitude. Learning from the mistakes of others is an essential part of the training of the high-altitude traveler.

Wickwire (1988), Curran (1987, 1995), and Roskelley (1987) all provide good analyses of the consequences of decision making at altitude.

CHAPTER 12

Boukreev (2001) should be required reading for those training for the Death Zone.

Delavier (2006) is a great reference for weight workouts.

Ilg (1999) treats the body holistically; see his other books as well.

Twight and Martin (1999) provide good overall advice for training.

CHAPTER 13

Coffey (2003) discusses post-trip letdown.

Waterhouse et al. (2004) provides specific recommendations for treating jet lag.

Index

aspirin, 101
athletes, 68, 81
atmosphere, 263–66
atmospheric pressure, 14–15
ATP (adenosine triphosphate), 56, 111, 124–27
atria, 27
atrial natriuretic peptide. See ANP (atrial natriuretic peptide)

B

backcountry travel, 252–55
backpacking, overnight, 85, 130
bacteria, 143, 145
balaclava, 159
Baltoro Glacier, 100
barometric pressure. See atmospheric pressure
Barrard, Maurice and Liliane, 249, 252
basal metabolic rate (BMR), 128–29, 156
Base Camp
    food needs, 130–32
    value of longer approach to, 87
Bashkirov, Vladimir, 91–92
Bates, Bob, 256
Bauer, Willi, 195
Baxter-Jones, Roger, 254
behavior and altitude, 111–13
benzonatate, 109
bicarbonate, 29
biochemical pathway, 272–73
biology
    exercise, 47–69
    fundamental concepts, 15, 266–73
biomechanics, 57–58
Bishop, Barry, 89
blood, 23, 26, 28, 29
blood acid-base balance, 197
blood oxygen saturation. See SaO₂
blood pressure, 28, 155
blood vessels, 26

Blum, Arlene, 185
body temperature, 153, 155, 161
body weight management, 244–45
Bonington, Christian, 180
boots, 159
boredom, 64
Boskoff, Christine, 185
Boukreev, Anatoli, 83, 88, 177, 197, 199, 227, 255
brain, 125
    dysfunction, 110
    and exercise, 56–57
    and fatigue, 62
Breashears, Dave, 176–77, 218
breathing, 23–24, 24–25, 107–8, 113, 243
Bremer-Kamp, Cherie, 185, 192
bronchi, 21
Buhl, Herman, 89, 112, 157
bureaucracy, 63–64
Burgess, Al, 188

C

calcium channel blockers, 157
canker sores, 168
capillaries, 21, 27
capsule style climbing, 86
carbamazepine, 157
carbamino compound, 30
carbohydrates, 89, 125, 129
carbon dioxide, 24, 25, 29–31, 43–44
carbon monoxide, 31, 106–7
carbonic anhydrase, 30
cardiac output, 28, 75, 155
cardiovascular system, 26–29, 236–37
carbonic acid, 29
carotid body, 24
catalysts, 273
cells, 15, 124–28
cellular respiration, 124–28
central chemoreceptors, 23, 25
central command fatigue, 56–57

vision problems, 99, 168–69
VO₂ max, 54–55, 59, 236–37

W
wakeup time, 255–56
water loss, 137
water safety, 143–51
wavelength, 165
weather, 256–57
Weathers, Beck, 158
Webster, Ed, 112, 184, 211
weight loss, 121–36, 139, 244–45, 260
Welzenbach, Willo, 221
willpower, 60–68, 209–12
windbriefs, 159

windchill, 155, 158
Wolf, Mrufka, 115–16, 216
Wolfe, Dudley, 178
women
    effects of high altitude, 77–78
    die in Pamirs, 214
    and local cultures, 191–92
    as team members, 185–86
Workman, William and Fanny, 189

Y
yoga, 244

About the Author

Mike Farris began studying biology in 1975. His original research interests included the effects of natural selection on gas-exchange characters in plants. As Professor of Biology at Hamline University, he has taught human biology to hundreds of non-scientists over the past 20 years. Mike has been hiking and climbing at high altitude for over 30 years and has completed many technical alpine rock and ice climbs in the USA and Canada, climbed Kilimanjaro and Aconcagua, reached 26,000 ft on Kangchenjunga and Broad Peak, and summited Gasherbrum II (26,362 ft). Since 2002 he has spent nearly eight months above 17,000 ft. Mike has also completed over 40 marathons and ultramarathons, including two finishes of the Hardrock 100.

FEET AND METERS CONVERSION TABLE

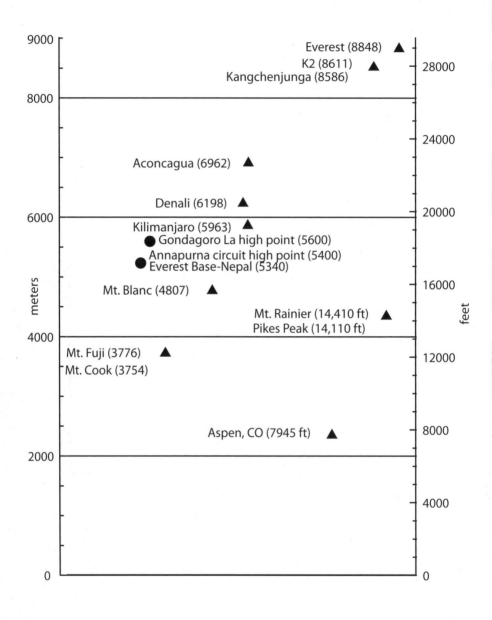